CW00766040

Thinking in Education Research

Also available from Bloomsbury

Educational Research, Jerry Wellington

Educational Research and Inquiry, edited by Dimitra Hartas

Philosophy of Educational Research, Richard Pring

Rethinking the Education Improvement Agenda, Kevin J. Flint and Nick Peim

Thinking in Education Research

Applying Philosophy and Theory

Nick Peim

Bloomsbury Academic
An imprint of Bloomsbury Publishing Plc

BLOOMSBURY ACADEMIC
LONDON • NEW YORK • OXFORD • NEW DELHI • SYDNEY

BLOOMSBURY ACADEMIC
Bloomsbury Publishing Plc
50 Bedford Square, London, WC1B 3DP, UK

BLOOMSBURY, BLOOMSBURY ACADEMIC and the Diana logo are trademarks of Bloomsbury Publishing Plc

First published in Great Britain 2018

© Nick Peim, 2018

Nick Peim has asserted his right under the Copyright, Designs and Patents Act, 1988, to be identified as Author of this work.

Cover design: Nick Evans
Cover image © Shutterstock

All rights reserved. No part of this publication may be reproduced or transmitted in any form or by any means, electronic or mechanical, including photocopying, recording, or any information storage or retrieval system, without prior permission in writing from the publishers.

Bloomsbury Publishing Plc does not have any control over, or responsibility for, any third-party websites referred to or in this book. All internet addresses given in this book were correct at the time of going to press. The author and publisher regret any inconvenience caused if addresses have changed or sites have ceased to exist, but can accept no responsibility for any such changes.

A catalogue record for this book is available from the British Library.
A catalog record for this book is available from the Library of Congress.

ISBN: HB: 978-1-4725-9108-1
PB: 978-1-4725-9107-4
ePDF: 978-1-4725-9109-8
ePub: 978-1-4725-9110-4

Typeset by Integra Software Services Pvt. Ltd.
Printed and bound in Great Britain

To find out more about our authors and books visit www.bloomsbury.com and sign up for our newsletters.

Contents

List of Figures

Preface

This book has been written from a point of view that is rare in philosophy of education. It takes the injunction that the question is the piety of thinking seriously. It calls into question therefore not only the dominant format for research ('research by numbers' as I term it) in education, the model peddled by the handbooks, but also the hardly ever questioned idea that education is necessarily a force for good. In other words, it pushes ontological thinking about research, philosophy and education to its limits.

The book was conceived from a practice of teaching on research courses for masters and doctoral students. It grew out of the conviction that not only was the way of thinking I was offering right, but that it was experienced by students as enriching and productive: much more so than the drab formulae of the handbooks. Generations of students, then, have informed the thinking and the ethic of this book, and I owe thanks to them, their interest, their patience and their enthusiasm. For me, teaching has been an essential element in thinking, and especially in the processes of rethinking that I associate with deconstruction. Of course, teaching can't be done alone, and I want to acknowledge the quality and verve of the many students with whom I have spent so many hours in discussion in supervisions, lectures and seminars.

This book also grew out of a reading of modern and contemporary philosophy, starting with the realization that deconstruction – now a commonly used, though not necessarily well-understood, term – has a special and very important meaning. This meaning concerns the future of philosophy as an essential dimension of the future of thinking. Deconstruction teaches that neither philosophy nor thinking is over and done with and that the tradition of formal engagement with metaphysics still has a great deal to offer, still offers a rich affordance. What's more, deconstruction and its allies have produced new directions for philosophy, some only touched on lightly in this book. I believe we are fortunate in that we live in a time that is very rich in philosophy, if we know where to look for the sources of renewal. For educational researchers – and others in the social sciences – the contemporary regeneration of philosophy is rich in practical possibilities for knowledge. Here I have tried to show how going back to some of the origins of thinking (engaging 'What is ...?' type of questions) offers a great deal more than the research manuals and what passes for educational philosophy in its dominant form can dream of.

None of this, though, is offered in the spirit of absolute certainty. That ethic – the ethic informing the quest for constant, rationally driven improvement – must be displaced by one more attuned to the actual conditions of knowledge and thinking. If this means giving up on the remorseless, misguided quest for impact, then let that be understood as a welcome liberation.

Introduction

What kind of book is this?

This book is an invitation to throw away the handbooks that tell you, falsely, how to do research. Often taking the form of research 'by numbers', such manuals promote a limited idea of research. The element of thinking, the most significant dimension of research, is reduced to a series of choices among fabricated options. This book is an antidote to that formulaic approach. It offers to engage thinking to enable research in social science and in education to come alive.

Thinking is the vital dimension of method – method itself. Starting with thinking enables the researcher to begin to articulate their specific project, engaging immediately with themselves, their dominant interests and the worlds they care about. This book explores some resources from philosophy and theory as essential resources for any social science research endeavour. The clichéd divide between theory and the empirical is unhelpful. The usual binaries offered to social science researchers are irrelevant – and can't provide an effective stimulus for the thinking that can productively inform research.

Some of the following are the exhausted binary oppositions of research handbooks:

empirical/theoretical;

realist/constructivist;

qualitative/quantitative;

positivist/interpretivist;

and others ....

By refusing these binary oppositions this book rejects sterile anxieties deeply familiar in debates about the state, function and essence of educational research. It tackles questions that dominate current thinking about educational and social science research: about relevance, impact and the very meaning of education in our time. This ontological dimension is implicit throughout and surfaces now and again as the crucial issue at stake in educational research. It is alarmingly the case that, despite the proliferation of educational research, it rarely addresses the most serious and far-reaching ontological questions. This book is written from a conviction that the ontological question attending education is the most pressing – and the most interesting – question in contemporary social science, as well as the least well understood and least frequently addressed. It also suggests that the questions that attend educational research are really questions that attend all forms of research and that what we refer to now as education – or educational studies – embraces all questions concerning knowledge, research and the meaning of science.

Starting with a basic phenomenology of research relations, this book explores major lines of thinking in modern European philosophy and theory as a resource for the conduct of research. Essential dimensions of the research endeavour will be addressed, including: defining the object; exploring one's subjectivity and subject position; giving an account of the field, its structure, its history; examining the relation of the research issue to truth; addressing the process of writing, constructing and claiming a case; addressing questions of meaning and relevance; addressing the contemporary field of educational knowledge and its institutions. New ways of thinking arising from contemporary philosophy are also considered in their relevance to educational research.

With its emphasis on thinking, this book challenges commonly held features of the research process expressed in handbooks. This book sees research as thinking written into an essentially open genre that requires the decision-making competence of the researcher. This approach privileges the researcher as thinker, not in the sense of some dreamy theorist, but rather in the sense of a someone who can summon a range of ideas and perspectives. This researcher is aware that there are resources for original and expansive thinking ready to hand. The thinking in question consists of the heritage of modern philosophy. To emphasize modern philosophy (i.e. philosophy since Descartes, 1596–1650) is not to suggest that other philosophy is of less relevance or value. Modern philosophy is conceived of as a running commentary on previous philosophies. What's more, philosophy is not confined to what is separated into a special domain of knowledge or writing; philosophy is, as I will hope to demonstrate, intricated in the most everyday workings of our thinking as well as in the larger frameworks of ideas that consciously or unconsciously shape our apprehension and experience of our worlds. All research is a kind of philosophy. Nevertheless, towards the end of the book I will claim that our time is a particularly rich time for thinking. Philosophy is alive and well and finding exciting, provocative new ways of realizing itself.

Despite recent arguments seeking to subordinate, marginalize or even to banish or theory in social science research, the dimension of thinking is important to every aspect of research at every stage in the research process. It is important because the modern divide between knowledge and thinking is both false and unhelpful. Thinking provides a general methodology from the start, without having to wrestle with techniques of research, with the fraught difference between method and methodology and without having to commit precipitously to an epistemological stance. The approach here will identify key issues for the researcher whatever their object, orientation and context. Starting from the basic scenario of a researcher confronting an object within a context, the research process can begin by using a phenomenology of research relations to articulate a real position drawing on the researcher's own experience and world – with a rich promise of expansion, development and possibly change from there via a hermeneutic of horizons.

The book will reinterpret the relations between philosophy, theory and research drawing on contemporary resources, linking them into the traditions of 'Western metaphysics'. While it will not pretend to provide an exhaustive summary of such positions (who could do that anyway?), it will indicate sources for the mode of thinking being applied. The intention is to suggest occasions for productive engagement with research thinking to enhance research practice for researchers who are starting out not, necessarily with a background of philosophy, but who need to think, and probably to rethink, their own relation to the object, whatever it may be, that they intend to research.

Philosophy, theory, metaphysics and research

Much research philosophy need not be explicitly formulated as philosophy per se. Philosophy, formal or, most usually, otherwise, is nonetheless evident in every aspect of research focus and practice, if by philosophy we include the business of making statements about how things are. All research must do that. Fundamental, introductory questions are philosophical, such as the following: What is the object of this research? From what position is this research being conducted? What is the data relevant to this research? How might this data be accessed, selected, organized? How does this research interpret its data? What field does this research occupy and what positions have been established and what is their claim to authority? What has scholarship had to say about this topic, this object, this field? Why does this accumulated body of 'knowledge' have this particular character, and what might this research contribute that's new to a field of knowledge? What other ways of thinking from what sources might be available

to re-examine and know this object anew? These questions are fundamental to any research enterprise and engage powerful philosophical issues.

Further questions concern purposes: What's the point of this research? How does this research contribute to or challenge the stock of knowledge and understanding? How does it stand in relation to the conventions of research production and knowledge classification? What contribution does it make in a larger sense? To the 'world'? Few researchers engage in a serious project without confronting big questions concerning the nature of science, the nature of knowledge and without considering what ideas permeate contemporary understandings of these vital phenomena. None of the questions in the above series is without a potential richness of engagement. Indeed, it is that very potentiality – the space of possibility – that makes research possible and can make it an exciting enterprise.

The research process necessarily generates questions that carry significant philosophical potential. That potential in research is enhanced by paying attention to philosophical questions, positions and modes of exploration. Fundamental philosophical aspects of research – object, context, data, interpretation, knowledge, relevance, community and world – will be made explicit in dialogue with some currents in modern (post-Cartesian) and contemporary European and analytical philosophy. This book will follow Derrida's assertion that 'metaphysics' is not only the property of formal discourses of philosophy, but is ingrained in the most everyday and worldly utterances and practices. This necessary metaphysical dimension will not be represented as other to method and data, but will be presented as an always-available space for development in the research enterprise.

Rather, the book will acknowledge the necessary, indissoluble relations between theory and philosophy. Thinking, theory, language, metaphysics and philosophy stand in a complex and indissoluble relation. The philosophical dimension of research is not so much a menu of optional positions – usually cast in the form of handy oppositions – but a complex process of orientation to fundamental dimensions of research thinking and practice. The philosophical dimension of social science thinking will be considered as an example of the necessity of metaphysics but will include examples of sociological theory to illustrate how social theory, as an inexplicit form of philosophy, must also always already be at least implicated in research practices. Thus, one major effect of the approach will be to constantly deconstruct the assumed divide between practice and metaphysics. In other words, like it or not, theory, philosophy, metaphysics are always already there, an inescapable dimension.

The fear of theory often takes the form of anxiety of being dominated by one overarching, systematic way of thinking. In seeing everything from a single perspective, so the story goes, we run the risk of losing touch with the complexity of lived experience. But this is just an indictment really of poor theory or poor application of theory not of theory itself. Theory may become a kind of straightjacket for thinking when it is disconnected from that sensitivity to issues and complexities that is characterized by determinism. In effect, thinking is, as deconstruction clearly demonstrates, interminable. And as I will hope to demonstrate through the book, the big philosophical issues have not been settled once and for all. The history of philosophy, from a perspective of deconstruction, is the history of partial answers, partial solutions, partial insights and explorations into those issues that remain live for us in all our present efforts to wrestle with knowledge and its production as researchers.

Another realization is that theory is there anyhow. It is one of the triumphs of deconstruction, to demonstrate that everyday language – and everyday thinking therefore – is always already freighted with theory. In this sense, there can be no 'ordinary' language free from the taint of ideas that expresses some direct relation with how things are. Language itself *is* metaphysics. Its semantics and syntax both express relations with the world and implicit understandings of the nature of things. To eschew theory as mere 'jargon' is to fall into the trap of thinking that there can be language free from metaphysics. While some philosophical language presented here is different and uncommon, it is offered as necessary extensions to expression. A new or different language is required to go beyond a wilful adherence to a 'common-sense' view of things. The no-jargon, no-nonsense approach suffers from the tendency to simplify things in the rich complexities of the social world. Those complexities will not only serve to render research more plausible but may enrich understandings of the nature of the thing in question.

The common-sense approach runs the risk of leaving everything as it is. It has the potential to annihilate real questioning. The familiar is laden with cherished assumptions. Why would we want to run the risk of not testing these? Without this element of risk, research arising from a formulaic project must belong to the order of the already known or at least to the order of the blindingly obvious. A great deal of educational research follows this pattern, of course, and it has to, in order to sustain the very world that it purports to be investigating.

While this book draws on the resources of contemporary continental theory, including some of its most recent cynosures, it will consider ideas from the broad history of modern philosophy from Descartes. It will also make limited use of the tradition of analytic philosophy spawned by Wittgenstein. In recognition of the metaphysical contribution of forms of thought other than what is formally designated as philosophy, the book will also draw on major theoretical positions such as anthropology, psychoanalysis, sociology and the theory of science. Throughout mention will be made of key philosophical positions, texts and authors: but without resorting to an overly technical language. Some key philosophical terminology will be careful introduced. The main focus will be on the ideas and their impact on research thinking and practice.

This means that there will be quite a bit of name-dropping and this probably needs some explanation. The use of proper names in the book is to signify certain positions that are, in certain fields of knowledge and thinking, more or less established, although invariably retaining dynamic possibilities for change and renewal. So, for example, if the text refers to Bourdieu or Spinoza, the point is to signify some of the key themes and problematics associated with these names. It is not to evoke the spirit of some actual person. The use of proper names works as a kind of shorthand to signify recurring and useful ideas. The reader who comes across a reference to Heidegger's 'fundamental ontology' will be able to extend their understanding by exploring further key themes associated with that phrase, considering terms and the ideas they signify such as 'care', 'being-in-the-world' 'mood', 'anxiety'. These words have their own rich associations but when coupled with Heidegger signify a chain of associations offering a challenging way of looking at the world.

The resources of the legacy of European or Western philosophy, particularly that philosophy following Descartes and Spinoza, are assumed to be highly relevant to contemporary projects. The history of modern philosophy after Descartes is regarded not so much as a source to mine for established and received wisdom, but rather as providing provocations for thinking. Important connections between philosophy, metaphysics and thinking can be explored through knowledge of the strong tendencies and illustrative examples that major figures in philosophy epitomize.

Readers are invited in relation to the various sections of this book to consider their own research focus, interests, objects, contexts, orientations, data and purposes from these various perspectives and in relation to these various ideas. The idea is that the book can carry the reader through the process of research – in a specific project, for example – by exploring how fundamental features of any research structure might be addressed.

Beginning? But where does research begin?

In answer to the question 'What is philosophical about research?' this book is strongly inclined to say, 'Well, everything, of course, from beginning to end'. And the very fact of beginning itself opens up a philosophical theme, a theme for thinking and rethinking.

The very beginning is itself an interesting point for enquiry. This might be especially the case with research that is, at the very least, an attempt to move from not knowing to knowing. During the course of Plato's *Meno*, Socrates and Meno discuss virtue, with Socrates claiming that he wants to examine its nature but insisting that he doesn't know what it is:

> SOCRATES So now, for my part, I have no idea what virtue is, whilst you, though perhaps you may have known before you came in touch with me, are now as good as ignorant of it also. But none the less I am willing to join you in examining it and inquiring into its nature.
>
> MENO Why, on what lines will you look, Socrates, for a thing of whose nature you know nothing at all? Pray, what sort of thing, amongst those that you know not, will you treat as the object of your search? Or even supposing, at the best, that you hit upon it, how will you know it is the thing that you did not know?

Plato's *Meno* thus poses a fundamental problem for research. Unless the quest, in terms of an object or objective, is known from the start, how can it be pursued? If the nature of the object in question is what the research claims to be exploring, that nature cannot be known in advance. Of course, that's the point of the research: to contribute to what's known. Does this suggest that research – even in its most mundane, unphilosophical form – recognizes from the outset that the object cannot be determined in advance? And that what is being pursued is not the 'very' nature of the 'sort of thing' being treated as the object of the search? Is research therefore necessarily dedicated to partial knowledge, partial understanding, partial revelation? What about the claims, then, of empirical research? Are they also subject to this 'law of partial revelation'?

Something – many things, in reality – must be known in advance for enquiry to begin or to be awakened. Research proposals are required to make clear statements about focus and method. They are also required to give some indication of the framework of ideas the research will take place within to reveal the object – or the nature of the object – in question. They must always betray a sense, at least, of what they are examining or re-examining, and they may well have a stronger inkling, a hypothesis perhaps, concerning the as-yet unrevealed truth of the thing.

The question concerning where a research enterprise begins is significant in terms of the known and the unknown, touching on the very provenance of knowledge. The field of epistemology – or theory of knowledge – is concerned not only with how we know what we know but also with the process of acquiring knowledge and with what knowledge *is*. And any research enterprise, surely, to be engaged on a quest for knowledge at all, must operate within some understanding – not necessarily very conscious – of what knowledge is. This itself is a metaphysical question of the most far-reaching kind, surely?

The state of questioning may be disturbing to our sense of what knowledge is. The element of uncertainty – of not knowing – here seems to play a crucial, founding role in knowledge. Slavoj Zizek has a useful neat angle on this fundamental uncertainty that attends the nature of knowledge. Zizek reminds us of Donald Rumsfeld's epistemological categories: 'the known knowns', 'the known unknowns' and the 'unknown unknowns'. Zizek points out that this catalogue misses out the most important element: the unknown knowns. The unknown knowns constitute all the background knowledge, understanding, ways of seeing and sense of purpose that we unconsciously bring to bear upon a research question or topic. This is no mere set of assumptions but, as we shall see, is the vast accumulated sense of things that comes with being-in-the-world in a very specific way. Our knowledge and our quest for new knowledge or for the expansion or refinement of knowledge can't be detached from this reservoir of 'unknown knowns'.

To begin at the beginning is never as easy as it first sounds. This is as true of research as it is of anything. So much will have taken place before the beginning: so much that will have made any beginning possible. What of this 'so much'? Is this not then the 'real' beginning? In any attempt to provide an account of the beginning, would not this pre-material that has had its hand in shaping the beginning itself be the beginning or the point at which the beginning must be accounted for? The trouble is that the problem of the beginning besets the pre-beginning as much as any other beginning. The beginning appears to be an ever-receding point that we can never reach.

More practically, perhaps, where do I begin to give an account of my research? Do I attempt to give an account of its genesis and its genealogy and its progress and development? How far should this account go and in what specific directions? We still refer to the beginning, and, to render an account of the impetus for our project, we still need to define a point of origin. What if this point of beginning was somehow a necessary fiction? Derrida writes of the disappearance or delay of the origin (Derrida, 1976). It is as though we must create or fictionalize a point of origin. Such questions concerning the point of origin or the place to begin are both tactical and philosophical. In fact, it is easy to see how research arises from conditions of practice in social contexts – where meanings and effects may contain elements of uncertainty.

A teacher practises in the classroom, say, and is deeply familiar with that environment. A question arises concerning the merits of a mode of teaching. How might such a research endeavour begin? Someone might suggest an 'action-research' project for a small, limited context. An empirical model might suffice to gauge the effectiveness of the mode of practice via a small range of measures. Results could be produced and judgement made. On the other hand, it is difficult to determine where the question either begins or comes to an end. There is an ontological dimension to this, surely. It might begin with questions concerning the context. What is a classroom? To understand the most basic element of context it might be necessary to undertake an historical analysis of the evolution of the classroom. Where to begin that, though? When – and how – does the classroom appear as an essential component of the school? Are we referring here to the emergence in the nineteenth century of the modern school? Are we referring here to the classroom as an apparatus of schooling in modernity? Several significant dimensions open. Lest we think these take us away from our original question concerning a specific mode of teaching, actually we might say that understanding the environment teaching occurs in – and this might include historical, sociological, topographic, linguistic dimensions among others – might be vital for understanding the work of the teacher and the possibilities of pedagogic interventions.

Many other questions arise from the original question: questions of pedagogic history, for instance, subject history, curriculum development and organizational, institutional histories. These touch on wider social issues including the rise of the schooled society, the changing configuration of public knowledge in modernity. None of these matters, surely, can be discounted as irrelevant in advance unless we claim that our investigation is to begin with a refusal to explore the ontological dimension. If so, we are left with much that is taken for granted and established. Are we not then saying that these dimensions lie beyond question in some sense? How can that be legitimate for research?

Of course, real research projects do limit their scope. They do so precisely because they choose, not necessarily consciously, to discount certain perspectives and to adopt inbuilt assumptions. A great deal of research dedicated in recent times to school improvement, often heavily funded, discounts questions concerning the fundamental nature of schooling in modernity and never questions the nature of the apparatus, the school, that is the context of its explorations. Its empirical urge to make decisive judgements about existing practices and to make recommendations for possible reforms mean that these things have to be put aside as though irrelevant (Gorard, 2013).

Of course, it would be possible to search for origins in an ever-receding mission. This quest cannot reach a decisive point of origin, but must settle, hopefully both cautiously and provisionally, on a point, duly set in quotation marks, as the modest point for a beginning. Already, even before we have specified anything, we are in the midst of interesting and surely important questions.

How do we begin then, having defined a possible point of beginning more or less arbitrary, given that we might have started elsewhere, if only a little earlie, later or differently positioned? The possibilities, in fact, are dizzyingly rich. Let's imagine a researcher in the social sciences who wants to provide an introduction, to give an account of the origin and genesis of the thesis in hand. Our researcher must introduce a topic, a theme or a subject that enfolds the object of the research. In addition, the researcher will need to consider the particular orientation towards both subject and object that the research entails and must also consider the researcher's orientation within the topic or theme. This process entails a series of significant decisions that must be made and owned.

Where to begin? A moment in time, a point in a history, an account of that history. A particular experience? Whose? And what defines the particularity of that experience and how does that particularity relate to a generality that renders the exploration of the experience of more than individual interest?

Where we are and the event of research

Beginning from where we are sounds rather like trite advice. But it may be more useful and more interesting. Heidegger's fundamental ontology seeks to address the biggest question of all – the 'question of questions'. In order to address this question, Heidegger begins to interrogate existence of the 'being' that ask the question. What, in the conditions this 'being' inhabits, might give rise to this question and what in addition might give this strange perhaps unanswerable question its force and import? The answer that Heidegger comes up with is far too lengthy to summarize here. It is, in fact, the substance of the voluminous *Being and Time*. It was this book that marked in twentieth-century Western philosophy a 'return' to or at least the opening up of seriously ontological questions. In it Heidegger never really got round to addressing the question of questions itself, but rather dwelt on giving an account of the important dimensions of the questioner that might illuminate the import of the question. And this model might serve here as one way of looking at some of the kinds of issues that can be addressed in the process of giving an account of one's beginning even where that beginning might be indeterminate and elusive of definition. What factors are involved in the initiation of a project? This question might in fact apply to any project – large or small.

What Heidegger's model offers is a way of giving an account of the situation, in a broad and complex sense, of the 'being' – or researcher – who puts the question. Borrowing Heidegger's terminology, we might begin to define the situation of the researcher in terms of being positioned in a 'world' of practice. This world is likely to be more or less organized with a specific belief system, harbouring an orientation to meaning and way of doing things. It will have its own repertoire of things that it sustains. It will have its own language practices; it will distribute identities in a more or less systematic way. It will provide a framework of meaning for the practices it sustains. It will, in Foucault's surprising formulation, 'produce the objects of which it speaks' (Foucault, 1977b). Being within that domain of practice offers specific ways of being, both constraining and affording. That's why it makes sense to refer to such domains as 'worlds' as they constitute spaces for being in particular ways that make, understand and act upon things in their own specific fashion.

At the same time, the 'being' of the practitioner within that world is not entirely exhausted by its limits. The researcher comes with their own specific 'thrown' identity. We carry forward the accidental, contingent factors of our being that contribute to shaping how we are in whatever worlds we may appear in. Our substance is predicated on features of our 'thrownness'. These features include the time and place we come into the world, in the sense of historical era, culture, language, dominant world picture and so on. Our disposition and attitude, our very comportment is formed and fashioned by these conditions in encounter with the world. We inherit much. In language we inherit a symbolic order. The acquisition of language, according to Lacan, for instance, is a momentous transformation of our selves (Lacan,1997, 2006). It is what primarily places us within a specific symbolic order that carries with it the very categories available to us to make sense of the world.

Within a 'world' – or domain of practice – certain modes of sense-making will prevail, offering a range of options of ways of being. An important dimension of 'becoming' – in the sense of taking on a possible identity ascribed by the field of practice – is the process of becoming 'inward' with the values and ways of being afforded by our world. This inwardness is predicated on both belonging and attachment. It signifies an automatic, unconscious element of attachment. In *Being and Time*, Heidegger gives an account of the special meaning of 'care' in human existence, the kind of 'care' that arises from our belonging and attachment. Care signifies a kind of commitment, something essential about how we conduct our everyday lives in relation to our 'world'. We are caught up in the things and concerns of our world. The idea of care indicates how for 'dasein' – or the subject that experiences things – being-in-the-world is characterized by an immersion that carries with it a strong charge of interest. We are not neutral to our context. We are positioned within it in a motivated way.

This causes some problems for the idea of scientific approach to knowledge that must derive from our concern for our world and that must arise within the complex network of attachments that we forge – to things, people, ideas, ways of thinking, understanding and knowing. Enlightenment philosophers had sought to rationalize knowledge – to strip it back to an essential structure. Descartes used extreme doubt as a starting point. Kant sought to tease out the relation between understanding things-in-themselves and our perceptions of them. While they came up with interesting ways of thinking about knowledge, they forgot, it seems, that knowledge rises in specific contexts of living, that it is specifically situated, that it is saturated with 'care' and anxiety and that it often relates to a desire to sustain a 'world'. But we do not have to see this being positioned, caring and investing in the world of practice we belong to – or seek to belong to – as a negative drag on our potential for neutrality or disinterested objectivity. It connects rather to something fundamental in our very being.

Heidegger gave special attention to the mood of anxiety (fundamental mood or 'Grundstimmung') as the driving force of all forms of 'care', although for Nietzsche it was a more positive force that might impel one's commitment especially in relation to the field of knowledge. In both cases, knowledge could only be driven by investment, by the intensity of attachment and commitment. To be in the throes of some epistemological fatal attraction – or 'amor fati' in Nietzsche's terms – was precisely the condition required for any philosophy or knowledge worthy of the name.

Heidegger's anxiety is an essential underlying condition. It implies a break with everyday concerns or at least engenders a perspective on them. Anxiety positively is linked to how Heidegger considers the possibility of freedom. Anxiety is to be distinguished from fear, which may be fear of some*thing*. Anxiety is more generalized: ultimately about the possibility of nothing. Anxiety is the expression of a realization of the necessity of death. Anxiety acts as driving force, something to work against through absorption in our everyday concerns. We inhabit a world that is meaningful in terms of its everyday practices, and in this guise the world is homely ('heimlich'). Anxiety disturbs this equilibrium, threatening to render the everyday strange and possibly meaningless. Anxiety is the experience of being alone with one's finitude; separated, albeit temporarily, from the cares of the homely world. As this anxiety instigates a kind of separation from the everyday self, thus we may glimpse the possibility of freedom, freedom from the ties and limitations of the everyday. In this kind of break with everyday consciousness, thinking may intrude as instigative of questioning. This potential break with the everyday through the common experience of anxiety holds out the possibility for all of us to hold things in question. And for Heidegger, the question is the piety of thought. Alain Badiou, the contemporary French thinker, writes about the break with everyday consciousness as the 'event' – as the possibility of a transformative experience, like revolution or falling in love, whereby our sense of ourselves, our world and our commitments may be challenged and changed. One of the points of beginning that we might pursue as researchers is the question on the issue of our own orientation to the 'event' that defines our mode of being in the world that we seek to research.

Philosophy as a research resource

From a Heideggerian perspective, there is no possible elimination or avoidance of metaphysics. Many research manuals and educational research advocates have implied that the metaphysical dimension can be ignored or reduced in favour of a practical modality. This advocates research that must leave its basic premises untouched, that must assume the cares it sets out with are proper to its endeavour and treat the 'objects of which it speaks' as determinate and given.

The pre-Socratic philosopher Parmenides, one of the first identified formal thinkers in the European tradition, offers the idea that being itself must be one while our sense of things tends to posit differences between a multitude of entities. For Parmenides, the idea that all things are one is logically irrefutable – and indeed it is hard to argue against that position. The truth of things, according to this position, it would seem, is at odds with our immediate perception and with the common-sense 'metaphysics' that informs our everyday intercourse with the world. Parmenides illustrates that, even at its earliest, European thinking has been concerned to define the very nature of things and has been 'metaphysical' or ontotheological.

The concern with the fundamental nature of things continues in modern and contemporary thinking. Earlier philosophers had sought to determine the nature of the substance of this stuff of being, just as, in a different but startlingly related way, contemporary 'philosophers' of matter attempt to define the 'nature' of nature (reality) by determining the most fundamental materials of the universe, the so-called building blocks of reality. Quantum physicists – who may not identify themselves as philosophers, but who are, to a very significant degree, thinkers and metaphysicians, whatever else they are – have recently celebrated the triumph of the confirmation of the existence of the Higgs boson, the so-called God particle that confirms the theory that this special entity is what gives matter mass, and its revelation as a physically existing entity confirms a strongly held theory. What's being sought here, it seems, is not so different from what the pre-Socratics sought when they determined the essence of the substance of ıd as water or as compressed air. The desire to find a point of origin or erlying simplicity in the nature of things, paradoxically, has given rise to increasingly complicated accounts of the fundamental nature of physical reality, often with surprising and anti-common-sense findings, as is famously the case with quantum mechanics.

The example of Kant and the nature of research

Some of the trouble – useful trouble, actually – with questions concerning knowledge are seriously articulated in the texts attached to the name of Immanuel Kant. Kant's writings provide one of the most sophisticated accounts of the relations between the given faculty of understanding and knowledge.

Kant's thinking offers an important entry into thinking concerning the possibility of providing a 'realist' account of how things stand with the world. The intricacies of his phenomenology of knowledge still provide an incitement to rethink the foundations of current conceptions of science. Why go to Kant, though, for such an incitement? Not because Kant is uniquely a provocation and certainly not because Kant is an authority. Rather because Kant's writings are representative. He was both influenced and influential in strong currents of thought that remain live in the European inheritance. The 'phenomenon'/ 'noumenon' distinction that Kant works with and teases out at great length – the distinction between the-thing-as-we-perceive-it and the-thing-in-itself – is not yet an exhausted distinction. It recurs in various guises and provides a point of reference for both thinking and rethinking. This remains tricky ground. The question of the essence of 'things' has been beset by a range of perspectives in the history of Western philosophy. No resolution or coming to rest of this question concerning the nature of things or the question of what makes things what they 'are' has been arrived at. Nor has it been finally established whether it makes sense to speak or write of there being things that *are* in the simple and direct sense we habitually use. Philosophers, for instance in the contemporary scene, especially the so-called 'critical realists', argue intricately for the resolution of questions concerning the nature of the object, including the question of whether there is a 'nature' to or in the object (Harman, 2016; Meillasoux, 2009).

There are three main dimensions of Kant's work, all leading towards continuing concerns of Western philosophy. One is morality, asking about the basis for moral agency. Another is human freedom and its relations with social being. The other concerns the foundations of knowledge: asking about the conditions knowledge exists within. These areas remain relevant to contemporary collective life in general and to specific contexts of practice. It's not so much that Kant determines the future lines of development for Western philosophy to pursue such questions or issues. It's more that Kant comes to stand as the figure that philosophy both draws on and goes beyond. No doubt as a serious reader of philosophy works their way through the Western tradition, there will be some texts, some figures that are more resonant that others, but this process is hardly ever simply a matter of simply rejecting one wholesale while accepting another as authoritative. The business of doing philosophy, it seems, is not eschatological: it does not work to a determinate end. The interminable nature of reading and thinking is recognized in deconstruction as advocated and practised by Derrida (rather than the loosely thought through casual use of the term).

A note on method

The era of modern science is often represented as finding its first major coherent theoretical expression in Francis Bacon's *Novum Organon*. This polemical text, it's sometimes claimed, clinches a liberating and enabling way of thinking, articulating a new science, inaugurating a new relation between the human species and its world. *Novum Organon* promised liberation from the dominance of knowledge by the two key forms of authority of the middle ages: Aristotelean thinking and biblical revelation. The book's original title page presented the image of a galleon passing beyond the Pillars of Hercules, beyond the familiar waters of the Mediterranean into the uncharted Atlantic Ocean, opening a new world for exploration. According to the image, this breakout work heralds new possibilities for knowledge. Here the new emphasis on experimental research promises to offer a more certain grip on 'Nature'. This project set itself the task to rethink experience in combination with understanding within an ethic of testing to formulate 'a new and certain pathway from the perceptions of the senses themselves to the mind'.

Bacon's proclamations are aphoristic: they take the form of pithy, decisive statements of the truth of knowledge while claiming also to herald the true path to knowledge. Their confidence is appropriate for the 'new science' that was to inaugurate the era of scientific achievement still in progress. The stagnation of thought and practice that Bacon attributed to misguided reliance on unquestioned authorities and a limited logic that activated them was over. A new era of discovery, as the title page indicated, had arrived. Method, above all, was to supplant reliance on syllogism and become 'the pathway to truth'. The new form of knowledge, especially knowledge of the physical world, was to transform collective being and consciousness to an unprecedented extent, a dramatic change in the relations between human beings and their world. The new era of thought depended on a certain demystification. Self-generating human knowledge had no bounds. Its progress would be unlimited. The species would take possession of its world within this new ethic of knowledge.

The transformations new science produced continue to inform our world view enabling different ways of being in the world. Within a few hundred years, radically new and powerful forms of knowledge thrived. Contemporary commentators on globalization point to the huge changes in communications systems, for instance. In quite recent times, HDTV, satellite communications, fibre-optic cabling, digitalization and the exponential development of computer processing power followed from the scientific knowledge that informed the industrial revolution and the development of the modern world with its huge advances in fundamental knowledge in a staggering array of fields including biology, chemistry, physics and cosmology (Moreton, 2013). Characterized by speed of communication, the capacity to image the world in unprecedented detail and the high-speed movement of information of exceptionally high-quality enhanced strongly established scientific theories that had already changed fundamental aspects of the world: evolution, relativity, genetics. All bear witness to the massive transformative power of scientific knowledge, as well as the capacity to rethink the order of things in a more generalized way – producing new versions of world history, of the history of the cosmos, of the make-up of fundamental substance. The very laws of nature seem to have unfolded to the highly trained, rigorously disciplined gaze of science.

We might identify one significant element of our present condition – including the general condition of human understanding – as the zeitgeist that still, 400 years after Bacon, expresses faith in science. There are those who, like Sir Paul Nurse, the former president of the Royal Society, still claim that science is on the verge of solving the major problems that beset the world. For most, though, that faith, I think, is no longer unambiguous, if it ever was. Science, in alliance with machine technology, has wrought changes that, although inordinately powerful, have not been unambiguously good. A number of positions have challenged the claims of modernity to represent the triumph of knowledge and reason. Heidegger's 1950s essay 'The Question Concerning Technology' reveals the danger in the instrumental ethic that has accompanied a vision of the world and its inhabitants as potential resource. Weber's earlier account of 'instrumental rationality' served as a mostly unheeded warning to the dangers of bureaucratic systems detached from purposes and from fundamental thinking about purposes and meaning. Zygmunt Bauman's more recent accounts of modernity have shown how modern and contemporary conditions, as the products of a certain 'weltenschauung' and 'gemeinschaft', can give rise to appalling consequences as well as to a certain spiritual restlessness and radical uncertainty of being. Foucault's 'great transformation' and Deleuze's 'societies of control' articulate problems concerning human freedom that arise from modernity's forms of social organization.

What we might call the scientific revolution was also accompanied by a new consciousness of human being, including the emergence of scientific knowledge concerning the species, accompanied by attempts to get at the heart of species being. Pope had declared that 'the proper study of mankind is man' and Kant had sought to establish the basis for human morality and to define the very nature of enlightenment. Darker rumblings attended the nineteenth century's assertions that humans had evolved from humbler and decidedly animal origins. Nietzsche had berated the history of Western thought and had decried the platonic inheritance, while Freud had demonstrated that our conscious 'rational' selves were underpinned by a darker substratum of residual energies and desires that were too disturbing to own up to. The twentieth century demonstrated the provenance of dark forces in two cataclysmic – and for many catastrophic – world wars, fuelled and empowered by 'technological enframing' and finally revealing new depths of collective depravity, fuelled ironically by visions of perfectibility. All this occurred while the unimaginable vastness of the cosmos was gradually becoming evident – and the place of the human species within it was becoming more uncertain, more questionable, more contingent and more fragile.

An analyst looking at contemporary social science practices might be struck by the extent that research is dominated by a paradigm that privileges (1) a form of knowledge (2) a genre of representation that both carry strong traces of the inheritance of modernist faith in knowledge as essentially a means towards the ends of rational improvement. This ethic is hard to shake off but is not without serious problems, some of them being expressive of the misplaced faith of modernity that 'science' could itself, without the encumbrance of metaphysics, or philosophy, or thinking, provide answers to the huge problems that modernity had set itself. We perhaps now inhabit a world where there is less certainty about 'master narratives' and where, in spite of the residual traces of such thinking, a radical uncertainty confronts us, as Bauman dramatically tells us Bauman, 2000). This condition is ambiguous. While it may offer opportunities for rethinking collective being, it also suggests that the existing dominant paradigms (the present ethic of impact, for instance) for the production of knowledge and the meaning of research are exhausted. What it certainly signifies to me is that faith in modernist projects of renewal, reform and redemption that have beset educational research needs to be seriously reconsidered.

Method, after Bacon, promised to be the assurance that those troubling features of research – validity, reliability, truth – could be tamed and managed out of existence or at least to the point where they no longer represented a threat to the supremacy of the new knowledge and its increasingly powerful institutions. If we look at the research handbooks, that proliferating genre, we see that they are full of admonitions and procedures to address the question of validity. Each researcher, it seems, must face the problem or the question of what guarantees a claim to have a serious purchase on truth. Each project must lay bare its methodological soul and articulate the precise method that enables it to claim that it belongs properly to the special order of technological knowledge sanctioned by the powerful, often world-dominating institutions that decree what is in and what is out, whose work legitimately belongs. Method has been reduced to techniques for the production of data, data in turn coming to be seen as the decisive fulcrum for the revelation of new knowledge. Thinking is never represented as method in these accounts that separate method from design and design from the basic phenomenology of research relations that are never even considered as essential to the research process.

Thinking as method confronts what has become a limiting law of genre, to borrow Derrida's phrase. My contention is that thinking has the power to liberate the researcher from the spectral constraints of a genre that has gained force only through traditional authority. Just as Bacon had seen the possibility of going against and beyond established authority, breaking with the custom and practice represented as the necessary order of things by the research manuals may be enabling for modes of research that are more closely allied with the rich resources of thinking. The archons, those who guard academic processes and decree what is legitimate, stand for the established traditions and investments that, in the case of educational research, have not served the enterprise so well. The present condition of education research is indicative of tendencies in the contemporary university in the field of the social sciences in general. The rite de passage represented by the doctoral research thesis is seen as an essential precursor to becoming a qualified, authorized researcher – and is dominated still by the restricted genre promoted by the research handbooks.

Throw away the handbooks

Research handbooks organize the research thesis into component parts that have attained the status of essential elements: defining your issue, formulating your questions, literature review, method, methodology, ethics, analysis and conclusion (Thomas, 2013). While this approach provides a ready-to-hand structure, it proposes a restricted view of the research process.

This book is predicated on the idea that theory – or more properly, as I will hope to both explain and demonstrate, theorizing or 'thinking' – is an essential component of the practice of research. From this basic premise, it follows that the commonly held distinction between empirical and theoretical dimensions of research is not only incorrect but also limiting for the researcher. This book aims to show how resources for thinking that arise from modern and contemporary philosophy and theory enhance research. Thinking can help to avoid the conventional approach with its limited purchase on the social. Thinking can refine, extend and strengthen our understanding of the world in crucial ways. Rather than seeing theory or thinking or metaphysics of philosophy as an add-on to the essential business, directed towards practical improvement, this book will propose that theory, philosophy, metaphysics, thinking can be, productively, usefully, seen as essential elements in the process of expressing what it is that is going in any research project.

Theory is pragmatic. Most research handbooks reinforce the separation between theory and the practice. This difference is clinched in the special status accorded to 'method' touched on above – in the common assumption that method is a neutral technical (or 'craft') means to an objective end. Thinking is method and is more than a means to an end. If thinking is an ever-present component of research – explicitly aware of its own movements and grounds – it is demonstrative of the continuity between itself and its object, the subject who engages and the task of revelation that the research sets itself.

For many, research in social science is practically directed towards the improvement of the world. This book will not insist that research, to be valid, must be of practical significance – in any immediate sense. It will privilege thinking as an end in itself, as it were, although an end that can have unforeseen circumstances. This book argues against the common and powerful idea that the future both can and should be programmed and will argue that instrumental rationality has proven to be a double-edged stratagem at best. At worst, the ethic of improvement has led to some very negative consequences, especially in the field of education.

This book opens the possibility for any research project, however apparently limited in scope and focus, to engage with the 'metaphysical' dimension, the dimension of thinking that is always there whether consciously and explicitly or not. One significant point of beginning is represented as the experience of the researcher, not as a touchy-feely, sentimental or confessional mode of engagement; but as a necessary prelude to locating the focus of study in its proper context and in its inescapable relations with a given point or consciousness. This element of addressing one's own subjectivity I sometimes refer to as objectification of the subjective. It means that one comes to understand oneself as a researcher belonging to a particular world or mode of practice. That world, that mode, that belonging can be articulated, re-examined. It is a way of guaranteeing an important kind of originality, the originality that arises from engaging with the specificity of one's own historical being within an order or knowledge and framework of ideas that belongs not to oneself but to one's time and one's world. In drawing on your own experience as a researcher, you reframe it and understand it differently: this is a transformation of the self at the level of knowledge. This is an important move in the deconstruction of the false division between the objective and the subjective. That unthought division obfuscates much contemporary research thinking – often advocated by the handbooks – that asks for a position to be taken or that sees the world of knowledge in terms of the familiar binaries of research manuals: objective/subjective, quantitative/qualitative; positivist/interpretivist, science/social science and so on.

This book aims to approach what often appear to be complex ideas as resources rather than as barriers to understanding. Ideas, it proposes, are to be engaged with in the unfolding of a project and not simply in an introductory section, to be lightly touched on and then gone beyond to get to the real, empirical work. The approach and the ideas suggested here draw upon the very resources that enable us to renew our thinking potential. This is a function of addressing in an informed way the important differences and equally important connections between those big terms: metaphysics, theory, philosophy and thinking. The premise that the approach is based on claims that understanding aspects of philosophy in our time can help us also to understand our own thinking and our own potential for rethinking – and that is a significant aim, after all, of research. Contemporary thinking is rich with potential in the wake of far-reaching, revitalizing contributions (referred to in Chapter 7) that have stirred up thinking into new vitality.

Noam Chomsky's account of what it was that Galileo did addresses the thinking dimension of research. Galileo did not identify a new object to examine. His approach was to what was already known and familiar. He began to ask questions, essentially ontological questions, to interrogate assumptions, so that the phenomenon itself could no longer be explained only by received wisdom. It is this attitude that offers the promise of opening onto perspectives that are radically critical, that seek to renew thinking by thinking again and that seeks to redefine our sense of things, to regenerate knowledge. Any project that begins, seriously, to confront the ontological question must in one way or another give rise to thinking Any project that gives space and brings thinking resources to bear on this fundamental interrogative move must revisit, review and challenge received wisdom and common-sense perception. This kind of critical approach contrasts with what currently passes for 'critical educational studies' a field of research that (necessarily) neglects to interrogate its favoured understanding of what schooling is and what is its potential to be otherwise in order to retain its salvationist ethic. And, of course, the approach advocated here, as will be indicated, is problematic for a research that wants to simply offer evidence for the school improvement agenda or that wants to guarantee that it meets the impact factor criteria of university research departments, a problem that particularly attends those areas of research practice that see themselves as tied to a specific domain of social practice – education, being the prime example perhaps.

Chapter 1

Dimensions of Philosophy

Everyone is a philosopher

That research is necessarily philosophical may not seem obvious. Any research opens philosophical possibilities. The fact that much research disregards philosophical promptings reveals contemporary assumptions about 'real knowledge' and its sources. The role of thinking is essential in research, of whatever kind. It is particularly significant in terms of questions of truth, validity and rigour that are sometimes thought to belong to the dimension of 'method'. I want to demonstrate that thinking and method are not separate components of a process that can be broken down clearly into staged segments, as research manuals suggest.

This approach may complicate things, initially, in the name of a certain rigour of thinking; it will also offer specific ways of being productive. Thinking is not so easy. The history of philosophy and the resources of metaphysics fortunately offer an enormous resource bank for enabling thinking, often about those things that we automatically take for granted. Our deep-seated understanding of things is harder for us to access than surface beliefs we hold consciously (Heidegger, 1962; Wittgenstein, 1968). And yet, as Antonio Gramsci put it:

> Everyone is a philosopher, though in his [*sic*] own way and unconsciously, since even in the slightest manifestation of any intellectual activity whatever, in 'language', there is contained a specific conception of the world, one then moves on to the second level, which is that of awareness and criticism. (Gramsci, 1991, 323–324)

Our certainties are the very elements of our knowledge that we may know least about, in fact. It is the things that we don't call into question that most organize our thinking and influence our very seeing and understanding of the world.

When we refer to 'our world', we should include in that apparently easy phrase an understanding of our thinking about that world and its 'nature'. Kant was at great pains to demonstrate that we don't simply see things that are in front of our eyes. The most familiar objects and entities that populate our knowledge and our understanding are not present to view in any simple, direct way.

We rarely come face to face with our own understanding of things. More usually, we come to an understanding of our understanding through a painstaking process of reconstruction, drawing inferences from the bits and pieces of knowledge that we have and the ideas that we express. We must postulate something separate from our knowledge and ideas that we might call 'understanding' if we want to talk in Kantian terms. On that view, our perception and understanding are more than contingently related. We can't separate one from the other. This is an epistemological law of contamination. Our most rigorous attempts to see things dispassionately are already organized by forces framing our world view. Similarly, our perception/understanding and the things we perceive are not the same. This epistemological law of difference is at the heart of Kant's critical philosophy (Kant, 2003).

The implications of this insight for research are enormous. The questions that arise by simply asking how we perceive or know things seem very basic. They are fundamental, of course. At the same time, they are both complex and interesting. They provide the occasion for extended engagement. They are not questions that only arise in special contexts, either – in philosophy classrooms, for example. They are questions that have far-reaching practical implications. How we determine the nature of things, as Heidegger came to insist, determines the destiny of the world (Heidegger, 1962). Questions concerning 'Being' (for that is what they are in effect) have far-reaching import for knowledge and research. When we ask what something is, we open out possibilities for exploration. We cease to hold the thing in a taken-for-granted understanding. Such identity questions force us to reconsider the relations between thinking and knowledge production, an important relation if ever there was one in research practice. After all, doesn't research always aim, in some rigorous way, to engage with the *nature* of things, or at least with the nature of some specific *thing*? Considering the very nature of anything necessarily implicates intensive interrogation and complexity, surely? And that word 'nature' evokes significant complexities for developing our thinking, as the philosophical stance known as 'deconstruction' demonstrates (Derrida, 1978). Already the possibilities for expansive thinking have been released.

Thinking philosophically isn't just a matter of pausing and ruminating. The kind of thinking that merely reflects on things without recourse to any other stimulus makes it hard to get beyond the confines of our own already established, given understanding of the nature of things. Common-sense reflection has limitations, especially in research where we are honour-bound to seek the new, although in educational research common sense has come to enjoy a fashionable status. Reflection will struggle to see or understand things anew without some nudge or prompting from elsewhere. We can't rely on our already-developed and solidified understanding of things to make a significant shift in knowledge.

This is a major issue in educational research. Consider the fact that a great deal of educational research simply evades or forecloses ontological questions concerning the very essence of its object, education. So much educational research takes for granted what education *is*, in spite of a myriad of reasons to put this very 'thing' into question and to wonder, perhaps in both senses of the word, what education has become in our world. Education is an enormous question. What's more, research in the name of 'school improvement', and research done in the name of 'critical education studies', has never bothered to ask itself What is a school? What is this strikingly modern institution? Education studies has hardly ever asked the vital question concerning the form of the school that we confront in our researches as educationalist in the modern and contemporary era, that deeply embedded and ubiquitous institution that is almost always assumed to be the bearer of positive social processes or civilizing work (Peim, 2013a). Not to put this extensive and highly specific, carefully historically crafted apparatus into question seems to me, from the point of view of anyone aspiring to a serious understanding of what education is, to be a grave omission.

The apparent urgency and immediacy of the assumed task – improvement, say – is felt to sweep such questions aside in the name of practical utility. Yet surely, the practical value of research that does not yet understand the essence or the historical ontology of the very institution it seeks to improve must surely be doubted. Such doubt is borne out by the annual repetitions of the same questions: how to improve performance, how to enhance the puissance of the institution, how to redistribute educational success more justly. These apparently urgent questions are predicated themselves on premises that are, to say the least, dubious. The assumed benefits to the social order of schooling are by no means given, in spite of what common sense might suggest and in spite of the dominant understanding of education studies that claim to be based in rigorous research techniques (Gorard, 2002).

If research begins with what is not known, as surely it must if it is to be any kind of genuine enquiry, we must allow ourselves to become open to new way of apprehending what we are interested in. The problem is that new ways of understanding, grasping or apprehending, even simply new ways of seeing, are not easy to access. Our habitual ways of seeing are habitual for good reason. We already live within a particular horizon of understanding. Our ways of knowing things are already caught up in a systematic, strongly established network of ideas and oppositions. Our thinking tends to be habituated to particular ways of seeing things. This is the point that Gramsci makes when he declares quite seriously and sensibly that everyone is a philosopher (Gramsci, 1991). Everyone has ideas about the world. Everyone has ideas that constitute a 'metaphysics', a way of understanding the nature of things. We owe to twentieth-century philosophy's obsession with language the insight that everyday language is itself a kind of metaphysics. To state that something is the case is not simply to state that something is the case. It is in effect also to express an epistemological stance, inevitably with ontological undertones.

For the researcher standing on the precipice of a research project's beginning, the metaphysics of the thing under enquiry opens urgent questions: how to understand that familiar thing anew; how to articulate one's own relation to the thing; how to produce a systematic way of knowing that thing and its context in a new but systematic way; what sensitivities might need to be taken into consideration; and the question of what knotty, thorny problems might arise in the process.

While a fully formulated, carefully crafted research question might not be easy to produce, a series of important questions arise almost automatically when fundamental dimensions of philosophy are brought into play. A more or less systematic approach is possible deploying what I have identified as six dimensions of philosophy for research. These identify specific ways of thinking that allow the researcher, of whatever object in whatever context, to pose questions and to identify essential issues. These dimensions are offered here as possible starting points for beginning a process of research thinking. Thinking is always enhanced by the researcher's reading, but that reading can't be easily contained and defined to what is proper to an object. Research reading can't be reduced to the status of what the research manuals refer to as a 'literature review' (a misleading, although strongly established, idea) – as if all the literature concerned with a research endeavour could be gathered together and sifted. That model denies the role of thinking. The process implicit in what follows in this chapter is more creative and more open. It requires significant acts of decision-making that tax the researcher's will but that – because of the nature of decision-making – provide productive occasions for articulating the research project's 'metaphysic' and provoke engagement with the research project's fundamental questions.

Ontology (being) 'nature'/essence

Perhaps the first dimension the researcher may approach and will certainly already have pondered, albeit unconsciously, perhaps, is the very nature of the thing that the research project brings into scrutiny. It is perhaps surprising the extent that the 'What is ...?' type of question can engender thought and can demand careful exploration. At the same time, it has to be said that this 'What is ...?' dimension is among the most seriously neglected in social science research. In the field of education research frequently bypasses this question. The urgent need for improvement or for redemption, so the logic seems to go, requires practical engagement with what is currently there. Findings must be generated urgently to satiate the demand for impact. In educational research – as with other professional and practical fields – impact is often deemed to be the principal location of meaning. The effect of this is to short-circuit the research process so that the ontological dimension gets suppressed, forgotten, unrealized. In fact, impact is a highly questionable idea that threatens to distort social science research with current priorities.

The significance of ontology, or of the ontological dimension, resides in its fundamental nature. Classically, ontology is first philosophy. In other words, it belongs to what must be considered first in philosophical engagements. Sometimes ontological questions can appear banal or absurd. What is a table? The question seems irrelevant and to belong to a parody of what philosophy is. To ask this kind of question seems to suggest a merely indulgent desire to problematize what doesn't need to be scrutinized. After all, its blindingly obvious, isn't it, what a table is?

The apparent absurdity of the 'What is ...' question belongs to the apparently mundane nature of the object in question. If we know what something is, surely asking such a question serves no useful purpose. Mostly, we live in the world without troubling the objects that we encounter with questions about their identity or their provenance. Heidegger refers to this mode of engagement in terms of things being ready-to-hand (Heidegger, 1962). We don't ask what a table is very often because most of the time we are using it, putting things on it, writing on it, manoeuvring round it, cleaning it, polishing it. It is familiar and it is obvious what it is. But there are times when things puzzle or bemuse us. Sometimes these are relatively trivial things, like tables, but sometimes they are more important, less obvious and sometimes powerfully complex things that we don't fully grasp, although they are familiar features of our everyday world and experience. If we think of some of the complex objects that inhabit the world of education, their identity is not necessarily given. Although a great deal of educational research does treat such objects as though their ontological status can be taken for granted, occasionally groundbreaking work can be achieved by going back to ontological basics and asking fundamental questions about fundamental objects. In my own experience, everyday complex components of education – the classroom, the school, for example – will bear the kind of scrutiny that ontological interrogation will offer (Peim, 2001). The meaning and identity of these things, after all, cannot be said to have finally been settled, in spite of common-sense impulses to think the contrary. This openness in the identity of things is a very common property of key entities addressed by social science research.

A good and far-reaching example of the possibilities that ontological interrogation may afford is available in Heidegger's later essay 'The Question Concerning Technology'. In this still-influential 1954 paper, Heidegger, as the title suggests, sought to comment on the role of technology in modernity. The interrogation includes an analysis of the meaning of technology. So, the central concept at stake in the paper, the object of its concern, is revealed by argument – and with reference to some tactically selected reading. Much of the paper in fact is designed to reveal a way of thinking that defines what technology is in a new, startling, innovative but quite convincing way. In seeking to explore what the essence of technology *is*, Heidegger is able to advance an argument that makes significant distinctions between modes of technology, thus providing fresh ways of thinking about what is an already deeply familiar entity. We soon find, following Heidegger again, that our basic common-sense understanding of what things are, ways of thinking that are embedded often more in practices than in conscious or explicit thinking, are laden with assumptions, often assumptions that are roughly 'knotted into a system'. We could claim quite plausibly in relation to this semi-articulated system that it constitutes some of our most fundamental beliefs about the world and about the nature of things, things that might include tables and technology. We tend to develop a more or less systematic way of understanding the nature of things based on culture and education. Most of the time, the system and the way it shapes our understanding of the nature of things operates at an unconscious level: it tends to work in terms of 'unknown knowns' to borrow Zizek's take on Donald Rumsfeld's famous epistemology again. In the realm of the unknown knowns, we are most likely to be in the grip of what Heidegger sometimes referred to as ontotheology: our beliefs about the nature of things having a theological cast.

Phenomenology (things) perception/experience

Actually determining the nature of what something – or some thing – *is* turns out to be more difficult than at first it may appear. This is true even of tables but is much more the case with complex entities. It touches on some quite fundamental – interesting and productive – realizations about knowledge, what it is and how research relates to it. One of the most famous cases of an explicit interest in our relation to the nature of things arises in late nineteenth-century philosophy in the guise of phenomenology (Moran, 2000). Phenomenology is essentially concerned with the way that we apprehend things, with the relations involved in an articulation of how we stand relative to things. Phenomenology returns to basic questions of Western philosophy concerning the difference between 'the-thing-in- itself' ('noumenon') and our understanding or knowledge of the thing ('phenomenon'). It has a bearing on classic Cartesian questions of certainty and the grand quest of epistemology for grounding real knowledge. Phenomenology is often surprisingly foreclosed in texts on social science research and the so-called essential texts in educational research. Addressing the phenomenological dimension provides clearly defined lines of development that can ensure that research is both rigorous in relation to questions of history and context but that also avoid the pitfalls of simply offering a naively positioned view without addressing the matter of position. Ultimately, the absence of a phenomenological dimension suggests that research knowledge must be unaware of its relation to the conditions that shape it.

In the twentieth century, phenomenology came to signify a specific project associated with a group of philosophers. Its most famous exponent was Edmund Husserl, although significant others were involved, whose name is forever linked with 'phenomenology' as though phenomenology were something that he invented (Husserl, 1970, 1973). But phenomenology has a deeper history and can be better understood in terms of a concern with how phenomena appear to consciousness, a concern with the relations between 'subjects' – knowers – and objects – knowns – and a concern with the thinking arising from identifying the basic components and relationships involved in our encounters with the stuff of the world. Heidegger, Husserl's student, remained concerned with phenomenology, albeit from an essentially ontological point of view. For Heidegger, following Husserl, but going beyond the scope of Husserl's thinking, phenomenology inevitably led into ontology that would provide an account of the most fundamental conditions of possibility for knowledge (Heidegger, 1962).

Recent concern with what has come to be known as 'the Higgs boson' would provide an interesting, multifaceted example of a phenomenological case study with ontological implications. To ask bluntly what it is would probably perplex even the most sophisticated physicist. We might rather need to go into the history of quantum mechanics, the emerging catalogue of fundamental particles, the story of Higgs's speculative claim and the subsequent history of particle physics, leading to the construction of the Large Hadron Collider. This would require entering the world of modern physics, understanding its arcane way of looking at the world and engaging with some of the positions within it.

Perhaps to really know what 'the Higgs boson' is we would have to become a 'subject' of the world of modern physics in a fuller sense. Once in and of that world, our vista of understanding would be framed by its established horizons. We would be caught up in its logic, attuned to its general way of thinking. The Higgs bosun would be known to us in this way – and not in some other possible way (as might be illustrated by innumerable Higgs bosun jokes). This example illustrates some of the possible complexity – and attendant expansions – that a phenomenological approach can open.

As a way of thinking concerned with coming to an understanding of and providing a descriptive language for basic relations between subjects and objects and their mutual world, phenomenology can be seen as an inevitable part of a philosophical turn. Phenomenology follows an essentially enlightenment concern with defining both limits and possibilities of human knowledge. This concern goes back to Kant's negotiation of the differences between empiricism and idealism, where empiricism wants to privilege the immediate presence and reality of the object and where idealism wants to insist on the supervention of the mind as prime source of perception, understanding and knowledge. Phenomenology leads into Maurice Merleau-Ponty's concern to articulate the intricacies of perception: as a powerful reminder that there is more to seeing than meets the eye (Merleau-Ponty, 2002). In its desire to both interrogate and articulate our relation to 'things-in-themselves', philosophy also takes an anthropological turn, seeking to understand the various conditions – historical, social, cultural – framing our world, our knowledge.

You don't have to be Immanuel Kant to engage in a productive phenomenology of subject–object relations in some field of research or in relation to a research project that knows what it is it is interested in but wants to carefully elaborate, construct, explore and reconstruct its approach to that object. For the researcher in social science, a basic phenomenology can begin to elaborate fundamental relations: a subject (researcher) in relation to its object (topic/issue). A basic phenomenology can begin by giving an account of the relations between constituent components of the setting of a project.

In the beginning, a subject, let's say a researcher, confronts an object. This is the most basic research situation: the object 'stands' before the subject. The subject knows the object, but has determined to seek to know it, or an aspect of it, differently. This might be a researcher standing before an element of education, say, for example, assessment. The situation at first glance is simple. And yet a complication immediately arises in relation to the word and concept 'research'. Research implies production or the creation (invention/discovery?) of new knowledge. What might be new though in this crushingly familiar confrontation? The researcher must have a sense, at least, an inkling, perhaps, that there is something unknown, or not fully known, or partially known, or known and understood wrongly, about the object. The researcher, that is, confronts the familiar, known object quizzically. In one way or another, the researcher's stance indicates that the object is not entirely transparent to view, that it is not known exhaustively or correctly in its present manifestation. Something important about the nature of the object is not immediately open to a full and exhaustive view. While we might say that the researcher knows fully well what the object *is*, at the same time the 'being' of the object is not fully available. As a consequence, the researcher's knowledge of what the object is not in perfect accord with what the object *is*. There is a curious double logic about this insight, but it is one that pertains to all our knowledge. And really all our knowledge must in some way be constituted by this difference between our knowledge of the object and what the object is. This difference is intensely interesting and at the same time elusive of definition. It opens the possibility for rethinking, lending a productive mobility to our apprehension of things. It belongs to the order of what Derrida has referred to as 'the spectral' (Derrida, 1994). It is the basis for what has come to be known as object-oriented ontology (Harman, 2016). In education, its implications are far-reaching for so many familiar, fundamental objects: assessment, for example. If we probe this thing, this entity, this object, assessment, its automatic identity in education might begin to seem odd, perverse, even (Flint and Peim, 2011).

Both Kant and Husserl, writing at very different times, posited the idea of 'the object-in-itself'. This entity or idea has interesting ontological status. It must exist if we want to avoid the pitfalls and impossibilities of an idealist view of the world, a view that suggests reality is the projection of our minds. In other words, whatever we might say about the state of our knowledge of the object (in-itself), it must exist. On the other hand, we acknowledge in the phrase 'object-in-itself' something that differs from 'the object' pure and simple or the object as we apprehend it. There is no way round this spectral difference. It is there whenever we make claims about the essence of anything (as commentators frequently do about education, for instance), as though we could abstract some pure version of the thing from the brute reality of its manifest appearance.

A spatial representation or diagram can help us to articulate the nature of this 'spectral difference' and its importance. Let's imagine a drawing that represents the subject as separate from the object. Let's say, for the sake of argument and illustration, that the subject stands before the object or stands in some determinate spatial position in relation to the position of the object. Immediately here we begin to introduce new elements into our descriptive model.

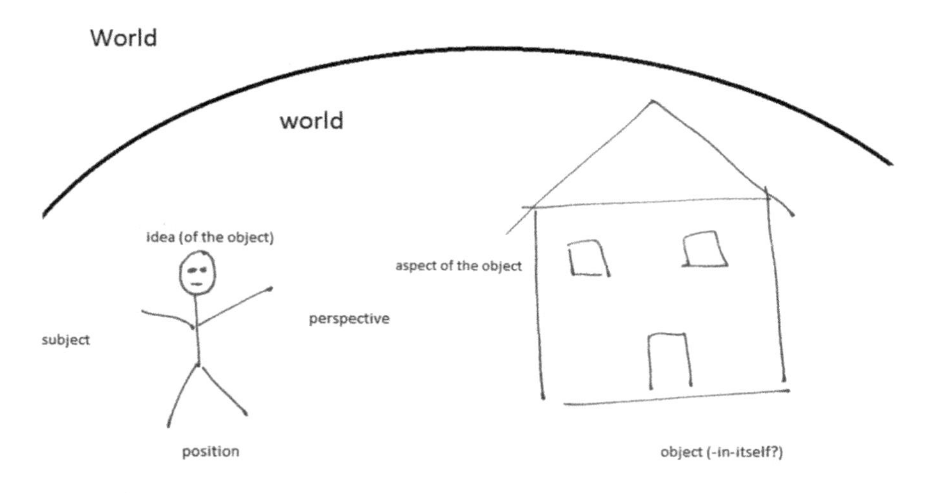

Figure 1.1 Phenomenology

At present, our subject and our object occupy some abstract space, but of course, we don't have to be Martin Heidegger to realize that no such abstracted subject and object have ever existed. Apart from the fact that the subject we have posited is naked and alone, as it were, and the object has no identity whatsoever, they both must occupy some determinate space. And this space is not just a neutral container for their separate existences. It is both the occasion of their coming together into some relation of encounter and what has contributed to their existence in the first place as well as to their specific character, formation, identity. This space is essential for there to be any possibility of a dynamic relation between them. We might, albeit provisionally, characterize it as the *context* for the subject and object encounter. We might be tempted to use the word 'world', and if we are, as we shall see, we will need to exercise care, caution in the account we give of that world. In fact, we will probably have to reach for some complicating language of 'world-within-world' to begin to account for the characteristics of that space. The immediate world of the subject–object encounter is in turn framed by the larger world that all three inhabit – the world at large, as it were. And while our representation refers to 'space', it should also be obvious that what is perhaps not easily represented in a diagram is the dimension of time. So, in addition, our description or analysis of the encounter of subject and object will need to make reference to the element or dimension of time. In what way, though? There is the time of the object and the time of the subject and the time of the encounter, for starters, to contend with – and these three differ from one another often in subtle and interesting ways. Time also encompasses the idea of the specificity of an era: 'my time', 'our time', 'modern times', for example.

The spatial representation of the encounter between subject and object opens another crucial dimension for exploration. It is clear from the diagram that the subject occupies a position in relation to the object. Similarly, the object offers an aspect of itself to the subject. This double relation has dizzying complications, but is essential in giving an account of the relation. At stake are the identities of both subject and object.

The point of these initial elaborations is to suggest that a phenomenological approach, reduced to an apparently simple formula that asks us to give an account of subject, object and context and the relations between these things is not merely a philosophical game. Some such account is essential to any kind of research.

The traditional literature review advocated by research handbooks suggests that there will be a determinate body of writing that can give an account of significant knowledge of the object. This approach assumes that the object and the knowledge so far acquired of the object both can have a stable identity and are likely to have a consistent kind of relation to one another. A moment's thought is enough to problematize this assumption. If we think of any complex object that is likely to be the object of a research project in education – literacy, for example, or some feature of the classroom – it's likely that what it *is* will either be underresearched or will be contested with many decisively different accounts of its identity and nature. Such differences are not trivial. They indicate fundamental ontological conditions of our familiar world. For research, it is the role of structured, informed thinking to explore the research object necessitating critical decisions that have to be confronted concerning the identity of the object, what it *is* and what might be appropriate modes of approaching it and engaging with it. Such matters can't be settled by a 'literature review' without erasing the role of thinking.

Epistemology: Theory of knowledge

Consideration of the object in the ontological mood – in the quizzical, 'What is ...?' mode – is a necessary phase in the research process. It is likely to recur, especially in relation to complex social objects. Much research asks questions about the nature of already-existing complex objects in the social field. Present understandings, of course, need to be considered if new understandings are to emerge or to be generated. These can usually be accessed by various kinds of reading of existing accounts or accessing languages of usage or observations of current practices, existing determinations. To produce new knowledge or a new take or purchase on the nature of the object in question usually requires some account of the process to effect such change. In the sixteenth century, Michel de Montaigne claimed that most forms of knowledge were 'false conceit', and that we struggle as beings to know even ourselves (Montaigne, 1993). It is the effort of science, including social science, to obviate that feeling of radical scepticism regarding knowledge and its production. And, of course, with perhaps questionable and certainly varying degrees of success, both science and social science have produced considerable quantities of knowledge so far. Both have also furnished an array of techniques for the production of knowledge of a kind that can confront or, ideally, defeat the sceptics' assertion that knowledge is mostly founded in delusion.

Questions concerning how we know what we know and how we might extend the knowledge that we have belong to the branch of philosophy usually referred to as epistemology. According to the Charles Taylor, epistemology is no longer the foremost dimension of philosophy (Taylor, 1995). It has 'fallen into the sere', although it must be said that some very recent energetic renewals of philosophy have returned again to epistemological questions in order to rethink foundations. Quentin Meillassoux and his followers have reviewed the European epistemological heritage so that some secure grounding for the possibility of knowledge that does not depend on human consciousness can be posited (Meillassoux, 2009). The jury is out on whether this attempt to circumvent what Meillassoux refers to as 'correlationism' is successful. After Kant, some would say, the rationalist epistemological spirit finds its apotheosis in Hegel for whom history is driven by a dynamic process of constant self-transformation in the direction of higher states of being and knowledge (Hegel, 1998). In the wake of such German idealism appear what may seem like much darker philosophies, reflecting a gloomy turn to parallel some of the eighteenth- and nineteenth century's scientific and technological triumphs as well as the clinching of the European domination of the world in the latter stages of a brutal colonialism that had nothing to do with enlightenment in its simplest sense. Western knowledge then appears much less certain and much darker.

For a good while, epistemological questions were at the forefront of Western metaphysics from the rise of science charted by Bacon to the problematization and affirmation of certainty in Descartes and beyond. Perhaps the high point of European philosophy's concern with questions of knowledge is in the work of the meticulous, remorselessly logical Kant. Fuelled by the scepticism Kant found in David Hume's insistence that only experience could ultimately be the grounds for any kind of epistemological certainty, Kant's magisterial *Critique of Pure Reason* explored the tricky terrain of the relations between knowledge, understanding, intuition, perception and 'objects-in-themselves', the latter problematic term returning to haunt Western metaphysics at the turn of the twentieth century. Kant was not merely concerned with highfalutin forms of knowledge or academic practices or science. He sought to get to philosophical grips with everyday knowledge and wrestled with questions concerning the kind of knowledge that informs our mundane encounters with the things that surround us, as well as the kind of knowledge that informs our more formally expressed beliefs. Kant's excitement at Hume's deeply sceptical turn of mind is balanced by his cool appraisal of Bishop Berkeley's idealism. Berkeley had ingeniously sought to salvage reason's necessary attachment to God by demonstrating that all that we took for material substance was logically traceable back to the operations of the mind: no mind, no matter (Berkeley, 2009). Kant addressed Hume's scepticism and Berkeley's idealism with a deliberative energy dedicated to teasing out the minutiae of thought concerning the grounds of human knowledge. We might note that Kant's engagement with idealism and scepticism occurs during the high enlightenment. Kant's resolution acknowledges that our thinking is always dependent on 'a priori truths', rather like Zizek's 'unknown knowns', those habituated ways of thinking we can't do without that provide logical frameworks. One important upshot from this synthesis is that there can be no purely empirical knowledge. We cannot claim to simply know things based on the facts. Our thinking is always already contaminated with 'intuitions' and frameworks that we cannot put to the test of some rigorous method. For Kant, then, human knowledge has limits and reason has limits. Kant's enlightenment is 'man's [*sic*] emergence from immaturity to a point that acknowledges the complications of knowledge and reason, rather than the attainment to a realm where those vital things can be secured once and for all (Kant, 2003).

After Kant, enlightenment confronts turbulent history. The optimism of Hegel's positive dialectics is offset by Schopenhauer, the gloomy anti-Kant, for whom the will to knowledge is blindly driven, purposeless. Nietzsche followed with an attempt to renew knowledge by disengaging it from truth: in order to remake the world as creative project. Twentieth-century modernity in turn witnessed the runaway – and potentially fatal – triumphs of science-based technology. Humanist confidence no longer applies after the depredations of twentieth-century history. Subsequent history, knowledge and thinking tended equally to suggest that the 'human project' was not destined to inevitable progress and that both human being and human consciousness were essentially contingent, shot through with what Meillassoux has called 'radical finitude' (Meillassoux, 2009).

Contemporary understandings of knowledge of veers between (1) confidence in techniques for the production of knowledge, the technologies of social science, for instance and (2) radical uncertainty in terms of how to make sense of that knowledge. What's more, an apocalyptic tone dominates much philosophy (Haraway, 2016; Latour, 2013; Moreton, 2013; Stiegler, 2013), warning that the survival of the species is in danger at least partly as a consequence of the hubris of human science and technological puissance. It is ironic that an era of epistemic uncertainty seems to have generated a new insistence in universities (alleged powerhouses of knowledge production) on 'impact'. Knowledge is required to account for itself in an immediate way and in terms of its use-value. All universities now publicly subscribe to this dubious ethic. University research web pages are full of it, extolling their own achievements in relation to its now uncontested demands.

For the researcher, questions arise concerning one's orientation to the business of knowledge production and its relation to the pursuit of truth or validity or use. The technology of knowledge production is there for all to access in countless research manuals. Giving an account of method usually requires some details of the specific technologies deployed, their validity status and the kind of knowledge they might give rise to. Research handbooks endlessly rehearse the repertoire of techniques, the general technology of knowledge as now practised in social science and in education. Methodology, however, requires a kind of meta account of why this particular ensemble of techniques was deployed – and how it stands with the general conceptualization of the project in hand. Methodology may even require some engagement with questions concerning the provenance and the value of knowledge. A major problem for the researcher wrestling with relations between method and methodology is the discontinuity implied in the conventional organization of a research thesis. For example, already-existing knowledge, addressed in the poorly entitled 'literature review', cannot be properly understood as already given and over and done with, static and dormant. While intended to delimit a research project's focus, actually engaging with what has already been written in relation to the object of that research is more likely to open than to close issues. This 'review' dimension must generate as well as reflect upon knowledge.

What's more, it is unlikely that many of us have a ready-to-hand epistemology or epistemological stance that we can elaborate before proceeding to implement it in our research. An epistemological stance is more likely to be crafted from the implicit procedures outlined above in terms of giving an account of one's subjectivity in relation to the object of one's research desire. So epistemology will have to take into account that desire. It will also have to engage with questions about the kind of knowledge already attained by a subject who exists in some determinate relation to an object. Most research in education relates to or arises in a specific institutional setting where understandings of the object already exist and already exert some determining force. These considerations suggest that an epistemological approach will need to be layered in some way to account for the different overlapping dimensions that determine present and specific understandings of what the object is and what is appropriate to explore in terms of producing new knowledge of it and through what means.

Practical knowledge ('phronesis') is sometimes cited as an alternative to abstract knowledge, often cited as a kind of 'clean' alternative to the labyrinth of speculative knowledge that might attend any complex object of research, and that is likely to be the grounds for epistemological torsions, confusions and uncertainties. In fact, seeking to engage with epistemological issues that relate the practical knowledge of institutions with more abstract, reflective, speculative kinds of thinking can have extremely productive consequences for research practice. Mapping out and exploring those relations is a productive activity – not only in terms of providing words for the thesis but also in terms of doing more or less essential groundwork.

While approaches that take an epistemological stance that privileges the speculative (the domain of thinking) may be less in favour than those that privilege the empirical, there is much cause to question this hierarchy. Research handbooks frequently represent the empirical dimension – fieldwork or data gathering – as central to research. This is a seriously limiting myth, albeit a powerful one. The point about the significance or otherwise of data and data production in research is fundamentally epistemological. Any sketch of a social practice will attempt to identify its surface features. Those features that immediately present themselves for our apprehension can be readily articulated. We know that our knowledge of them, though, will be coloured by our position in relation to them as outlined briefly above in the section on phenomenology. At the same time, we know that what we see before us can't be defined only in terms of its surface features. It won't reveal its not-so-surface features immediately to us. And there are likely to be many of these for any object. The question or the issue of non-present elements that are dimensions of what the object is presents an issue for knowledge, of course. We cannot rely on immediate observation and, as reference to the dimension of the subject suggests, we can't wholly rely on that anyhow. The question concerning what the object of our enquiry *is* even at this very starting point is complicated by a metaphysical dimension that poses issues for epistemology. Knowing the object differently from its surface modality may demand the intervention of theory – or thinking – to reveal dimensions that no amount of data production can give access to.

If knowledge of the object requires that we engage with non-present elements, how do we render such elements present? According to Plato's dialogue, *Meno*, this is an essential question. For if the elements we seek are not present, how might we know what they are? What's perhaps more troubling is how might we know where or how to look for them, let alone come to some understanding of them or give some authoritative account of them? Marjorie Grene in *The Knower and the Known* claims in effect that the question posed in the *Meno*, the question that puts into doubt the quest for knowledge – how to seek for what we don't already know and how to know that we have found it should we do so – is not so much a declaration of the impossibility of knowledge as an affirmation of something fundamental about the very conditions of knowledge, something about the nature of knowledge itself and its very conditions of possibility. Grene offers hints of an interesting ontology here where 'an object' is not to be understood as something entirely or even very clearly separable from the context it inhabits. Reality, she suggests, is composed of contexts that give meaning to the things we designate as discrete objects. Rather like Peter Sloterdijk's image of 'spheres', objects are always relations and always inhabit discrete worlds (Sloterdijk, 2011).

> whatever we seek it is not some definite thing which will reveal itself self-sufficient and complete, but a point of entry to a reality that is in some sense more than any one object we aspire to know. (Grene, 1966, 34)

But, of course, we don't set off on a quest for knowledge like intrepid and daring explorers approaching some strange terrain always for the first time. One of the problems for the researcher entering into the world of a given field of practice or into an already-established space of knowledge is that many have been there before. The field of knowledge is already peopled by established figures, concepts, data, interpretations, position, perspectives. Epistemology implies that the researcher must take this already-existing state of affairs into mind and, in some way, must find a point of entry and clear some ground to begin a fresh exploration. A critical epistemology will seek to call into question what is already fixed and determined.

In Derrida's curious approach to questions of knowledge, the archive guards against the intrusion of improper elements. Knowledge belongs to what is established and needs to be protected against unruly or wayward disturbances. The 'archons' (perhaps another name for universities in the modern era) protect not only the store of received knowledge but also the rituals of entry into the world of knowledge. The archons guard over the form of the doctoral thesis. They decide what is publishable and what is not. But whatever protections they may impose with whatever degree of strictness, there is always the possibility of a break with the genre, of something new emerging, in a new form, despite the increasing attempts of research handbooks to constrain and predetermine the shape of research productions.

Hermeneutics: Interpretation as exploration

Grene insists that there can be no clear distinction between knowing and learning. This is rather like insisting that our knowledge of things is a kind of reading of the world. As situated beings subject to the restrictions and specificities of being-in-the-world, we have one particular vantage point from which to grasp knowledge. This takes us back to the phenomenological mapping that insists that we must 'see', know, understand and make sense of from a particular position. How then might we gain a new purchase on a familiar object of knowledge in a systematic or rigorous way?

One question we face as researchers at a very fundamental level concerns certain features of our being positioned that are not so easy to account for. We may know who we are, where we come from and how we are positioned in terms of time, place and institutional context, but the powerful undercurrents of our knowledge are often harder to give an account of. This is not only the case for the unconscious motivations, predilections we might have as individual subjects. It is also a product of more intractable, more difficult to get access to dimensions of our knowledge. This is the domain of what Hans Georg Gadamer referred to as pre-understanding. Pre-understanding is not a property of only the individual knower. All the taken-for-granted accumulated knowledge that hangs around the object imposes a challenge to the knower to break through and reach towards something as yet unrealized. Such pre-understandings cannot easily be swept aside to reveal the object-in-itself, the much desired but elusive entity in modern Western epistemology. And there is another – perhaps seductive, perhaps treacherous – dimension of pre-understanding. It is the case that our sense of what constitutes appropriate and useful procedures for forging new knowledge are also freighted with already-established understanding. For the researcher seeking to find a way to produce something new (the demand of research), this double hermeneutic bind may be experienced as a barrier on the path to knowledge.

The problem may reside more in the language that we use. The idea that there could be a 'smooth path' to knowledge may be exactly what would best be deconstructed in the knowledge generating process. In addition to personal factors, the dimensions of the subject, there is also the historical contingency of the object's contextual situation to consider. Both subject and context provide opportunities for rethinking, for exploration and to produce new knowledge. This is where attention to the philosophical dimension of research comes into its own. The particularity of my orientation towards the object is essential to situating it and therefore giving an account of it. This basic encounter opens onto further issues and questions furnishing potential material for the knowledge production enterprise. As we saw earlier with the determination of the subject, knowledge of objects, contexts, fields is historical, culturally specific and also, surely and inescapably, political. Most fields of practice that constitute arenas for social science research are fraught with often-conflicting differences in relation to ideas. Identities are always in play whether that be the identities of things, subjects, fields of practice, forms of knowledge, modes of research.

One of the difficulties we have as human subjects is that while we often refer to reality and have an understanding that reality is 'there' somehow and while we frequently bump up against reality in a variety of ways, when we get down to it we must submit to the fact that, on reflection, we simply don't have direct access to reality as such, in all its richness and complexity. That's not to say that we don't experience reality at all. We do in an obvious and embodied sense all the time. It is however to acknowledge that our apprehension of reality, particularly at the level of mindful understanding, is always already mediated for us through the cultural lenses that organize our vision, through language that constitutes a symbolic order that powerful enframes our being-in-the-world. Language and discourse provide us with ready-made modes of understanding and articulations of the nature of things. Language carries metaphysics with it. It stages meaning. But the metaphysics of language is not entirely stable. Because language itself is predicated on difference and relies on spacing – terms applied here in a sense derived from Derrida – there is an essential mobility in language. One of the consequences of this is that meanings are frequently contested – and this happens to be most the case for the words that are laden with the most symbolic significance. That's one reason why the language of identity is so important and so frequently subject to dispute.

Language constitutes metaphysics in several ways. One obvious way is that language determines what things are! This doesn't just mean that language articulates the world, although that is important enough. Language designates and makes differences between things: think of the work of taxonomy in science that seeks to define beings in their essential differences from one another. But it is also the case, interestingly, and in a far-reaching way, as Wittgenstein declared: 'The limits of my language are the limits of my world' (1961, 5.6). On this view, language is world creating, but also world delimiting. But as Wittgenstein and Derrida concur: my language is not mine. A language is the product of and the property of a way of life, certainly never of an individual. Individuals use language and may put their own stamp on their usage. But language is, interestingly, both internal and external to human beings. It is where the outside meets and constitutes the inside. Language is collective. To know a language is to know a way of life, as Wittgenstein affirmed, recognizing also that language was the bearer of mythology or metaphysics. If I am able to make subtle distinctions between certain kinds of fir trees and certain kinds of larches and certain kinds of hemlock trees, it is not because I as an individual decide to do so. Nor is it because my tree-obsessed friends and I have decided that these are significant categories. These distinctions are written into our collective language and are available to anyone who wants to pursue them. Every now and then someone may want to contest whether or not such and such tree belongs to the hemlock or fir categories. Some particular trees make categorization difficult. But the designations that do get made are public not private. And this is as true for emotions and ideas as it is for dominant forms of plant life.

The idea that language and way of life are so intricated as to be utterly interdependent has far-reaching consequences for the nature and the logic of knowledge. When we encounter a tree, we don't see it for the first time and then go through a process of relating sense data to form to the scientific categorization system of plant life. In Husserl's terms, our knowledge and our perception are 'intentional'. We live in world that's already sorted out for us – and we grow into it. Mostly, we don't puzzle over what the things in front of us are in some painstakingly epistemological sense. We know because we live in a world with others who know. In some sense, the world has always already been interpreted for us, sorted and ordered in the symbolic system that is language. And that system operates significantly in the register of the unconscious. We grow up to be readers of the world so attuned that we rarely have to speak the words out; we can mostly read the world automatically and make sense of where we are and what we see in an instant. This clearly has advantages in terms of enabling us to orient ourselves.

For the pursuit of knowledge, our strongly embedded unconscious understanding presents a deep problem. Our language is not language itself and is not at one with the world either, although we are likely to experience it as such. Languages order the world. They carry a metaphysic with them. What's more, languages are usually divided into separate if overlapping discourses that 'produce the objects of which they speak' (Foucault, 1977b, 48–49). If language gives us access to a ready-made order, it also at the same time represents a kind of barrier between the world and our understanding of it. And if languages do offer symbolic systems, those systems are never entire and complete unto themselves; they are never static. The logic of language clearly demonstrates that they can't be. Language is an order and an ordering, but it is at the same time, mobile, plastic and enormously differentiated.

Language opens an immensely complex and productive issue. Languages constitute dynamic systems that are also sites of conflict where the struggle may concern the very nature of things. How can we even begin to understand our own understanding of things, given that understanding in language is deeply habituated and includes a significant unconscious component? According to Gadamer, we simply have to acknowledge that this is always a starting point for us and we cannot get outside or suspend or bracket out our 'fore-understandings'. According to Gadamer, the enlightenment goal of eliminating all prejudices is a prejudice. But Gadamer has a series of insights that offer a productive answer to the problem of 'the hermeneutic circle', the idea that we are locked up in our own understanding and can't get out (Gadamer, 1989). As noted above, systems of languages are not closed. In order to exist at all, they must have two important kinds of 'spacing': a spacing between the elements that constitute the bits and pieces of language (syntax) and, of course, a spacing between the elements of language and what they signify (semantics). Spacing introduces an element into language that problematizes both stability and presence of meaning. This essential insight of deconstruction highlights how language may enact its own destabilizations.

So if language constitutes the horizon of our being, it is not a closed horizon. What's more, as Gadamer is keen to indicate, we may make ourselves aware of other horizons that may react with the open sections of our own (Gadamer, 1989). Language is not a complete unity. Different discourses operate different vocabularies, relating to different entities and activating different modes of apprehension. Discourses may interfere with one another, destabilizing the borders between themselves and enabling new, hybrid forms of knowledge and understanding to appear. We can see his happening historically as new forms of knowledge emerge from the coming together of hitherto disparate discourses. Examples include the emergence of psychology, linguistics and, more recently, cultural studies.

In the field of English studies, it was the incursion of new forms of knowledge that disturbed for a while the central assumptions of subject identity. During the

1980s, English (in higher education, at least) discovered 'theory', a varied body of thought that included social theory, media theory, cultural studies, philosophy, psychoanalysis and history (especially its own history), among others. The impact of this varied intrusion was felt in some quarters to be considerable. The subject tended to split between the traditionalist who wanted to hold onto the time-honoured versions of subject identity and the radicals who – drunk with the heady mix of new ideas – wanted to dissolve that traditional model or at least reform it beyond recognition, some declaring the emergence of a new subject altogether (Belsey, 1980; Dollimore and Sinfield, 1985; Easthope, 1991; Macherey, 1978; Moi, 1985; Peim, 1993).

Gadamer, the hermeneuticist follower of Heidegger, might express the arrival of a problematization of subject identity in terms of horizons (1989). The existing and relatively stable historical outline of English studies had been broken open by the intrusion of other ways of thinking that had belonged within other horizons. English had met its Other or others. As a consequence, the very idea of a pure subject with self-policing, natural borders was deconstructed. Conflicts arose in various arenas about subject identity. It was thus revealed that the subject was fractured not only in terms of its contents, but also in terms of its place in different institutions of learning. So English existed in the specific forms it took according to the Bernstein principle of recontextualization as well as according to subject ideology (Bernstein, 1995). The meeting or collision of different horizons then had the effect of enabling English to be approached and understood in a range of quite different ways.

The point of this excursion is to illustrate the Gadamer principle that horizons of knowledge are both permeable and overlapping. And the very process of bringing different horizons together allows differences in possibility to reveal themselves. The nature of these differences can be far-reaching. The thing in question may no longer be what it was. The given 'nature' of subject identity, for example, is challenged by the existence and possible intrusion of other ideas that might exert a force for change. The other ideas may allow alternatives to come into view. They may suggest specific types of expansion, revision, radical change – or they may have more revolutionary effects, depending on how they get read and how their impact on the field in question gets read and implemented in thought. This is the point of much knowledge generation in the social sciences and humanities: the reinterpretation of what is already known and familiar, but may for one reason or another be presenting problems or that may come to attention for contingent reasons. Some aggravating factor can trigger an urge towards rethinking, reinterpretation, repositioning, destabilizing of what had hitherto seemed secure and given, established, archived and solid.

Considerations of the different horizons that knowledge exists within and of how relations between different horizons may shift knowledge suggest something powerful I think concerning knowledge ontology. This is a topic not much addressed and certainly not addressed in research handbooks that tend to eschew such 'metaphysical' matters as distractions or unnecessary complications that might interfere with the practical business of research progress. But the very word progress introduces a necessary complication. Many of the examples we can think of key knowledge in the social sciences don't move from one stage to the next in simply incremental stages as one outmoded mode of knowing is superseded by its successor.

To a very significant extent the role of theory – or thinking – is to provide a hermeneutic lever or aggravation. Worlds of practice tend to be dominated by ways of understanding and acting that have become authoritative, embedded, naturalized even. That is to say that established knowledge and practice carry a certain kind of weight and authority by inertia. Practices that are strongly embedded and taken for granted may seem to be natural. They are what they are by force of natural necessity and they continue because 'that's just the way we do things' or 'that's just the way things are'. Resistance to theory is often a symptom of this feeling that the order of things is the order of things by virtue of natural authority and that this knowledge has evolved through a process of rigorous and necessary social selection.

To think ontologically is to open the possibility of difference. And one major difference at stake in much social science research is the difference between how things are in practice and how they have to be. There are many aspects to this difference. It is a difference that leads onto many differences in a complex play of differences. It is the business of thinking – to articulate significant differences at play in our knowledge and in the practices that relate to knowledge. Nowhere perhaps is this complexity of difference more evident than in education where practices are constrained by specific conditions and arrangements: the institutional framework, the building, the allocation of numbers, ideas about what good teaching is, the available social technologies, the demands of the curriculum, assessment processes and many other institutional, trans-institutional but also local and individual factors. Putting all these things together we can understand at a glance how difficult it is to speak of an essential nature of things. Any practice is the product of intersecting histories operating at different levels, of intersecting ideas and, in effect, of intersecting worlds. While some differences can be accommodated against one another, others may give rise to conflict and ultimately to what Jean-Francois Lyotard refers to as 'the differend': the kind of situation where thoroughly incompatible differences pertain (Lyotard, 1988).

The hermeneutic dimension means recognition of differences – even if these differences are ontological differences that imply incompatible determinations of the very nature of things. Even if we determine where we stand in relation to differences, we must acknowledge that the hermeneutic dimension is active in our decisions to define the reality of a practice in a certain kind of way. When these collisions seem irresolvable – as often they must – we are in the domain of the aporetic (see below). Paradoxically, perhaps, this is often the domain of the new, the creative, the unpredictable and unprogrammable.

And as Lyotard recognized implicitly in the very idea of 'the differend', powerful ethical issues arise from contemporary conditions of knowledge production. How do we use the technologies of knowledge production at our disposal? What claims do we make for the knowledge we thus produce? But also, where do we stand in relation to questions concerning truth? And how do we, collectively, individually, in our affiliated groups, deploy our knowledge in the world especially in relation to that difficult but persistent factor that confronts us in the guise of the Other? These questions introduce, for educational researchers, ethical issues that are a far cry from the usual, prophylactic view offered by universities and their research committees.

Ethics: Beyond the checklist

The 'ethics' in question here is an expanded understanding of the term. It doesn't refer to research ethics understood in the narrow sense represented by the research handbooks where a series of checks and balances is designed to ensure that empirical data collection doesn't offend its participants. That is a merely negative or prophylactic idea of research ethics. The sensitivity that such an approach to ethics insists on may be perfectly proper, but ethics conceived of in that narrow, procedural sense does not do justice to the ethical dimension of research. It is my contention here that that ethical dimension is immensely significant not only for the individual educational researcher but also for the field of research in general.

In the expanded sense, ethics touches on questions of meaning, purpose and value. We may imagine, rightly or wrongly, that research conducted in the social sciences exists within an ethical framing. Whether this is conscious, involving explicit articulation, we might well say that the ethical is *there* in research insofar as research seeks to make a claim on truth – and seeks to do so with some (albeit borrowed, negotiated) authority. The assumption of a relation to truth is written in perhaps to the research 'ethic' at large – certainly in modernity and beyond. Research institutions, mostly universities, claim in varying degrees but always to a significant extent, that their very right to exist arises from a commitment to be purveyors of truth ('facteurs de la verite' in Lacan's terms) in both teaching and research functions. In fact these two functions, teaching and research, must both claim their right to exist by an ethical commitment to the truth. Famous – and sometimes disturbingly dark – scandals have arisen where academic institutions or individuals have knowingly engineered false claims. Such scandals attest to the prevalence of this ethical commitment to the truth (whether it be appropriate or not).

At the same time, as with epistemological questions, the very nature of truth and the proper procedures for achieving it are both strongly contested. It may seem paradoxical that the sacred value put on truth exists alongside some recognition that truth is essentially agonistic, a site for contest, struggle and change. According to some contemporary versions, the enormous significance of truth is precisely that it can't be – and mustn't be – determined or specified. This is not, however, to suggest that truth is somehow relative nor is it to suggest that truth is dispensable. It is rather to commit to the idea that truth is an empty space that must at all costs be defended against all those dogmatisms or totalitarianisms that might seek to occupy it with their own determination of what it is. This is what some serious versions of science determine as truth: scientific truths, being always provisional, are subject to the possibility of falsifiability; otherwise, they are not scientific (Popper, 1992).

For Plato, there is an interesting version of this orientation to truth. Truth exists but not in palpable form. The reality that we are familiar with through lived experience is not equivalent to truth. That reality is rather like a fallen version of the ideal truth that exists in a ghostly, paradigmatic state above and beyond actuality. As living subjects, we have access to the reality of things in their material form but do not have direct access to their ideal form.

This difference between reality and paradigm is an interesting one and is also one that has haunted Western metaphysics in all cases where we may be aware of some abstract notion or form that corresponds more or less to real, actual cases of the thing in question. It serves to remind us that the truth claims we make are gestures in the direction of the paradigm rather than the truth itself. If the model of truth proposed in Plato seems alien to modern consciousness, it may not actually be so far removed. Ideal objects are frequently posited as units of abstract thought, in modernity and beyond as much as in Plato. It may be the case that there is a strong parallel between how language works – with its generalized categories of things that find instantiation in reality but that also at the same time, as Kant might have it, organize that reality for us to understand in the first place. We can have no apprehension of reality without its representation.

For us, truth has a strong tendency to be a matter of 'correspondence' between what we assume to be 'out there' somehow and how we represent what is out there. This correspondence depends also on a difference, of course, meaning that the expression of truth must always be distinct from truth 'itself'. These brief observations here suggest that the questions of truth and its pursuit touch on both abiding and new lines of thinking in Western philosophy (Meillassoux, 2009; Plato, 1997).

Commitment to the pursuit of truth is felt as an ethical commitment in general for researchers. It is interesting to ask though where that commitment comes from? Is it through an attachment to an ideal of knowledge? If so, how much is that ideal of knowledge articulated? Where would one find its most apt expression? Or is the commitment to truth more the function of an attachment to a community, or to an ideal community? What community exactly is it that claims our allegiance as researchers? A wider community for whom our commitment to truth would be in the long run significant? Or a community of scholars whose ideals we must embrace – and do embrace willingly – in order to belong? In one way or another, these questions touch upon the ethical and – certainly within the world of academic endeavour – relate to questions concerning the good life where good is understood as more than merely comfortable or happy. Somewhere lurking in these questions and issues is the perhaps disturbing thought that our commitment to the pursuit of truth through knowledge may be the function of an ontotheological metaphysics – or may only have been vaguely thought through.

It's often alleged that for Plato the good life must be reflective, given that 'the unexamined life is not worth living'. Much has been made of this alleged assertion of Socrates, who is often considered to be the mouthpiece of Plato. Whether that is the case is a 'knotty point', perhaps: but the idea has currency, and especially resonates in modernity when the grounds for ethical existence become more problematic and uncertain. On this view, to be ethical, to begin with at least, means that we must be reflective, self-examining and questioning, above all of ourselves.

One of the most interesting claims for the grounding of the ethical comes from Kant, who was quite content, perhaps even somewhat ecstatic, to acknowledge that although he didn't know where it came from, 'the moral sense within' was a certain feature of his very being. Kant also understood the essence of the ethical to be entrammeled with the nature of reason and its relation to duty, understood as a moral imperative that would require any subject to follow its demands. In fact, Kant claims that ethical conduct is always informed by reason as a form of attachment or agreement to an imperative. In other words, when we are being ethical, we act under the sway of an injunction that cannot be refused, even if we happen to refuse it for some contingent reason. What's more, this is not, in the end, a question of weighing consequence, of deciding that if an action is taken, a result or outcome will follow. Kant's mighty contribution to the thinking of ethics resides in the affirmation of the 'categorical imperative' that erases the means–ends logic of ethical decision-making. The categorical imperative demands that an action be taken because it is the right action; at the same time, it provides the criterion that will ensure that action falls properly within its remit. The categorical imperative demands that any action can be moral only if it is in accord with the consideration that it could become universalizable. This move is as it were designed to cut out the intrusion of contingencies – the awkward demands that might be made by specific cases. Kantian ethics, for all its complications (that I have grossly simplified here), is robustly clear and strong, tied both to reason and to the expression of a human essence.

Nineteenth-century thinking saw various problematizations of Kant's relative humanist optimism. In the figure of Nietzsche, ethics took an unanticipated turn, in the rejection of the ethical as understood in much of the inheritance of Western thought. Nietzsche sought to produce a 'genealogy' of morals, so that ethics itself could be historicized with a view to rethinking its place in the world and in the pursuit of meaning detached from the dead weight of inherited morality. Ethics, in Nietzsche's sense, should be life affirming.

The turn that thinking took with the emergence of the work of Martin Heidegger is not always considered in ethical terms (except, of course, and quite rightly, to condemn Heidegger's disastrous involvement in Nazism). Heidegger's 'fundamental ontology', however, has radical and positive implications for how the ethical might be conceived. In *Being and Time*, Heidegger's lengthy account of the conditions of existence for 'dasein' ('being there' or human being) includes key terms that cannot but have ethical implications. In this sense, the ethical is not, as for Kant, the wondrously unaccountable, mysterious force from within. In Heidegger's account, the ethical arises from the condition of 'care' that accompanies our engagements with the world, the very specific portion of the world, always already configured in a particular mode, - we inhabit. In this account, the ethical is not separated from our way of life. It associates with our anxieties, our belonging to others and with the practices we engage in to make a world that is specifically 'ours'. On this view, we are ethical in specifically situated ways that accord with contingent factors that determine who, what, when and where we are (Heidegger, 1962).

There is another, existential dimension to the ethical. Heidegger grants 'dasein' a certain freedom to think above and beyond the everyday concerns of our immediate 'world'. This relates to the condition of anxiety. In our daily commerce with the world, we are beset by mundane anxieties, but Heidegger identifies a more general mood of anxiety: a powerful force constantly murmuring in the background to our lives. It is not something we can overcome. It is fundamental to our very being. It is associated with knowledge of mortality and the associated fear of nothing. Its driving force, although grounded in the negative, is generative. Anxiety towards death drives us to distraction. Our intense, if not always conscious, awareness of our own radical finitude impels our actions, dispositions, affections. At times, we become conscious of this dimension of our lives. Choices, decisions or commitments are made in the shadow of this awareness. In such moments, we can claim a certain purchase on freedom. For Heidegger, freedom is not an ongoing and inescapable condition: it is glimpsed at now and then. Freedom is a possibility that arises from our ability to acknowledge our anxiety-driven sense of things. This freedom is precisely where the ethical comes into play. After all it is only where we can make decisions that arise from a condition of freedom that we can possibly claim the status of ethical beings.

For Heidegger, the dimension of the ethical arises out of the account of fundamental ontology, the condition of our being-in-the-world. It has far-reaching implications for our orientation towards knowledge. In later work, the ethical dimension gets closely associated with thinking, where 'thinking' was distinguished from philosophy or metaphysics. The inherited tradition had seen the domination of the world by Western metaphysics that had delimited thinking and that had suppressed the question of Being. Heidegger posed the possibility of thinking outside of or differently from this tradition, although finding such a vantage point is not so straightforward. Derrida would later insist that there may be no way out of the enclosure of Western metaphysics, which doesn't mean that we must remain its prisoners. We can think (in fact, we have to think) both within it and against it: deconstruction, for Derrida, following Heidegger, means a restless commitment to thinking (Derrida, 1978; Heidegger, 1993e). What Heidegger understood probably better than anyone since and including Plato is the extent that all our thinking is ontological, always already grounded in an understanding, albeit implicit, of what holds together 'beings' and their relation to Being. That is why Heidegger privileges the question as the most essential mode of thinking.

The point of this detour is to suggest that for Heidegger and Derrida thinking calls on a certain responsibility to truth – although not (as in the sense outlined briefly above) as a determinate end point or discrete goal. Thinking means an ability to dwell in a kind of questioning, questing mood. There is, it seems, a doubleness to this implication. First, there is a negative requirement not to assume that the dominant order of the day is necessarily how and where truth is to be found. But this negative also engenders a positive: it means privileging thinking above simply adopting the ready-to-hand techniques of research to provide a 'warrant' for a truth that can be put to use in some direct project of improvement. Knowledge needs thinking to engender what we might call a scientific rather than a dogmatic stance. It is almost as though we need to remind ourselves that – as impressive, extensive, powerful and secure as our knowledge may be – there is always thinking intricated intimately in it. As Parmenides adjured at the very beginnings of Western philosophy, 'Thinking and being are one.' The thinking that arises from what knowledge we may feel we have secured is far from done with. According to Heidegger, we are only just beginning to grope towards some possible understanding of what we are and how we stand in the order of things, in spite of a certain metaphysical hubris. There is nothing more ethical that this relation to thinking.

An alternative, perhaps less metaphysical, twentieth-century view of ethics is offered by Wittgenstein's insistence that social practices, including ideas, are born from and within 'forms of life'. Eschewing any truck with transcendental questions concerning the origin of the ethical dimension, Wittgenstein proposes that ethical being is in fact a matter of following the implicit rules of a game, a game we know because we are what we are in relation to a specific form of life. This is because for Wittgenstein, it seems, much conduct, thinking and language use (these three things being closely intricated) concerns following 'the rules of the game'. It turns out that following a rule is never a simple application of an unambiguous procedure. Some commentators here claim that Wittgenstein is vastly extending the meaning or application of the world 'rule' (Wittgenstein, 1968). This may be so, but we can see the value of this way of thinking easily, I think, if we consider how language works. Language is always rule bound and yet we do not speak like automata. This is due to what we might call the subtle dimension of 'play' (Derrida, 1978).

In some ways, Wittgenstein's approach seems to drain ethics of its ethical component: to suggest that our actions are strongly related to pre-existing codes. And yet the element of freedom doesn't vanish here. It remains significant. In some ways, this is a radically hermeneutic interpretation of being-in-the-world: it suggests that at each step of our way we are obliged to make interpretative moves to forge on. Wittgenstein certainly seems to have abandoned his early idea that ethical statements, insofar as they cannot be verified or otherwise by natural science, are meaningless. They are necessarily meaningful in the flow of life that they belong to and arise from. While they may not have transcendental significance above and beyond that specific flow, they share that fate with all manifestations of meaning. The fact that in his later philosophy, Wittgenstein's favourite metaphor is the game, doesn't mean that the activities or practices that are analogized in this way are trivial. Far from it, for Wittgenstein the world itself is organized into discrete, overlapping language games that give shape to and organize social life – or life. Insofar as philosophy attempts to elevate the ethical – or any other dimension of being – into another domain or attempts to give it a space of existence above and beyond the specificities of lived experience ('way of life'), it is misleading. The attempt to think about fundamental terms of existence outside specific forms of life leads to mystification, and gives rise to the knotty problems that philosophy throws up. According to Wittgenstein, these problems are of philosophy's own making. Something of this general way of thinking can be seen in the work and thought of Jean-Francois Lyotard who provides examples of irresolvable ethical conflicts arising from the collision of different forms of life. On this view, the ethical comes into play most strongly in conflict, and invariably engages knotty and intricate questions of justice (Lyotard, 1988). Lyotard's account of 'the differend' – the principle of difference informing collisions whereby different forms of life cannot understand or negotiate with one another – is sometimes associated with the peculiar condition of modernity and beyond. We have become familiar with accounts of the 'clash of civilizations' thesis that proposes a simple split between competing ideologies in global struggles.

Where forms of life clash as with, for example, ethnic struggles for political recognition it is often the case that quite different, often opposing ethical positions collide that cannot be settled by appeal to some enlightenment version of universal rationality. This faith held out the promise of progress in terms of the scope of knowledge, the power of thought, but also in terms of material and social problems facing the world. Radical disturbances have contributed to the problematization of this faith in enlightenment rationality. Rationality itself has come under suspicion. Early in the twentieth century, the sociologist Max Weber had warned of the tendencies of bureaucratic rationality to take on a monstrous life of its own, draining activity of meaning to privilege institutional purposes above and beyond the interests of individuals or particular groups, especially those who find themselves outside the magic circle of what later became known as 'social inclusion'. Various crises, some of monstrous proportions, contributed to a suspicion of the very possibility that rationality could be the key to progress and could be the effective driver of knowledge, social organization, progress and salvation.

Along with Weber's forebodings concerning 'instrumental rationality', Freud had suggested that rationality was always necessarily accompanied by and driven by unconscious forces (Bauman, 2000). Modernity experienced a major crisis in the First World War's destructive mixture of science-based technology, rationalized mobilizations of mass populations and technologically enhanced destruction. Underlying this, many felt, like Freud, that there must be a powerful negative force in the collective human psyche (Freud, 1921). Bureaucratic rationality found its darkest apotheosis in the mechanized murder of millions in the Second World War – according to some, the ultimate expression of biopower (Agamben, 1997; Bauman, 1991). With its capacity to organize millions and the emotional distance of the trained bureaucrat, as Hannah Arendt realized, monstrous evil required merely ordinary everyday people and habits for its realization (Arendt, 1964). Foucault's account of modernity as the era of biopower referred to 'the great transformation' in terms or more and more rationalized ways of ordering and managing large numbers of people including determining their very comportment within the bureaucratized and normatively ordered spaces of modernity (Foucault, 1977a). The very triumphs of modernity – including the great discoveries of physics – seemed to turn against and threaten the future of a humanity that in its proliferation threatened the nature of nature. The recent annunciation of the geological era of the 'anthropocene' has signalled panic in the face of the radical transformation of the world. Human presence itself has brought still unresolved ecological crisis and the destruction of species, habitats and possibly the ecosystem itself. No one, not even the most rational rationalist, knows how to deal with this condition. Similarly, no one can think of any other solutions that don't rely on the very processes that seem to have brought about the crisis (Bonneuil and Fressoz, 2016).

A good deal of social science within an ethic of improvement continues to express faith in rational development. In the field of education, the ethic of improvement is strongly associated with an assumption that education is an unqualified good – for the individual, for disadvantaged groups, say, and for societies. The history of education as grounds for inequality, as mechanism for the production of self-managing, norm-saturated populations never gets taken properly into account here and is most usually represented as a mere prelude to the proper realization of education's redemptive power. Many continue to express an ethical commitment to the idea of education as a vehicle or apparatus for social improvement, in spite of the massive evidence to the contrary. We can see here how the dimension of the ethical belongs to a 'community of practice'. In the case of education, there is an automatic assumption that research is likely to be fundamentally and positively ethical in character, even though this may contradict the available knowledge. Here we can see how the ethical and forms of knowledge – especially in relation to what we might call the ontological dimension – are inseparable, but not always positively so.

That is not to say or suggest that we might escape from our commitments to a world view or community of practice into some pure space of the ethical, but it is to suggest that ethical issues are present in the determinations we make about the perspectives we adopt, about our ontological stance, as it were, and about what kinds of knowledge we will seek to bring to bear upon the object we seek to know further through research.

Aporia: The dimension of paradox, difficulty and productivity

It is apt that aporia, an important and perhaps neglected dimension of philosophy, should follow on from ethics. The domain of 'aporia' can be characterized by conflicting positions and conflicting understandings, or else can be understood as a place or a space where understanding breaks down, or cannot find a clear way through. Ethics is rightly associated with this domain, for the aporetic signifies often what cannot be resolved. Such impasses call forth the ethical self that must make decisions.

Aporia has recently been foregrounded especially in the work of Jacques Derrida. Derrida's practice of philosophy almost entirely involved readings of key philosophical texts in the light of questions raised concerning the provenance and possibilities of Western metaphysics. Derrida has also addressed everyday concepts that have a bearing on our culture and thinking. Derrida explores a number of 'aporias' from both a philosophical and an experiential point of view, touching on vital ethical questions such as hospitality as it relates to cosmopolitanism (Derrida, 1996).

The decision, as Derrida demonstrates, is problematic. To be a decision, it must escape the enclosure of rational calculation. The good news is that occasions for breakdown in research momentum can, paradoxically, perhaps be the occasion for rethinking – and indeed, this has been the practice of much of the productive political and ethical work that has gone on in the name of deconstruction where questions concerning hospitality and cosmopolitanism, forgiveness and reconciliation, the relations between law and justice have been revisited. The experience of aporia is common enough in everyday contexts of practice and might be said to characterize all those intractable problems of the day. The experience of aporia is also likely to problematize all positions that lay claim to unproblematic progress: say, from research question through method towards solution. Above all, I would claim the experience of aporia is ground for rethinking: in other words, grounds for reviewing our relations to the object in question.

Earlier in this chapter, I mentioned Lyotard's idea of the *differend*. Lyotard's concern here relates to questions that arise in relation to aporia in politics and aesthetics. Perhaps the most interesting examples address cases where specific objects are addressed from different perspectives that take the form of different language games or 'phrase-regimes' to borrow Lyotard's own term. Such language games are incompatible. They may be so radically different from one another as to belong to different ways of being-in-the-world and different orientations to knowledge. Such language games constitute 'the objects of which they speak' differently, according to the insight on discourse offered by Foucault. Often cited is the case of aboriginal land claims for repossession based on tribal custom set against a mining company's possession of land held under modern law. A formal court of appeal could only operate from within one of those contrasting positions. We know that official courts in Australia will represent modern, European-based law and will judge in favour of those occupying the land rather than deferring to the primordial claim. So, the logic of that situation gives rise to a wrong that cannot be represented as an injustice within the recognized field of justice: a differend. It is in cases such as this where we can see more clearly the relation between justice as a more than legal idea of right and justice as used in a linguistic or representational sense, as in to do something justice by description or by giving an account of what it is. The phenomenological, the ontological, the discursive and the ethical meet dramatically in such an instance. Underlying all research (that claims to produce some new understanding or knowledge) lies this relation.

Lyotard's position has some discomfiting implications, some of them teased out in his discourse on Auschwitz. Lyotard asks about the meaning of names and claims that names are meaningful in relation to the phrases that embrace them and that they enter into a grammatical relation with (Lyotard, 1988). How we understand the meaning of Auschwitz depends on our awareness of a network of phrases that constitute a phrase regimen. To those that are enculturated into this phrase regimen, the claims of a holocaust denier are meaningless. On the other hand, the denier can make demands – for empirical evidence, for eyewitness testimony, for proof – that miss the point about Auschwitz and its significance that belongs to another ethic (or phrase regiment) entirely. In an important and perhaps upsetting way, we can see how Auschwitz becomes an ontological issue in such a case. What is it? What is the meaning of Auschwitz? Clearly, there are many dimensions to this question. But the case reveals again that ethical, ontological and phenomenological issues are intricated into a politics of knowledge – a mode of politics that is in play in all instances of knowledge claims, if to a much less visible degree.

The present condition of education gives rise to many aporia that are evident in much discourse arising from educational research. In a time when there is almost universal agreement that education is a force for good and an essential desideratum of any modern society (Wolf, 2002), educational discourses and practices are overwhelmingly locked into a series of oppositions that carry with them considerable historical, political baggage.

Philosophy now

To understand the contemporary conditions or context of thought is a massively complex business. And yet all our thinking derives from this context whether we know it or not. Mostly we are likely to be unconscious of the genealogy of ideas, expressions, turns of thought that inform what we are. Our legacy is elusive to ourselves, since it precedes us and shapes us. It doesn't immediately reveal itself to us, but insinuates its order into our very being as we acquire, use and get used by language (Lacan, 2006). This dimension is the unconscious of knowledge. It includes the sedimented layers of the history of thinking that at some levels we may have transcended and gone beyond but that in other ways may also haunt our consciousness of things. According to much twentieth-century thinking, there is a tradition of Western metaphysics – going back to its more or less Greek origins or emergence – that carries this spectral dimension. Modern and contemporary philosophers and commentators have made much of this inheritance since it patterns our thinking and draws a limit to our possibilities for thinking further. While this idea of a predetermined limit might give us cause for modesty in terms of the claims we might make for our conceptual ventures, our awareness of it may enable us to rethink its structures and effects and negotiate new pathways through its knotty tangle. We may regard this heritage as enclosure, but, at the same time, as resource. This is the lesson of deconstruction: that the tradition of philosophy is not dead, but is available to us as reservoir of our own inherited metaphysics that we can reread, reinterpret, change and produce something new from. We can take this renewal further, as I believe Catherine Malabou has done in her recent work. Taking seriously the idea that metaphysics is everywhere, she has used insights from changes in biological sciences to rethink questions concerning biopower and identity (Malabou, 2015).

We live still in the context of the enlightenment legacy, hence perhaps our collective faith in the ministrations of education and in the power of science. While elements of the legacy of scholastic thinking remain, in the field of knowledge the ongoing influence of the Copernican revolution, the Baconian privileging of method, the rise of rationality, the alliance of science with technology can be felt in much of our now institutionalized attitudes towards knowledge and the practices that go along with them. Epistemological questions remain significant to Western thought (the legacy of Descartes and Kant). Knowledge is still being addressed, rethought and reconfigured (Meillassoux, 2008). But it is worth recalling, always, that the history of thought is caught up in the history of the changing world order, as Hegel forcefully made us aware and Marx reinforced in the famous slogan 'being determines consciousness' (Hegel, 1998; Marx, 1970, 47). The emergence of modern science and the enlightenment accompany a drastically changing world order. The title page of Bacon's *Novum Organon* (1620) depicts a ship passing through the Pillars of Hercules out into the uncharted waters beyond the Mediterranean. This may represent the opening onto a new world, the great period of 'discovery' but may also represent the domination and exploitation of long-ago-inhabited lands and peoples by European powers. The emergence of science, and later social science, and the enlightenment are accompanied by the world dominating expansion of Western power. Enlightenment and the triumphs of rationality are accompanied by brutal conquest and destruction (Hochschild, 1999). While Hegel had heralded the idea of history as essential progress, Darwin later revealed a less-flattering image of evolution. Ideas about progress were beset by doubts about the very nature of things prompted by the annunciation of 'the death of God' and Freud's promethean discovery of the unconscious. Cosmology continued to radically decentre the earth and to propose that creation, far from emanating from the mind of a supreme being was determined by still inexplicable contingency. Einstein's revision of Newton made the world, and its environs seem like a much less stable place. The First World War left Europe – 'an old bitch gone in the teeth', in Ezra Pound's phrase (Pound, 2009). The United States emerged as world industrial power and introduced new, rationalized modes of production that left the workers, though for a while economically more secure, more alienated from their work (Harvey, 1991). Various versions of catastrophe emerged, exacerbated by the shattering revelations of the Second World War, including, most troublingly, the bureaucratic rationality that contributed to unprecedented mass murder, and the demonstration of the destructive potential of scientific knowledge in the atom bomb, soon to be reconfigured as the apocalyptic hydrogen bomb. Was this the end of the dream of enlightenment, the more-than-rude awakening to a darker history to come? Increasingly, anthropologically oriented knowledge problematized the idea of a collective human essence, while history seemed to prognosticate a less-than-transcendental future. The philosophy of science struggled to determine any serious philosophical foundations for knowledge that some saw as fatally allied to technology and dominant economic interests (Feyerabend, 1975b; Heidegger, 1993c). As language came to be increasingly thought of as fundamental to human being, its essence seemed more elusive. The illusion of the picture theory of meaning gave way to the recognition that language reflects back our own imaginings of reality to us.

Many philosophers sought to rethink everything in the wake of crisis after crisis – a condition that Walter Benjamin had foretold was actually the norm, as the wreckage of history piled up (Benjamin, 1999). Heidegger had adjured philosophy to seek to revive a meaningfulness to itself by returning to the question of Being, or more properly, as the later Heidegger would put it, the question of ~~Being~~ – in other words, to start again and to try to find a way to thinking (Heidegger, 1993e). But as Derrida pointed out, the legacy of enlightenment and what follows is precisely the key resource that we have. Not so much despite the depredations of history but rather because of them, thinking must seek to renew itself with the resources it has. Recognizing that we are all necessarily historical 'bricoleurs', we must engage with what is ready to hand, after all, following Levinas, Derrida promoted the idea that we have an inbuilt ethical commitment to the Other, who, as Other, calls forth our ethical selves (Derrida, 1999). For Derrida, deconstruction is interminable. It can never come to a final closure. Thinking goes on. And deconstruction is – in a way that is related to its interminability – a matter of justice, of doing things, ideas, ways of thinking, ourselves and others justice.

Chapter 2

The Elusive Object of Desire

Introduction: The object in question

In *Philosophical Investigations*, Wittgenstein wrestles with questions about other peoples' pain and how we represent states that may not be visible but nonetheless exist in language. In a series of statements that carry the exploration this way, and in an undirected but apparently purposeful movement of thought, Wittgenstein considers an individual who claims to know what pain is only from his own case. Apparently shocked by this possibility of his own making, Wittgenstein offers this analogy:

> Suppose everyone had a box with something in it: we call it a 'beetle'. No one can look into anyone else's box, and everyone says he knows what a beetle is only by looking at *his* beetle. – Here it would be quite possible for everyone to have something else in his box. One might even imagine such a thing constantly changing. – But suppose the word 'beetle' had a use in these people's language? – If so it would not be used as the name of a thing. The thing in the box has no place in the language-game at all; not even a *something*: for the box might even be empty. (Wittgenstein, 1968, 293)

In this case, Wittgenstein claims to be addressing 'the grammar of sensation' (1968, 293). Much has been made of this passage; it seems to me to have reverberations for phenomenology particularly in terms of discussions around the determination of 'the object'. As Foucault put it, 'words and things' is the name of a compelling problem that forces us to acknowledge that discourses 'form the objects of which they speak' (Foucault, 1977b, 49). What are we to make of questions concerning things relation to our articulation of them?

To say that we live in a world of things is both obvious and uninteresting, trite even. Things get more interesting, however, when we ask what we mean by a 'thing' or an 'object'. Most of us would agree that things play a significant role in our experience of life. We frequently refer to our world as a kind of 'meta-thing' that organizes and gives shape and meaning to the various entities that we live among. There are interesting contemporary theories that take a very animated view of the role of things in our worlds. Bruno Latour's Actor Network Theory credits things with the power of agency – a move that makes sense when we consider the symbolic, cultural and practical value that certain things have in our world. Things are intricated with our sense of ourselves, our cultural identity, our status and even our capacity to manoeuvre our way socially, professionally and otherwise (Latour, 2011). Bernard Stiegler's 'prosthetic ontology' privileges the human–thing relation as fundamental to any understanding of past, present and future (Stiegler, 2013).

What things, objects, entities appear as significant in research and how can we define that significance? For most of us, most of the time even the most key items that constitute our world do not appear as problematic or as in need of description or definition. And yet the problematization of the familiar – 'verfremdung' in Bertolt Brecht's term – is what enables us to review our current knowledge, to expand it, add to it or transform it. 'Making strange' implies a calculated effort to look again at something that seems familiar, that has perhaps become 'unseen' in its 'familiarity'. To make strange in the Brechtian sense is to enable us to see again, to see differently and to know the thing anew (Willett, 1964, 91).

We might ponder some of the kinds of objects that arise in social science research: the history of literacy in England; school-leaving age policy; simulation in nursing pedagogy; displaced persons camps for Jewish refugees in post-war Cyprus; religious thought in international relations; the experiences and social trajectories of working-class boys on assisted places schemes; the cultural politics of English teaching in the late twentieth century; how home-schooled children learn to read without being taught. These have been research topics undertaken at doctoral level. All of them – even in the brief titles I've given for convenience's sake here – suggest the address of a complex entity requiring accounting for. A major research effort is necessary to establish the complexity of such entities. Complexities multiply when we consider how such significant objects are caught up in dynamic social practices and engaged with by a range of social and technical actors (Latour, 2011).

Much work in the social sciences can be described in terms of rethinking the already known. This is true of education where recurring themes undergo research; familiar 'objects' reappear for review, for further understanding or for a change of understanding. There is something strongly metaphysical in the constant effort to rethink the nature of deeply familiar things. It recalls the Kantian distinction between *noumenon* and *phenomenon*, suggesting research be directed towards a constant review of the 'thing-in-itself', that obscure object of our desire. At the same time, it is often alarming that familiar objects of the world of education are taken for granted in their identity and in their 'form of existence'. Consider the school, the most far-reaching social technology of modernity. Its object-being is poorly understood by the most lauded researchers; its phenomenology is rarely addressed (Peim, 2001).

As researchers, we stand before an entity seeking to determine something about its essential nature, or its inherent possibilities. In historical studies, we may address an object that has fallen from view, or been forgotten or neglected. Objects are never self-evidently what they are, in spite of what common sense may insinuate. The thing-in-itself, the 'noumenal' object, is much more elusive than common sense would have it. The object appears in the register of the phenomenal and as such is always subject to movement and difference. Consider again the school: its complex history, its different architecture, its organization of time, its social functions and more. Each dimension can be understood in different ways. What it is constitutes a live and important question hardly explored by educational research (Peim and Flint, 2011).

Whatever the object, we stand in some relation to it. Most usually we stand in a relation of 'care': we are not neutral observers. We take an interest. We may seek to adopt a properly scientific attitude; at the same time, we approach the object with commitment. Wittgenstein recognizes this primacy of desire at the beginning of *Philosophical Investigations*. Citing St Augustine's account of language acquisition, he notes that desire is crucial. Desire is there in language from the beginning as it is for Lacan. The research process in its articulation of an object is inevitably beset by desire.

For Bernard Stiegler, human life is always strongly characterized by a 'prosthetic ontology' (2013). The objects and apparatuses of meaning-making have a strong bearing on our psychological anchoring in the world, touching on questions of social fidelity. We experience the world through such 'prosthetic' means insofar as we experience life as 'worth living'. Our being in the world is organized by the things that surround us, things we invest in, things that enable us to be what we are: we are faithful to such a world.

For Stiegler, the real significance of the renaissance is the transformation of memory via the prosthetic apparatus of the printing press producing the 'grammatization' that leads into modernity. Recently, the digital revolution transfigures the 'hypermaterial structure' of the contemporary lifeworld producing 'an internet of things' (Stiegler, 2013, 60). The paraphernalia of life is not merely flotsam and jetsam; it makes us what we are. Our very actions – including the most intimate and meaningful – are caught up with the objects and their structuring that constitute our world (Latour, 2011). Things can only get more complex, but are always beset by desire.

Stiegler's work foregrounds a decisive relation between 'things' and human existence; it draws on Heidegger's account of technology as the expression of Being, a quite far-reaching and significant development in modern thinking. Heidegger's redefinition of technology engages with Aristotle's account of the metaphysics of production and its relation to truth. Heidegger proposes that production is a kind of 'bringing forth', or *poeisis*, in the sense that things are made; but, equally, insofar as things manifest possibilities of Being, production is also a kind of *revealing*. Means–ends technology is a way of revealing, and in its global reach has become a way of revealing the world. For Heidegger, the upshot of this line of thought is that the essence of technology, as a mode of revealing, is the realm of truth (Heidegger, 1993c). In this sense, things are massively important.

In this guise, as a form of revealing, technology determines or brings to light something that has the potential to be there but is not already there: to use a commonplace example from everyday educational practices, when a student's work is designated through the procedures of assessment as *being* within a category. The technology of assessment produces the category, defines the work and expresses what it takes to be some essential truth of its identity. Considered in this way, Heidegger's account of technology is looking to preserve a more original sense of *techne* as first and foremost a way of *revealing*.

Taking this idea – of technology as revealing – we can see how technology opens the 'real' to us in a certain way. Using the above example of grading, the technology of assessment reveals a truth about the student's work, and by implication about the student, but at the same time *conceals* other dimensions of truth about the student's work and, by implication, about the student.

Heidegger's way of thinking concerning technology draws a distinction between more ancient, local forms of 'handwork technology' and the 'machine' technology of modernity – hydroelectric plants, aeroplanes, and radar stations – and suggests that they are different not just in terms of *degree* but in terms of *kind*. It is in its relations with Being that modern technology differs so radically. The desire of modern technology is to manipulate and organize Being, and to impose upon it a symbolic order (Lacan, 2006). In its most extreme guise, modern technology marshals the knowledge of science to interrogate, dissect, expose and organize every aspect of the world. In modern technology, we are seduced into the false assumption that we control, that through technological control we master the world. It may seem obvious that modern technology's revelatory directives are created and controlled by human purposes and human will; however, Heidegger's position indicates something powerful to the contrary: human beings do not control technological activity and development.

For Heidegger, technology constitutes a framing for human activity and knowledge, not the only one, but in modernity the dominant one. We do not govern or control the mode of 'unconcealment' of modern technology. This idea of a limit to human knowledge and control is a recurring theme in Heidegger's work. It concerns the manner of our access to truth and raises fundamental questions about how we relate to the world around us, and the status of knowledge we produce. That truth is to be understood, as a specific way of revealing belongs to Heidegger's attempt to think differently from Western metaphysics – where the exalted human subject is the epistemological centre of the world (1968, 1991, 1998).

Contemporary assessment systems in education can be understood as exemplifying Heidegger's rethinking of modern technology, truth and knowledge. Assessment, even in its most humble, mundane classroom operations, can be defined as a technology. Assessment partakes of the scientific absolutism of Western metaphysics: it is implicated in its delimited determination of truth – the truth of the student's work, the truth of the student's Being, the truth of the subject. From this perspective, assessment stands precisely as the kind of 'thing', 'object' or 'entity' that stands in need of urgent rethinking in educational research.

Objects from the everyday to the ultimate

Wittgenstein's beetle has relevance for thinking about the relations between language and 'mental' objects, or ideas. This problematizes the idea that we may each have our own understanding of some thing or other, even in relation to complex significant objects that are fraught with the complexities and intensities of desire. But it also problematizes the integrity of the thing we suppose that language refers to. The thing we refer to in language is more elusive, more interesting. Consider the empirical object, education. Where would we even begin to look for it? Everywhere? What kind of thing would it be that we might look at? We might look at some of its components: schools, universities, nurseries, perhaps; then we might consider the psychological dimension of education. Even if we gathered together all the various institutional spaces, places and contexts that we might associate with education, would we then say that we had grasped education in its essence or in its fullness of being? What about the experience? For some dubious humanisms, education is the defining element of the human (Biesta, 2006).

There is something curious about asking, What is education? This question is rarely asked in either professional or academic educational discourses. Isn't there something strange about this omission? Given that both professional and academic educational discourses make frequent references to education, the essence of their discourse? We might return to Wittgenstein's 'beetle in the box' to consider different ways of knowing or understanding what education *is* or what the school *is* but that model is designed to illustrate something about language, the way we commonly refer to any entity that we might know, experience and understand differently without bothering about the ontological complexities of its exact identity. We might ask even if 'exact identity' is at all appropriate in this case. The implications of Wittgenstein's' beetle in the box are dizzying and that is perhaps the value of the analogy: not to reveal how language refers to an entity, but to reveal the questions and complications that attend such an everyday component of our lives. Such questions have a strong bearing on knowledge. Something of this ontological and linguistic complexity is indicated perhaps in the elementary school practice of the 'object lesson' alleged to have originated with Pestalozzi (1746–1827) and imported into early mass schooling in the United Kingdom. The object lesson consists of interrogating a physical object with a view to determining how it might be accounted for – a basic exercise in phenomenology. That this practice was instituted on a mass scale is interesting, to say the least. That it hardly applies to the fundamental objects of educational studies – education itself or the school – is both fascinating and alarming.

Everyday objects reveal something significant of the 'world' they inhabit. Heidegger's engagement with what are sometimes called 'the big' or 'ultimate' questions starts with an understanding or at least an approach to the everyday things that make up our world. If we can understand them we might have a chance with understanding the world both they and we occupy. This is the basic task, if you like, of phenomenology, although Heidegger always wants to give these kinds of exploration – basic thinking about 'things' – an ontological turn. And surely this is right, given that any 'thing' we address, be it ever so humble and ordinary, partakes of Being in the big sense? When we ask what something 'is', we can't count the 'is' part (that pertains to being) out of the question. The humblest entity stands in a relation to the world and may become the occasion for rethinking of the nature of that world (Heidegger, 1962).

This approach, while perhaps odd in everyday terms, is productive in research terms, particularly in social sciences where we are often confronted by a deeply familiar everyday element of the social world. My favourite example, the school, is scandalously under-addressed. If this basic apparatus is not approached through fundamental thinking (or fundamental ontology), all the pronunciations of school-oriented research, policy, legislation and even standard practices must have no secure understanding of what they are referring to, surely? Unless, of course, they are content to work with some ingrained, unspecified, less-than-conscious and less-than-fully articulated model of the entity they most speak of.

Fundamental thinking about *Things*

While Heidegger's approach to 'things' follows the tradition of Kant's *Critique of Pure Reason*, the emphasis is rather different. Heidegger doesn't begin with the assumption of a neutral world populated by neutral objects being engaged with by an actively seeking and knowing subject. Heidegger's focus is on the mutually determining relations *between* ourselves ('dasein') and the things around us. We are born into a world of things that are already laden with significance by our active engagement with them. For Heidegger, the things-in-themselves are not so much in question; there is a logical priority to the interdependence of 'dasein' and things. There has never been a pure human subject encountering a pure objective object before the intervention of culture, or 'world' (Heidegger, 1962).

In drawing a distinction between worldly engagements with 'everyday' things and science, Heidegger affirms that there can be no founding knowledge behind the conventional way we know things (Heidegger, 1967, 249). Science is concerned with universalities – how things are according to patterned rules; particular things are to be understood as manifestations of universals. Science seeks to get at 'the nature' of things according to its own premises and principles: it is axiomatic. Extracting things from their context of lived experience modern science investigates them abstractly. Science has little to say about objects in their relationality: about gifts, for example, works of art or diaries. Things are also caught up in the web of our being, engaging with and intricated in our symbolic projections. Not that a thing depends on our idea alone to be what it is. Aircraft are not mere projections. They are creations, informed by consistently tested properties of materials.

We can think of things as existing in two ways: as members of a class but also as unique individual entities that occupy time and place with absolute singularity. Some entities, like a school for example, or a classroom, are physical entities but are certainly not exhausted by that categorization. A school or classroom includes material elements that are essential to its being: but carries with it symbolic meanings that are equally essential. Drawing out the material and symbolic features of an entity can help us to determine what seems universal and what seems particular in the way that entity appears before us, although we must be wary of assuming that these categories are fixed aspects of reality, of course. Reality is dynamic.

One important consequence of thinking about the difference between the universal and the particular, in relation to objects, is that it forces us to acknowledge the dimensions of time and space that frame the entity in question. These dimensions are never incidental: as we shall see in the chapter that considers questions concerning context and world, the dimensions of time and space are defining to a significant degree. Any object for instance has a history. Unravelling that history can be immensely informative, even when that history is contested.

For Heidegger, how we approach an object is vital. The distinction to be made between science and common sense (or other kinds of 'given') suggests that things stand in 'different truths'. What that truth might be always involves some relation to our world. By this, Heidegger does not mean to reiterate the commonly held idea that what things are depends on your viewpoint and that we are all individuals and therefore everyone potentially experiences things differently. In concrete situations, the things that we bump into have other dimensions also that are not dependent on our viewpoint or on our idea of what they are. This is rather like claiming that things have a certain determinate specificity that comes before us, a certain 'givenness' even when they might be the products of our own making. Things have an existence independent of our understanding of them. In Lacanian terms, the rather frightening realm of things independent of our symbolic ordering is the Real. Our 'world'-making tendencies involve strenuous efforts to both read and construct so as organize the horrifyingly brute Real for us (Lacan, 2006).

Our relations with objects are mediated in language. Language provides a model for this essential but extremely complex relation. In language we speak of ourselves, from the point of view of and that is the subject of our discourse. But at the same time, we speak of things that are 'predicated' on this subject: things or objects that are distinct from it but related to it. In language, our concourse with things is always caught up in this subject–object/subject–predicate relation: and we cannot escape it as searchers seeking perhaps to minimize our specificity as subjects in order to claim objective authority for our findings and for our claims for significance.

This attitude has far-reaching implications – especially for some of the more simple-minded approaches to empirical research. Such approaches still enjoy a privileged status in educational social science research in general. The question of perception that has been significant in modern Western thinking must be foreclosed in such approaches to research. The relations between perception and concepts, between perception and something different that we might call understanding or knowing, is slippery. It would be a brave metaphysician who would claim to be able strictly to define the differences between them. It is easier for the researcher under pressure to produce 'impact' to continue as though such issues did not exist.

In modernity, this difference remains a key problematic in our collective understanding of basic questions about knowledge, certainty and historical paradigm shifts. Descartes and Leibnitz didn't really distinguish between perception and knowledge. In some important ways, seeing was knowing – with all the implications this might have. With Kant, there's more to seeing than meets the eye: and there's more to knowing, by a long chalk, than there is to seeing. Kant's *Critique of Pure Reason* is a critique of the view that reason has limitless power to determine the nature of things. For Kant, things have an existence of their own that is never going to be wholly amenable to our perceptual–conceptual apparatus. This sets a necessary limit to the rational. We might consider this to have been a very wise move: rationality not always having enjoyed a positive history. Pure rationality, in fact, is synonymous with idealism that strips the Real, to borrow Lacan's term, of its inalienable otherness and materiality.

Relations between subjects, their worlds and the things of the world ultimately lead towards far-reaching insights essential to any understanding of research. Questions arise over big ideas that haunt research thinking, like paradigms, objectivity, validity and truth. Thinking has a powerful bearing on these issues. Certain strands of philosophy continue to trouble the relations between subjects and object and consequently between science and its objects and science and the world. These are big issues for modern knowledge, none bigger in fact. The essential move of Heidegger's fundamental ontology – a rethinking in effect of the basic conditions of existence for 'dasein' – is that the things that we tend to separate as subjects and objects must also been seen and understood in their interdependence, an interdependence that constitutes the totality of things. What's more, on this view, when we believe we are thinking 'purely' rationally, the axioms that rational thought posits operate only within some approach or orientation that has already taken place or played its role in constituting our possibilities for knowing anything. The orientation means that we do not and cannot stand as naked, naïve subjects before the thing that we apprehend or seek to apprehend. We always already carry with us a dimension of thought that shapes the mode we can apprehend the thing in. Things in the world are revealed to us, but always within a mode of revealing.

So, for Heidegger it is important to affirm that modern science is not scientific because of its deployment of the scientific experiment (in social science often substituted by the random control trial), but rather that it is axiomatic: an experiment always sets up a hypothetical framework. The procedures and conditions, even the language and conceptual framework, are all set up in advance and only within them is 'nature' – or the things under interrogation – allowed to respond. The meaning of this is partly captured in Bacon's rather chilling phrase that we must do more than observe nature: we must 'torture' nature to force it to reveal its hidden secrets.

The Differend: Objects in difference and dispute

Jean Francois Lyotard's original concept of 'the differend' introduces another way of thinking about the representation of reality in discourse. Lyotard takes language to be a mobile open system that is frequently characterized by 'phrases in dispute' (Lyotard, 1988). We'll shortly see how this expression has epistemological and ontological implications. The immediate point is to make the connection between language, reality and injustice. This connects Lyotard's thinking with some elements of Derrida's deconstruction: the intrication of language and justice. At a straightforward level, I think we can get a sense of this connection if we think in terms of a just representation. Does our way of representing what is in language justly recognize what is? Here we open onto questions of the 'nature' of *things*, our access to that 'nature'. For how can we judge the justness, or justice of a representation of something or of anything without some idea or sense or evidence for what it 'really' – or properly – *is*.

Lyotard expresses interest in language and justice, in two senses. There is the idea of a just representation; also, the idea that questions of social justice are caught up with questions of the determination of things. This idea, little explored in the field of educational studies, has far-reaching implications for education – and especially for any claims for education to be a site for social justice. Lyotard has an agonistic view of language: he certainly doesn't ever entertain the possibility that language can express universally common interests, nor that language somehow is essentially concerned with communication. There is so much else going on: much in terms of conflict. In *The Differend*, a key distinction is made between what happens in litigation and in disputes that are predicated on 'the differend'. Disputes within the sphere of law have reference to a common language, the rules of which are more or less stabilized and open to public scrutiny. In the case of the 'differend', there is a victim whose interests or position is not merely wronged or neglected but who has lost or has had the power to be represented foreclosed.

Perhaps the most obvious kind of case that Lyotard presents is that of aboriginal land claims, where under ensconced, official Australian law aboriginal land claims have no recognition. In aboriginal law, they are perfectly legitimate. That legitimacy is not representable in modern Australian law. It is not expressible. It doesn't fall within the 'phrase regimen' of Australian law – certainly not as currently practised.

For Lyotard, a great deal hangs on this idea of the phrase. For him, a phrase can be any signifying event, although most commonly it will refer to language in use. A phrase is a unit of meaning but also signifies an event of meaning. We are constantly generating phrases. For Lyotard, the phrase is the privileged unit of meaning, but it doesn't stand alone. A phrase is a kind of theoretical fiction; it can represent a lengthy document or a pithy gesture. But a phrase cannot stand alone and make sense. Any phrase belongs to a flow, a 'concatenation of phrases'. Phrases mostly appear in series where one phrase links to another in the flow of meaning. On this view, a serious difficulty arises for the rationality of language – in the recognition that the laws of conjoining phrases allow recognizable 'concatenations' to appear. It is significant that Lyotard refers to the law of conjoining phrases as 'concatenation' as that again refers to the fact that phrases get organized in series but that the link(s) between phrases is never determinate. Such 'concatenations' are arbitrary, although they may have the power of convention to render them apparently 'natural' or 'appropriate' (Lyotard, 1988).

The common view of communication according to Lyotard is that phrases – or phrases in series, statements – are somehow determined or stabilized by their relation to some referent that signifies a portion of reality: some more or less palpable object or event – some 'thing'. Lyotard uses the phrase 'rigid designator' to depict this idea of a determinate relation to reality for statements organized in phrases. Drawing on various interpretations of Wittgenstein's discourse on naming, Lyotard problematizes this relation to 'reality' by reminding us that while proper names may consistently refer to certain individual objects or even categories of objects, this reference is essentially empty of content. When I refer to the University of Birmingham, we might say everyone knows what entity I invoke. But nobody knows for sure what I want to say about the University of Birmingham or what meaning I invest in it. Some designations are deeply problematic and fraught with conflict: Palestine–Israel for example.

How do we make sense of things within Lyotard's account of phrases regimens? Phrases gather meaning through usage to produce networks of meanings that Lyotard refers to as phrase universes: the complex possibilities of sense that enable meanings to be exchanged consistently. Every phrase presents a 'universe' on the basis of four elements: sense (possible meanings), referent (what's being referred to), addressor (from whom), and addressee (to whom). In its moment of enunciation, the meaning of the phrase is indeterminate, inchoate. It is the 'situation' of the phrase that renders any consistency of meaning. The situation refers to how the phrase appears in a 'concatenation of phrases' in any one of a vast number of 'phrase regimens'. Regimens bring together syntactic and semantic types that belong to particular linguistic operations – phrases can then be determined as constative or performative or as cognitive, descriptive, prescriptive, interrogative, evaluative and so on. Any phrase 'gathers' meaning from its insertion into a concatenation within a regimen. In another regimen, the phrase might have quite another meaning.

Phrase regimens are heterogeneous and incommensurable: radically different genres may bring different regimens together, but, at the same time, some phrase regimens will be at odds with others. Genres supply rules for linking phrases, but in a syntactic sense. Genres come into play in the larger functions of discourses. Genres themselves turn out to heterogeneous and incommensurable – and this gives rise to another level at which the differend may operate. Genres may also be seen in some significant ways to act hierarchically. In some spheres, some genres will supervene over others.

A differend occurs when a discourse inhibits links between phrases that would allow the representation of a foreclosed position. In the context of a dispute, the differend operates in relation to sense, referent, addressor and addressee. These elements may not be recognized by the dominant discourse and fall into a kind of silence. They cannot be represented.

The whole point about the differend is to draw attention to the fact that referents in the real world are often in dispute. Such disputes cannot be resolved by simply arranging for an occasion of conference or exchange. Power operates through discourses that may foreclose the discourse of the other.

> A case of differend between two parties takes place when the 'regulation' of the conflict that opposes them is done in the idiom of one of the parties while the wrong suffered by the other is not signified in that idiom. (Lyotard, 1988, 9)

The 'differend' exposes points of injustice where a powerful discourse improperly disqualifies or overwhelms a less powerful discourse within a situation of oppression. There are analogies with research and with the ethics of educational research here. At stake in Lyotard's discourse of the differend, it is often assumed, are matters of language: but there is another, ontological way of looking at it that suggests a more far-reaching issue. What is in question is the determination of 'the thing': the object does not reveal its nature, as it were, without some profound ambiguity. Understanding that ambiguity is at stake in how we describe and represent the world is an important perception for research that may give rise to a good deal of interrogative analyses and redescription. In educational research, strongly interrogative accounts of education – that call into question its sovereign authority and value – are foreclosed by dominant discourses of improvement and redemption.

Schooling and the differend of code theory

Basil Bernstein's code theory, addressing the case of language in education, indicates the hidden differend of schooling. This differend operates according to principles that are mostly unknown in their context of operation. Code theory exemplifies how thinking – rethinking, in effect – can change the meanings of phenomena we confront. It acts as disturbance to already-given understanding, perception and engagement with an everyday thing. In this case, the thing in question is the liberal model of the school – and of education in general. Code theory makes strange the established, everyday determinations enacted through education in our era. Code theory specifically forces us to think again about language and its relations with schooling social class differences – issues that don't automatically crop up either in the ontology of language or in the ontology of education (Bernstein, 1973).

Code theory developed from Bernstein's interest in how class differences translate into cultural differences and how these operate as power differences in educational institutions. What Bernstein was interested to explain was how perfectly intelligent and articulate people end up being rejected or deemed as failures by the education system – and why this negative process follows social class patterns. At the centre of Bernstein's findings are institutionalized judgements made about language. Such judgements are strongly patterned in favour of certain social class groups and against others.

Code theory began by identifying different patterns of linguistic usage according to different social class of users – social class in this sense is defined as a position in the social division of labour. Social class-patterned linguistic differences relate strongly to different family types that arise from different modes of interaction that in turn derive from different status positions within the social division of labour. They are not therefore simply linguistic differences, but linguistic differences determined by social class differences. They are not surface differences, either. Bernstein used the terms 'restricted' and 'elaborated' to refer to different types of language use – codes – that represent different orientations to meaning. These different orientations to meaning arise through social solidarity in the contexts of daily social life. Code theory explains how social class differences get manifested at the level of speech above and beyond dialect and individual differences. Drawing on and informing the emerging systemic functional linguistics of M.A.K. Halliday, code theory sees in the language of different class groups a significant difference at the level of 'social semiotic' (Halliday, 1973, 1979).

Bernstein's code theory research showed how in schooling power operates through linguistic social interaction, to translate cultural differences into differences of capacity and attainment. The school, then, is a vital mechanism for the social structure to effect this process: 'between language and speech is social structure'. This process is referred to as *reproduction*, although in Bernstein's sociology reproduction is a dynamic process sensitive to shifts in modes of production, cultural shifts in identity formation and the changing organization and ideas operative in its various institutions.

Code theory is an explanation of symbolic domination through language – where one form of language, referred to as 'elaborated code', is favoured above another, referred to as 'restricted code', within the formal and official institutional operation of the school. Bourideu would later refer to this phenomenon as symbolic violence. Language differences get translated as differences in aptitude, intelligence and rightness for academic progress and reward. Users of restricted code (in Bernstein's theory, this is the dominant code of the lower working class) are effectively excluded by their primary socialization in the home from the dominant codes of schooling. This does not mean that their language is itself 'restricted' in some absolute way or at all impoverished. It is differently coded. Middle-class children in contrast may have their values and habits of speaking and thinking reaffirmed by the dominant values of the school embedded in the elaborated speech code. Elaborated code takes a kind of symbolic precedence in certain contexts. On this view, there cannot be an objective judgement of linguistic performance against a normative standard across code modalities.

The example of code theory, surely, forces us to reconsider some familiar and very significant features of the world of modern education. It makes us look again at our understanding of language. It makes us reconsider how decisive judgements are made about social progress through academic attainment in relation to critical judgements about language. It makes us look again at the school as a linguistic environment suffused with utterly mistaken ideas that get translated into judgements that sort pupils or students into ranked categories. Code theory makes us look again particularly at the practices that schools deploy in the field of literacy where linguistic differences and cultural differences also come into play, differences that are also predicated on social class. Above all perhaps, code theory makes us look again – with shock and pain? – at the apparatus of assessment that runs through the process of schooling, begins before children enter the school and carries with it a ranking and ordering effect, and, as several commentators have noted, serves to reproduce social class differences rather than challenging them, which often works persistently in favour of certain groups that are deemed to have the most appropriate forms of speech and modes of expression. In a large sense, surely, code theory makes us look again at any easy assumptions about education offering opportunities for self-realization or for any kind of equality (Bernstein, 1970). Code theory should, in addition, force us to look very critically at the shallow discourses of ability that still dominate the everyday language of schooling, ideas that are shocking in their eugenicist ethic.

Bernstein's code theory is echoed and amplified by other studies that have identified cultural difference, expressed primarily through language, as the critical factor in educational differentiation, permanently giving the lie to assumptions about differences in intelligence. There has been an ongoing discourse concerning language and education relating to the schooling of African American children, for example a discourse in the United States that demonstrates the evident power of code theory but has little effect on persistent inequalities (Delpit, 1993, 1995; Labov, 2004; Smitherman, 2000). And while the sociology of Bourdieu – predicated on a similar concern with language and cultural differences – has been influential in some academic quarters, it has had little or no effect on the practices and outcomes delivered by schools and other educational institutions (Bourdieu, 1991). Bourdieu's powerful arguments concerning schooling, language and symbolic violence have made no difference whatsoever to the ongoing practices of schools in making judgements about the performance and abilities of whole groups of pupils.

Code theory helps to problematize the very idea of the school as purely and simply a context for learning. The school is above all always already a social environment in which class differences are caught up in operations of power. Neither learning nor teaching can be unrelated to this social fact. Social differences, expressed at the level of culture and realized in the symbolic domain via language, must always be in play in the most minute operations of the institution. This fundamental fact about the school cuts across any idea that access to schooling in itself can simply effect opportunity. The dominant 'liberal' position of much English teaching that claims to view all as equal and that claims to offer all equally the opportunity for response and for self-expression must suppress this fundamental sociological point (Peim, 2009).

Most research seeks to bring something that is not yet fully acknowledged in the order of things 'to light' – that is to spotlight its existence and its very particular way of manifesting itself so that it gets recognition anew. The example of Bernstein's code theory will serve here to indicate how the 'differend' may operate in effective terms in the field of education – and also of the value and potential of research to uncover and reveal the differend at work.

An object lesson

When we speak of 'a thing' or 'the thing', we often have in mind a concrete something that stands before us in time and space. However, that is certainly not the only or perhaps even the main way that we experience things. I now want to examine here the case of an object that appears in rather uncanny form to illustrate some principles of thinking in relation to our understanding of the thing, to illustrate also how the role of thinking can be decisive in our relation to key things in our world. Let's say our world is education. We are interested in exploring the world of education through an understanding of one of its most basic apparatuses, the school – the paradigm institution of modernity. How may we read such an object?

Here I want to examine the meaning of a photograph of a school to illustrate some considerations that might inform our understanding of key, complex objects in social contexts. The miniature case study I will explore here is a photograph found online when exploring some examples of private schooling for a module I was teaching to undergraduates. It happened to exert a certain fascination that partly stems I think from that fact that I have spent some time considering and writing about photographs in relation particularly to historical studies of education and that I have a long-term interest in the field of semiotics or the science of signs as inaugurated by Ferdinand de Saussure (Peim, 2005). The photograph invokes the logic of the 'trace' as articulated in Derrida's recasting of ontology as spectrality, a way of thinking that is particularly pertinent to the examination of visual images and that is also relevant to historical studies including 'the history of the present' – an understanding of the present as the repository and as the unfolding movement of history.

The photograph in Figure 2.1 is quite simple. It depicts a school. It is contemporary. Similar images may be found easily. Many things are striking about this image.

The provenance of the photograph is not given by its sources. It is not ascribed to an author in the way that a literary work might be. It seems recent but isn't dated. The image usually appears in the form of a news item, apparently neutrally reported as part of a trend. Information is usually brief and to the point: the image represents Wellington College, but Wellington College in China, in Tianjin, in fact. Tianjin is represented as China's third city, a port city 120 kilometres southeast of Beijing. It is interesting to note perhaps that when I

Figure 2.1 Wellington College, Tianjin

have presented this photograph at seminars or conferences and asked: What is it? Replies are not at all even or predictable. Some recognize it as a school, while some identify it as a prison. Others are bemused by its setting – urban and modern – and by its architecture, which appears dated while, at the same time, its patina is new. For me the key question to ask of this image or representation is: What is it? And it turns out that the answer to this apparently banal question is far from simple. It is a school, but that in itself is no simple entity; what we might ask is, what is this school, appearing in this particular guise, doing in the context of contemporary Tianjin? Of course, we would need to know something of the provenance of Wellington College, a famous, elite, expensive private school in Berkshire in England, a bastion of progressive private and again elite European-style education with a strong vein of 'Englishness' associated with its ethos.

The original Wellington College, of which the Tianjin version is claimed to be a clone, was opened in 1859; its foundation stone was laid by Queen Victoria, and it was initiated as a national memorial to the Duke of Wellington, who defeated Napoleon at Waterloo. The image is already freighted with history as soon as we catch its title or at least catch its reference to the object it represents. But this representation, surely, is complex and many layered. Carrying the name, and something of the style and the very architecture of Wellington College, Berkshire, Wellington College, Tianjin, bears the trace of that history. Recalling the history of the structure of education in England, 1859 is on the eve of the inauguration of the national education system that was to be founded formally by the 1871 Forster Education Act. In this way, we can trace a connection – albeit obscure, but nevertheless powerful – between the founding of Wellington College, conceived as a national monument and expression of elite culture, and the founding of the urban elementary school. The latter was conceived as national training ground for the relatively newly formed mass urban populations. The new social technology had been forged by pioneer bureaucrats such as James Kay Shuttleworth, the British arch exponent of the new form of biopower that was finding its material form and its spiritual character in the elementary school (Donald, 1992; Hunter, 1994; Jones, 1977; Wardle, 1974). Wellington College – in Berkshire and in Tianjin – is a reminder of the history of the separation between elite and mass education, a separation that continues of course in the contemporary scene.

This image recalls a 150-year history of the development of education as biopower (see Chapter 5). It also signifies the division between (1) education conceived of as training in character and engagement with the liberal curriculum and (2) mass education conceived of in terms of offering basic literacy and numeracy, a certain training of the body and the cultivation of a disposition towards self-management. The image then carries with it the traces of these movements: it speaks of something beyond itself, although this beyond is inscribed into what we might naively call 'the-thing-in-itself'. This realization, that the photograph calls forth something – many things – beyond itself, calls out for explanation. A basic phenomenology of this object in its context requires significant historical knowledge and social interpretation. Our own position is not without complications, either. How do we see this image? From what position do we view it? And, what sense do we make of it. We cannot see it through the eyes of the photographer (that obscure figure) that we might resort to in order to get some sense of its meaning. We may experience this uncertainty of meaning as a dislocation, one that is echoed in the strange provenance of the image: Wellington College in Tianjin. Does not this very designation disturb our sense of the order of things, of the world order of things? We might see the resemblance between this building, that appears to be newly constructed, and the architecture of the 'original' Wellington College. But what sense can we make of that? The scene presents an ordinary object, a school, but in a specific manifestation, Wellington College, but in an unexpected, dislocated location. The photograph does not, cannot, interpret itself. It appears as an instance of the Real that cries out for symbolic determination. It acts as a metonymic fragment of our world: we don't doubt its reality or authenticity. It is part of our world, but what can it mean in terms of our contemporary understandings of what it is: this instance of the paradigm institution, the school?

Ghostly things: Objects in time

The photograph, any photograph in fact, depends on many supplementary factors that are not within it to make sense of it, to read it, to see it even. Perhaps this photograph more than most requires some special kinds of knowledge, but even adding this dimension will not settle the question that hovers over the question of the meaning of the photograph. And I must confess that I think this is a photograph with a very powerful meaning. The meaning hovers somewhere between the manifest content of the photograph and what it conjures beyond itself. The inside–outside relation, as with any textual material, is vital. This is where we touch on some far-reaching issues concerning the object – and concerning the important issue of the objectivity of the object.

The whole of recognition involved in the reading of the photographs is rich and complex and cannot be described simply in terms of 'seeing' what is 'there'. Seeing is not an act or process that can escape the logic of representation: the visual field is organized for us and by us according to codes and conventions that give us an orientation and that allow for recognition as well as for active intervention in terms of meaning. A flat surface, differentiated by the shaped arrangement of a colour-varied continuum must be seen *as* a place, within a time, enfolding an event, revealing a social practice, a social milieu, a world. Recognition of this element of *seeing as* is equivalent to recognition of the 'unknown knowns' that we bring to bear upon our understanding, and perception, of the so-called everyday reality. As we have already acknowledged: Kant extensively articulated that there is more to seeing than meets the eye (Kant, 2003).

Although because its apparently iconic mode of representation, photography is often misunderstood as making more direct connection with reality than writing or speech. It can appear as 'light-writing', as though light itself were making a statement and the photograph were a more 'natural' mode of representation (Grosvenor, 1999). The operation of the aperture enables the image of what is apparently 'there' to be inscribed onto a light-sensitive surface. But this account of how photography works can be sustained only up to a point – and must foreclose so many other vital features involved in the 'reading' – or seeing – of a photograph. Elements such as framing, selection, perspective and the act of translation are required to read a three-dimensional reality from a two-dimensional surface. As we shall see below, there is the fourth dimension. Active work of mediation is required to render the photograph as sense-making, as in some way carrying the meaning of an entity in and of our world.

The fourth dimension here is time. A photograph is always a historical document that 'captures' (apparently) an instant of time that it doesn't always belong to.

In other words, there is some temporal dislocation in looking at a photograph no matter how recently taken and how much of our contemporary world. The photograph we might say is a historical document par excellence. It holds out the offer of data, but data, of course, always requires the supplement of sense-making to make it sensible. One interesting way of exploring the relations between data – in this case photographic data – and reality is through the concept of the 'spectre'. Initially concerned with questions concerning the alleged death of Marxism, Derrida articulates the logic of the spectre in terms of a thinking concerning the relations between past and present, the present being haunted by the spectral past. The past, like the photograph, is spectral because it is not, cannot be, fully present. The past is spectral also because it returns – as revenant. It comes back to haunt us. The past is also spectral as it signifies something incomplete, unfinished and, therefore, perhaps in a curious way, something that, although past, is yet to come (at least in its – impossible – full presence). The 'revenant' or returning spectre signifies a disturbance in the past that points towards or demands a resolution, just as photograph calls for resolution, or meaning-making – and signifies in doing so its own incompleteness. Addressing the spectral, Derrida coins the term 'hauntology' (Derrida, 1994) in a joke that makes a critical comment on the classic language of ontology; and that also summons an alternative set of principles from Derrida's earlier work concerning the deconstruction of the metaphysics of being-as-presence (Derrida, 1976, 1978, 1987). The spectre is an apt metaphor: the spectre is a presence that signifies an absence: it occupies ontological space differently from how we may imagine the everyday stuff of the world. In conjuring a present absence, the spectre plays with and disturbs this every metaphysics of presence: 'To be spectral is neither to be present nor absent; it is neither to be nor not to be. Indeed, the spectral, says Derrida, is what exceeds all ontological oppositions between absence and presence, visible and invisible, living and dead' (Rottenberg, 2002, 5). Derrida puts it thus:

> The concept of the spectral has a deconstructive dimension because it has much in common with the concepts of trace, of writing and differance, and a number of other undecidable motifs. The spectral is neither alive nor dead, neither present nor absent, so in a certain way every trace is spectral. We always have to do with spectrality, not simply when we experience ghosts coming back or when we have to deal with virtual images. Even here, there is some spectrality, when I touch something. (Derrida, 2001, 44)

Spectrality recalls the position Derrida elaborates in an earlier phase when, concerned with questions of meaning and being, Derrida proposes 'a new concept of writing', where writing comes to stand for the very operation of symbolization and acts as a metonymy for being. In other words, we experience the world in terms of its representation to us as a kind of writing, a concept that in Derrida's articulation emphasizes 'the play of differences' that disrupts any simple notion of presence. This takes us back to the phenomenology explored in Chapter 1 where the presence of any object or subject cannot be expressed or experienced as such:

> No element can function as a sign without referring to another element which itself is not simply present. This interweaving results in each 'element' – phoneme or grapheme – being constituted on the bases of the trace within it of the other elements of the chain or system. This interweaving, this textile, is the text produced only in the transformation of another text. Nothing, neither among the elements nor within the system, is anywhere ever simply present or absent. There are only, everywhere, differences and traces of traces. (Derrida, 1987, 26)

Derrida points her to an alternative logic, that is, the tendency of Western thought to make a clear distinction between presence and absence, being and representation, ideal and material. The spectre acts as metaphor for the logic of signification, while also providing a dramatic image of the critique of the metaphysics of presence. The spectre signifies the problematization of 'the living present' as singular, complete, self-present entity. In representation, something stands in for something it is not. The present signifier marks the absence while also conjuring the presence – never of course a 'real' or full presence – of what it points to. The sign, any sign, is haunted by this interplay of presence and absence. The sign can only stand in for what it signifies, depending for its own logic on the *absence* of the referent or the object. There can be no one-to-one relation between signifier and signified. All signs are subject to this logic of presence and absence. But this phenomenon that we can easily see at work in a photograph or written text purporting to represent itself is also pertinent to our sense of being-as-a-whole: the interplay of presence and absence applies to our direct apprehension of the world just as it does to visual material (photograph, say) or written material (text, say). It is the condition of possibility for our apprehension of any object, no matter how trivial or how significant. The research implications of this are, of course, momentous.

The spectre signifies a restless presence, both haunting and haunted, but also an absence or gap. There is something unanswered, something incomplete in the very nature of the spectre (Abraham, 1994). We might think of this space of incompleteness as the space of the quest for knowledge, or research. The spectre forces us to rethink our assumptions about present realities. Drawing on Kant, this logic of inheritance – an inheritance that carries an obligation for fulfilment or realization 'embodied' in the spectre – requires 'a decision and a responsibility'; no legacy can both express and deliver its own demands – it requires the responsible answer of a question that is not given (Kant, 1991, 110–111; Rottenberg, 2002, 6). According to this logic, no legacy of knowledge can be a simple, inert gift: 'truth' is always an incomplete project, always situated within a discourse, demanding a particular kind of work that cannot achieve final completion.

Let's imagine we could step inside the photo, as it were, and conduct some empirical research to find out what is going on. What would we experience? The immediate reality of a present presence? The logic of deconstruction says that isn't possible. Even if we were 'there', we could only bear witness to what was in terms of a representation that would also always be a translation – and that would necessarily carry with it the logic of the spectre. That is the problem with all claims that empirical data could settle the matter and determine the actual actuality of what there is and has been. That is also the problem with all forms of realism that might claim to have circumvented questions of representation and correspondence (Harman, 2016; Meillasoux, 2009)

The school as object

The photograph of Wellington College, Tianjin, discussed above, as an object raises questions relating to the main ontological themes tackled in this chapter, themes concerning the determination of the object, the differend, spectrality. These themes can't be neatly organized into a systematic order. They derive from various perspectives concerned to open our thinking about how we can know and represent our world, the world and the things that inhabit those virtual spaces. Such thinking offers opportunities for researchers to develop accounts of key objects they address in research projects. Here, I will reiterate a point I have made elsewhere and frequently that some of the key objects that fall significantly into the sphere of educational research have hardly been addressed as objects worthy of enquiry. Reasons for this must relate to the dominant ethic of research in education that assumes that it already knows what these key entities are in the very fabric of their fundamental being. Ontological accounts of the school are rare indeed. A few exist, but they do not inhabit mainstream educational research as points for departure or even as points for development (Donald, 1992; Hamilton, 1989; Hunter, 1994; Peim, 2001). Educational research has tended to remain blithely unconcerned with what education is and with what the school is, taken as an object to be explored, interpreted, given an account of, although so much educational research is – allegedly – school focused. In what follows I will briefly sketch out an account of the school in terms of its structure and function, by way of illustrating an ontological account of this paradigm apparatus (Peim and Flint, 2011).

The modern school (in the UK context) was born effectively 1870. The general institution that emerged was the state-funded elementary school. It was developed from and partly in reaction to some of the existing models, ideas and practices found across Western Europe. It was fashioned into a distinctive and unprecedented human technology. This emergence was not instant following the 1870 Education Act (Peim, 2001). That date constitutes, though, a useful rough starting point.

A number of key elements quickly came to comprise the architecture of the social spaces of the school – along with the clarification of their symbolic social functioning (Robson, 1972). The classroom, the playground and the hall signify symbolic, social functions essential to this new, extensive and powerful human technology. This new formation also included the definition of the figure of the teacher, the expansion of the curriculum and a powerful idea about the necessity for intervention into the lives of the 'people'. In total, the 'new' school represents an array of spaces, techniques and occasions for the transformation of populations. This is a vital process (1870–1900) in the constitution of biopower.

In 'Beacons of the Future', James Donald gives an account of the development of the elementary school from its precursor, the Lancasterian or monitorial school (Donald, 1992). These 'proto' schools are represented as being limited, if powerful, apparatuses. Their potential social function is limited by their monolithic architecture and arrangements of space. Conceived of as designed to manage the learning of large numbers via a rank and file ordering of all its pupils in a single space, the Lancasterian-monitorial school promoted a monumental version of learning via repetition. It proved an efficient teaching instrument utilizing the learning of its pupils as monitors in a chain of instruction. It was the proud boast of these schools that they could effect learning for large numbers of pupils with the presence of a single instructor. The monitorial-Lancasterian school, however, lacked the components of the elementary school that were being developed at the time. The new structure combined key elements to form an entirely new human technology, the modern school.

The elementary school depended for its biopolitical function on an amalgam of critical components. First, was the characteristic arrangement of space. In its classic form (and still, analogically today) the new governmental elementary school is constituted of the following symbolic/practical spaces:

the cellular classroom
the communal hall
the playground

The cellular classroom – distinct from the open schoolroom of the Lancasterian school – accompanies the introduction of the elementary schoolteacher, the bearer of the ethical technology characterized as pastoral discipline. The discursive roots of this emergence are generally traced to David Stow's account of the early model for the modern school in south Glasgow. In relation to this new modelling of the institutional apparatus of care, Stow begins to define the figure of the teacher as the pastoral figure who shares something of the character of the lives of the children he [*sic*] is to teach (Jones, 1990). The figure of the teacher – located in the space of the classroom – represents the emergence of the technique of pastoral surveillance that forms the core of the central social function of the school – the transformation of subjects into a self-regulating citizenry. The classroom is the location for the development of 'simultaneous instruction' that becomes – after several mutations – the system of organizing the school population into regulated segments that can be treated to the normative processes of training and examination that characterize the social function of the school.

The classroom engages relations of proximity as the necessary condition of the 'shepherd-flock game' (Donald, 1992). The figure of the teacher can transform urban populations, organized into discrete groups and age stratified, into a trained and self-disciplined citizenry of modernity through a pattern of normatively assessed development. The classroom is both the material and the institutional space for this relation, the necessary technology of the new form of state elementary school. This school population can be subjected to a regime of normative development and care – from statistical measurements of height, to the staged tested curriculum and the nit nurse.

The school hall being the site for general assemblies is the place where the idea of community can be expressed and enacted. Religious assemblies have been commonplace features of the modern school, though they have also been supplanted in more recent times by secular moral assemblies on conduct and values. The assembly hall is the place for the gathering of the population, for its daily routinized identification as a population subject to the shared rehearsal of values through exemplary moral tales, borrowing its style from religious practices of the sermon and concerned with the management of order in the institution and the inculcation of moral principles. In its most recent incarnation, the assembly hall is perhaps more likely to proffer secular moral guidance than religious and is likely to present moral dilemmas as occasions for the development of moral sensibility and the problematization of the self in relation to the ethical as a technique for reinforcing the development of ethical substance (Hull, 1975).

The playground – 'the carefully crafted milieu' – contributes to the school's function as moral training ground (Hunter, 1994). Both David Stow and Samuel Wilderspin, early nineteenth-century pioneers of the urban school, had advocated the significance of the playground. For Wilderspin, the playground is dedicated to the cultivation of self-government. In it, working-class children – 'rather filthy if not legislated for' – learn to manage their own conduct in the company of their 'fellows' who are learning to operate under similar principles of self-restraint (Hunter, 1994, 73). Sir James Kay-Shuttleworth, a key bureaucrat in the process of the development of the form of the elementary school, draws on David Stow's Glasgow Normal Seminary to account for the dual function of the playground where both exercise and recreation are significant features. The playground's importance also consists in the unobtrusive presence of the figure of the sympathetic, but disciplinary teacher to enable the development of 'propriety of demeanour' (Hunter, 1994, 75).

My sketch gives a very partial and limited account of the spaces of the school, conceived of as an object calling for a form of description that will enable its essential identity to be revealed. Of course, we all need to be wary of phrases like 'essential identity' as they might imply some noumenal essence that it would be impossible to pin down and delimit in any determinate way for all sorts of ontological, epistemological and hermeneutic reasons. The account I offer suggests a particular perspective, one that is keen to illustrate the enduring features of the school in its modern incarnation. It takes a view that the school cannot be simply regarded as a neutral instrument that might be directed towards quite different purposes. The history of the school in modernity suggests otherwise and belongs to, I would add, that huge change in social formation that Foucault refers to as 'the great transformation' involving the gradual transition, through the rise of certain apparatuses and practices, to a capillary form of power – one that is, I would insist, very much the order of day today. For this apparatus of modernity, learning is by no means the dominant function.

The school in ideal form

An alternative view is presented by Jan Maschelein and Maarten Simons, who represent their position as different from both reformers and restorers, those critics of the school who in their terms misunderstand its essential nature, according to its ancient, and specifically Greek, provenance. Once we realize this, 'what the school is and does becomes clear' so long as we attend to the school's 'radical and essential characteristics' (Masschelein and Simons, 2013, 9, 10). What's radical and essential about the school includes the provision of 'free time' and the sharing or making available of what is referred to as 'common goods' or knowledge and skills, although, interestingly, the book doesn't make it explicit what these are or might be with any specificity. According to this account, the school 'has the potential to give everyone … [the capacity and opportunity] to rise above themselves and renew the world' in what they claim is the language of Hannah Arendt, drawing on the concept of 'natality' (Arendt, 1958). This idealized vision focuses specifically on what it refers to as 'the scholastic years' as though there was no need to explore the age specificity (and obsessive age stratification) of the school.

For Maschelein's and Simons's account, the school is, as it is in my account above, 'a historical invention', with the difference that they trace its origin to the Greek polis, although not very explicitly and certainly not with any reference to the conditions it will have arisen into. This gesture seeks to define its emergence as being at one with the emergence of European culture rather than to associate it with the real socioeconomic conditions of the time. They are not claiming that the school's foundation depends on the co-existence of slavery, for instance. Rather they seek an ideal model to serve as template for 'reinventing the school' (I take this to mean conceptually). At the same time, they claim to act as advocates for its proper mode of being.

Maschelein and Simons do not shirk certain critics who present a series of accusations against the school – under the following headings: alienation, power consolidation, demotivation and lack of effectiveness. They categorize these critics into essentially two camps: reformers, who want to make the existing apparatus more effective, and the restorers, who want to return to some classical model of the school (a mythic ideal, it is implied). They do not however categorize themselves, but I would suggest that they appear in the guise of 'redeemers': their model is not the classic one that belongs to the restorers but the more ancient, more true and more proper model, they claim: it is the primordial essence, as they see it, of the school they wish to speak of in order to reclaim its right to exist but to exist in a new, and more radiant, form.

In their response to critics of the school, they make reference themselves to the 'fallen' school referring to its 'mad bureaucratization'. This actual, fallen school is essential for their call for the return of a redeemed school, a second coming for 'the quintessential school'. This is the project of renewal they call for as the special mission of the somewhat mystical vision of the school they present. And this vision is attractive, 'heterotopic' one might say, to borrow Foucault's powerful term. The school they promote, not actual, is still an everyday possibility, 'heterotopically normal'. It projects the vision of the mundane institution of the school transformed into a special, open space – free from the demands of worldly concern – a space for the very renewal of the world. On this view, the school (quintessential, mystical) effects a suspension of worldly concerns and allows a profanation of everything that is sacred. Its 'ownmost' possibility is to put everything into question in a protected space, although in this 'playground' (their word) the 'world' is made 'open' to the 'student' (Heidegger, 1962, 248–250; Masschelein and Simons, 2013, 138–139).

Even the most ordinary 'technology' of pedagogic practice, simply putting something in front of the students, on this view is seen as transformative – for the student and, ultimately, since their 'school' is the primary site for renewal, the world is thus made new. Maschelein and Simons argue for a retrieval of the *real* (although not real) school against its contemporary reduction. This is in effect a theological call for redemption. The fallen institution where learning outcomes, for example, and bureaucracy distort the proper mission of work against what is represented as the proper democratic function of the school (although, of course, there is nothing democratic about the school as we know it, and examples of democratic schools are extremely rare).

Maschelein's and Simons's school stages a vital openness to explore the relations between the world of formal knowledge and 'the lifeworld' of the students under the tutelage of the teacher as 'amateur', where 'amateur' is a positive term of approbation signifying the required openness. The task, as they see it, is to provide the conditions within the school for the requisite experiments towards the desired kind of openness. In a call to arms, they invite a rising of pedagogues: 'to stand up (again) and be heard' in a time when the 'voice of educators seems dimmer today than ever before'. This final call to arms, as it were, ends by acknowledging the loss or suppression or failure of the school to have realized its true mission (Maschelein and Simons, 2013, 140–141).

The object, then

In the cases outlined above, the most mundane object of education, the school, is, I believe, demonstrated to be not only a complex and difficult-to-define entity but also an object in dispute, subject to a 'differend'. What is in dispute here is not its existence. It remains a materially and historically manifest thing. What is crucially at stake in these different accounts is its essential being, its 'soul' as it were. It has for a long time seemed odd to me that this ubiquitous and massively significant social technology has not attracted much attention from educational researchers. Accounts of what the school is are rare indeed, as indicated above. Prompted by this realization, we may ask: Why this lacuna? Why this silence? It is tempting to suggest that the school and the larger education that it is metonymic of have become taken-for-granted elements of our social topography. The school occupies the status of the 'unthought', so much are its existence, function and value assumed. Education itself is just such another 'object' – in Timothy Moreton's phrase a 'hyperobject' – admittedly even more complex but at the same time 'an unknown known', a vastly powerful, global entity with its own force, laws, institutions, ideals and practices that is often felt to be beyond the reach of interrogation. Of course, arguments exist within and about education that promote their own versions of it, but the real business of putting education into question to examine its status as significant 'object' in our world has not yet begun.

It is unfortunate that the 'literature review' has become a standard component, an unthought dimension of research practice (Shields, 2000; Thomas, 2013). The premises of the standard form of the literature review are questionable, imposing a constraint on research thinking. It is as though a determinate body of work could represent ways of knowing and understanding a complex social phenomenon. This conception obviates a vital step in the logic of knowledge, avoids the metaphysical dimension, and negates thinking. Rethinking any object effectively entails engaging with a basic phenomenology.

The literature review is predicated on the projection of a determinate literature that defines the limit of the object in question. That projection distorts and delimits research from the perspective of thinking. The determination of the object cannot reside in a discrete, finite body of work. That approach is a recipe for the repetition of standardized practice to produce standardized outcomes, as so much educational research indicates.

Emphasis on the idea of 'literature review' might simplify the research process and might ensure that a project conforms to the standard genre, but it doesn't enrich knowledge or understanding of the object or topic in question. The generative capacity of research practice is more likely to be enhanced, even empowered, by the hermeneutic idea of a meeting of horizons.

What the literature review avoids – and does it do this deliberately? – is the likelihood of questions concerning the authority that accrues to established or canonical knowledge. Nor does the literature review as conventionally conceived address the means we deploy to make sense of texts and their accumulated value (Shields, 2000; Thomas, 2013). Both of those dimensions again offer ways of expanding the scope and knowledge base of a research enterprise. And both also offer the possibility of addressing both the accumulated knowledge and the form of that knowledge from a perspective that is informed about its conditions of existence. One of the key moves of Derridean deconstruction – a way of thinking that arises from a twentieth-century concern with ontological significance of language – is that it seeks to pose questions concerning limits, borders and given identities. It is important for thinking as researchers that we challenge the determine borders and categories of the research process, in order to reach further into the questions that can enrich our pursuit of the object we seek to know, even if in doing so, we find that the object-in-itself turns out to be more elusive and more complex to define and know that we might have thought at first approach. What's more, as indicated above, in the field of education the object in its ontological dimension is frequently (and willfully?) foreclosed.

Chapter 3

The Subject

Affirming the subject

The subject of my research, oddly though unavoidably, is myself. I find myself as it were at the centre of an enquiry that I have instigated, or, at least, that I claim ownership of that is mine to see through and manage. Although the world of knowledge it belongs to is not of my making, I appear within it with my own perspectives, my own understandings, although, in turn, these can never be fully my own: they have to have been – in order for me to be there at all – shaped by the protocols of that world. To distinguish myself within that world – as researcher, as producer of new knowledge – to that world, I must identify the credentials that authorize my contribution. I must justify the choices I've made and articulate my interpretation of that experience. In an obvious sense, there is no knowledge or world or meaning without subjectivity. The term 'subject' is rich in implication: coming to an understanding of that dimension means more than merely thinking or talking about myself (Moran, 2000). Surprisingly, giving an account of oneself as researcher has little to do with being subjective.

To give an account of oneself is trickier and more interesting than common sense may imagine. Complications intrude from the beginning. If the first task of the researcher is to give an account of oneself, a series of questions follow concerning in what discourse, what mode of understanding and from what position within what perspective I can articulate an account of myself. How am *I* qualified for such a complex enterprise? After all, isn't one's own subjectivity, for powerful and nontrivial reasons, itself a difficult topic? Am I not somewhat elusive to myself in certain important respects? And isn't one instantly obliged to reach beyond oneself for the resources to embark on an undertaking of self-analysis. That we know ourselves well is only one side of an intricate story. In one very important sense, we can only begin to know ourselves with the intervention of what is outside of ourselves, in forms of knowledge we may not necessarily possess (Williams, 2001).

The common-sense idea that we all already know ourselves, and know where we stand on things, hardly seems like a serious position for any serious knowledge-seeking enterprise. The familiar injunction to 'know thyself' appears shallow in relation to the complexities of psychology, social theory and contemporary theories of being and identity. Rich and varied ways of understanding the complexities of identity abound (Althusser, 1984a, b; Butler, 2005; Freud, 1921; Irigaray, 1993; Lacan, 1986, 2006).

Giving an account of oneself means articulating who we are in relation to the specific object and field of knowledge we are engaging with. This includes the relation between subject and world – in the sense of (1) the world of the research enterprise and (2) the larger world that enfolds that enterprise, including somewhere reference to (3) the world of knowledge. This complex field of thinking gives rise to temporal, spatial and socio-institutional questions: to explore one's orientation within those dimensions. The question of world is significant not only in terms of the grounds of one's understanding but also in terms of consciously contributing to knowledge, to the claim for the originality of one's discovery. This opens onto the question of meaning. The meaning of any work resides in its relation to its world, as well as in its relation to other worlds and to 'the World' (Harman, 2007, 46–47).

'The subject and research' announces a theme problematizing objectivity, queering any attempt to clearly separate objectivity and subjectivity. It also opens onto a series of vitally important questions that do not admit for ready-to-hand or formulaic answers and cannot be readily settled. Such questions resonate throughout the research, relating to the intervention into the history of thinking in modernity philosophy of ideas from psychology or 'metapsychology' (Boothby, 2001; Freud, 1921).

Modern and contemporary thinking have rearticulated the human subject: a key and constantly illustrative dimension being gender. In the field of gender, we see clearly how the subject is caught in a relation between discourses that operate outside of and independently of itself and its own engagements with such discourses. Where to locate and how to articulate the truth of this subject? Can an account of the subject begin in its own terms? The terms that articulate the subject can never be entirely its own. Such terms, to be available at all, must always precede and have an existence independently of the individual subject. On this view, the gendered subject looks as though it is not a stable entity from the beginning: its identity hovers between different ways of seeing itself or being seen – rather like the fundamental particle in quantum physics. The question of identity from the perspective of gender has opened up. This opening applies critically to questions of subject identity in general (Butler, 1990).

The enormous, fascinating discourse of subjectivity in modernity has been strongly influenced by ideas from the latter part of the nineteenth century and the early part of the twentieth century associated with Freud's 'promethean discovery'. The articulation of the unconscious as the other to consciousness has enormous implications for modern understandings of identity (Boothby, 2001). The psychodynamic element of subjectivity has become essential as constitutive of the subject. A certain mobility operates between subject, other and world, meaning that identity is mediated and not given. This insight is not merely abstract in its implications: recognition of the dynamism in subject formation problematizes the sovereignty of the self-conscious self. While we may imagine that conscious decision-making processes belong to a rational, stable ego, it turns out that rationality is a lot trickier and more interesting than common sense would suggest (Williams, 2001).

The psychoanalytic subject and the institution

The Freudian intervention suggests that all conscious decisions and consciously undertaken acts are always already informed by something else that can't be brought safely within the confines of rationality. The revelation of the unconscious strikes a blow to rational enlightenment. The positive effect of this 'discovery' is that it enables the constitution of the subject, its formation in social contexts, to be realized and more fully articulated. As both Freud and Heidegger reveal, the subject is newly, radically, to be understood in its relational being-in-the-world, occupied by its specific concerns that inform its mobile identity. The unconscious offers the occasion for rethinking the subject–object–world relation, bringing into play both the affective and the social dimensions (Boothby, 2001). The subject, on this view, is not singular but is multidimensional and mobile, as indicated above. The subject's achievement of whatever stability it attains, whether in terms of gender, status, self-consciousness or any other dimension of identity can then be traced. The subject on this view can never be said to be finished, finalized or fixed (Malabou, 2012).

An account of subjectivity after Freud is necessarily an account of one's relations to others, to things, to one's world and, for present purposes, to one's research. PhD research, for example, in the social sciences, is always conceived of as an individual project that belongs to oneself. Implicated, then, is one's inward, intimate relation to the object of one's desire for knowledge. And this relation of intimacy, surely an almost inevitable if not necessary condition, requires accounting for. For an adequate phenomenology of research relations, this element of subjectivity can't be foreclosed. An individual project demands an account of one's subjective relation with the object in question, meaning owning up to a specific attachment. One doesn't find oneself in a research context by accident. There may be accidental factors involved, but the undertaking of research into a specific object requires a commitment, not just to the object but to the world the object inhabits, to a mode of knowledge, a subject arena, perhaps – a rich and complex area of possibility. This is not some fluffy idea of self-expression. An awareness of the subject's relation to the established archive of knowledge demands hard-headed engagement and knowledge (Derrida, 1996).

The unconscious isn't only at work at the individual level. The unconscious inhabits the subject more intimately than the subject can ever know but also operates at a collective level. Collective being and identity is infused with unconscious forces. Language, for instance, operates at a significantly unconscious level. What's more, if we thought that individual structural irrationality could be offset somehow by the cool rationality of collectively established procedures, protocols, accumulated findings, we would be mistaken, as the twentieth century's history informs us. We all know and experience the authority of uncentred bureaucracies that issue edicts that come from nowhere and that we all follow. Rational bureaucracies, ostensibly instituted to improve procedures, guarantee impersonal judgements and secure proper and orderly adherence to necessary rules for communal conduct, can be experienced as nightmares of oppression, opacity and intransigence, as Max Weber (1864–1920) foresaw in his dark vision of the development of 'instrumental rationality'. In modernity, the subject is always, well before birth, a subject of this bureaucratic rationality that enfolds her being.

The bureaucratic embrace of existence that is a significant feature of modernity is also evident in the world of knowledge, the world of formal knowledge at least, with its powerful and global institutions. The public control of knowledge is exercised by and through these institutions, institutions that have the power to determine the validity or otherwise of knowledge and research. This fact touches on some major social and philosophical themes and carries with it – often unaddressed – far-reaching themes for the subject of research who is inevitably subject to the ethic and protocols of the institution (Peim, 2010). This is the institutional, bureaucratic dimension that both Kuhn and Feyerabend make much of in their accounts of the organization of knowledge in modernity (Feyerabend, 1975a; Kuhn, 1959, 1970). In both these influential accounts, it is the institution with its protocols, hierarchies and filtering procedures that determines what counts as knowledge. The stability of the order of knowledge is thus managed at the level of the social, an inescapable element in securing the borders. What we know, what we can know, stands in a constituent relation with the institutional unconscious of modern knowledge forms, unknown knowns in a far-reaching sense.

Formal, officially endorsed knowledge depends on the archive of what is established. New knowledge will always potentially carry a threat to disturb its security. The assurance of the archive and of the collective wisdom achieved through painstaking historical development operates as an authoritative power. The subject of research confronts that power and must seek its approbation. The subject of research is the subject of the institution of research – an identity that carries with it the requirement to accede to its demands. The relation can be seen in psychoanalytic terms whereby the subject of research is interpellated as a subject of the institution. The subject must transform its own desire to be in line with that interpellation. Ideally the subject will fashion itself to be as desired by the institution. The ego-ideal and the ideal-ego work together to ensure that we internalize the dictates of the world of research that confronts us in institutional form. We must fabricate our work, and our academic identity, accordingly. While we may be free to challenge the authorized version of the archive and challenge the authority of the 'archons' who watch over it, we must play that game cautiously. There is a law of genre that applies to what we produce as researchers but also to how we present ourselves (Derrida, 1996; Peim, 2010). The apparently rational, organized, procedural world of research, on this view, is fraught with unconscious forces, requiring acts of submission and faith as any other social context does. In the realms of research, conscious being is always accompanied by the unconscious.

Taking subjectivity into account means recognizing that any research endeavour concerns the psychodynamic apparatus variously articulated in psychoanalysis. Even from the most elementary questions, What do I seek? or Why do I seek what I seek? subjectivity and its psychodynamic structure are in play and must remain so to impel the endeavour. This dimension is important for essential reasons, including the necessity for a research project to demonstrate awareness of knowledge of the discursive domain it is emerging from and seeking to contribute to and to extend. The significance of the psychoanalytic dimension is not confined to the vagaries of the individual psyche and any (probably unlikely) intrusion of unconscious material into the detail of the research project. It is rather the structural and necessary relations between the symbolic order, the world of knowledge, say, the self-conscious intention of the individual subject of knowledge and that subject's necessarily imaginary relation to that world. Desire, in Lacanian terms, cannot be excluded from the objective 'pursuit of true judgement'; it can be usefully understood in terms of the impetus that drives the often arduous and apparently self-effacing work of research.

In other words, thinking through one's very primary research relations has rich potential for providing a discourse shaping an understanding of one's self-involvement in the topic, field and quest in hand. Giving an account of one's experience necessarily involves an analytic attitude. Language requires that one put oneself outside of oneself, as it were. I become the 'shifter' 'I' and thus have at least a dog's chance of some objectification of my own relation to what it is that I seek to know.

Articulating oneself thus is far from self-indulgent, or self-aggrandizing. In fact, it could be seen that giving an account of one's research relations, in terms of identifying one's historical situation, specific field and mode of interest, is necessary to the avoidance of intellectual hubris. After all, how many academics in the field of education claim that their position is the one true knowledge that can save education from its fallen condition (Gorard, 2002, 2013)? This can only be done by casting aside one's subjectivity and claiming that one speaks from some disinterested nowhere. If we imagine that all our decisions, including our academic and intellectual decisions, are taken on a purely rational and uncomplicated basis, we are deluding ourselves. We should be wary of overconfidence in the field of intellectual endeavour. Most celebrated cynosures of intellectual achievement have been modest about making absolute claims for their findings, acknowledging the necessity of provisionality of scientific knowledge and the rights of uncertainty.

To confront our subjectivity as knowledge bearers we must recognize the primacy of established discourse. The space that we operate within is the enabling space of a domain of knowledge that precedes us and enables us, as agents of knowledge, to be what we are within that field. We must work within the affordances of a domain or across domains. The desire of our subjective being must negotiate this terrain, with its requirements, protocols and established knowledge. Although research handbooks might like to render this confrontation neutral or anodyne, there remains a dynamic potential for change in both researcher and field. All knowledge, after all, exists in a zone of proximal development.

The subject *and* the object?

According to some recent philosophical positions, we are what we are through our confrontations: more specifically, through a dramatic, transformative meeting – or 'event' (Badiou, 2007). A transformative event, on this view, takes the form of a radical disturbance that calls forth our fidelity and ongoing commitment. We may all muse on some such 'event' shaping our lives: someone we met, a mind-changing read, a sudden realization. Examples apply to the world of knowledge, thought and intellectual activity. I will give personal examples of such events in my own professional life later in this chapter. How we experience the 'event', though, doesn't remain static. There's nothing lapidary about our experience. There may be a profound difference between an experience – our induction into field of knowledge or a profession, say – and our retrospective re-understanding of that experience. Our conscious intellectual lives are often disturbed by the difference between our experience of an event and our retrospective understanding of that event. Our personal histories do not follow the pattern of a coherent life story but are much more complicated by that shifting element as we reinterpret the meaning of our history, our place in history and history itself. Ourselves and our relations with specific objects or 'things' will have this always-shifting character, a dimension of our being that we must consider seriously in the business of giving an account of oneself (Butler, 2005).

All this emphasis on subjectivity surely problematizes the very possibility of pure objectivity? A subjective commitment is essential for a project to begin at all, to be driven forward, to inhabit one's consciousness and to make its demand for expression, development, solution. But this process itself entails objectification. To render what may be subjective in origin and in motivation objective, it must undergo the reflection, rethinking, redefinition and exploration that have been implicit in the model of research proposed in this book. The approach to subjectivity advocated here is one that enables subjectivity to be objectified.

The effect of this process is to deconstruct the division between subjectivity and objectivity. After all, much of the drive of twentieth-century rethinking of the formation of the subject – in Heidegger, Lacan, Althusser, Foucault, Bourdieu, Bernstein, Butler – is to indicate the objective character of subjectification as the process whereby 'the outside becomes the inside' to borrow Bernstein's phrasing (Bernstein, 1987, 563).

More importantly perhaps than the abstract assertion that research must necessarily involve a strong subjective component and more important than denying any claims of pure objectivity, the recognition of the significance of the subjective dimension constitutes an affordance: it provides a potentially rich component for exploration and discovery. This doesn't mean a descent into the self-regarding solipsism. On the contrary, this post-Heideggerian analysis (for that is what it is) is concerned to insist that the separation of the subjective from the objective is not possible to sustain. Both categories of being constantly contaminate one another. The relations between subject, object and field problematize pure subjectivity and pure objectivity. In other words, there is more subjectivity in objectivity and more objectivity in subjectivity than the conventional division allows. Addressing the subject–object relation offers an opening into an awareness of positionality. Any knowledge is subjective insofar as it inheres in a subject. For the researcher, knowledge must be seen to have been advanced by the researcher's intervention. To advance knowledge, the researcher must understand intricately their own position and the field of knowledge they are positioned within.

Heidegger's analysis of objectivity identifies strong tendencies in modern science with the destructive, limiting phenomenon called 'das gastell' (or 'enframing') – an alliance of science with machine technology that reduces Being and beings to things that stand separately from lived experience and that have value in utilitarian terms. Enframing sees the world as a set of entities to be manipulated, utilized, exploited, stored up and held in reserve. Against this technologico-Benthamite view of modernity, Heidegger sets the idea of a world that is intimately engaged with, lived in as world that discloses the truth of Being to its inhabitants. Such a world doesn't allow the subject to see itself as separate from it, as an administrator, an overseer or master. Heidegger refers to 'unworlding' as the project and condition of scientific knowledge in modernity. 'Unworlding' is the product of a legacy of the Platonic/Cartesian legacy, the legacy that seeks to abstract things from lived experience in a metaphysics of ordered and ranked identities (Heidegger, 1993c). On this view, we must acknowledge, as researchers, that we belong to a world that fashions us and that we cannot detach ourselves from as disinterested, spectral outsiders. Hence the call to give an account of ourselves.

Kant's critique of pure reason stands perhaps at the intersection of the enlightenment and modernity, but also seeks to give emphasis to the impossibility – and perhaps the undesirability also – of a purely objective knowledge. Achieved at a cost of considerable intellectual labour, Kant affirms that it is not given to human beings, as subjects of knowledge, to apprehend things-in-themselves. Such things are not only beyond the reach of human understanding, but beyond the reach, rather, of pure apprehension. The reason is due to the very fact of understanding. Our understanding always configures what we see, the object, but also the conditions the object is apprehended within. There is no direct mode of apprehending the object. We may posit the idea of things-in-themselves, and thus pay obeisance to the Real. While we cannot have any direct access to things-in-themselves and see them or know them in their own essence, we understand perfectly well that they exist independently of our knowledge of them. This is, therefore, an anti-essentialist view, one that says that it is not given to the scientist or the researcher or the humble everyday subject to know for sure that they have apprehended the thing-in-itself. But it is not an idealist view that says that only our idea of things gives them existence (Kant, 2003; Lacan, 2006; Meillassoux, 2009). We see things according to the faculties of mind that are inherent in being a human being, according to Kant. More than that, such faculties as we have are configured specifically in terms of time and place: one's own apprehension, understanding and even perception is affected by Being, in the Heidegger sense of a specific form of revealing that belongs to an epoch, a world, an era and a culturally specific context (Heidegger, 1962). Any specific form of subjectivity that we can think of must have its formation in some objective set of practices that are engaged in, administered and overseen collectively by others. Conversely, when we talk about seeing something objectively, our subjectivity has been fashioned by or given over to a certain form of subjectivity required by a super-subjective, collective, objective entity as embodied in a public institution like a university. But this objectivity requires a subject to realize itself in this required form: it is therefore a form of subjectivity, not a negation nor an erasure of subjectivity.

Subjectivity, objectivity and genre questions

It remains a common perception of research that objectivity is the order of the day and that this objectivity must somehow negate, banish or foreclose the intrusion of any subjective elements. Because of this heavily embedded assumption, the role of the subject in research – and its potential place as a major category for thinking and for articulation – is not much addressed, except in some specialist cases that acknowledge a role for personal narratives. The research manuals tend to begin rather with surface features that avoid the awkward considerations that can arise from serious engagement with the question of the role of the subject and the place of subjectivity in social science research.

The question of the role of the subject and the place of subjectivity in social science research however is worth considering, especially for the researcher in education who is likely to be addressing an object that they stand in some very determinate relation to. This is rather different from, say, a scientist who may be studying aspects of the molecular structure of manganese compounds or a biologist who may be studying genetic patterns in swallow populations. This book proposes beginning from a basic phenomenology of research relations, to enable the subjectivity of the research to be articulated without any loss of objective rigour. The basic phenomenology outlined in Chapter 1 suggests that we can find ways to rethink our own subjectivity as researchers that will avoid any loss of rigour and any tendency to present a 'merely personal' approach. The role of the personal in the acquisition and development of knowledge has long been known and articulated (Grene, 1966; Polanyi, 2015), but recent times – the past forty years or so – have seen a proliferation of high-level thinking concerning the nature of subjectivity with powerful implications for its intrication in knowledge and research (see above).

Educational research has been significantly shaped by a dominant model that restricts the genre. It proposes rather a genre all its own, a genre that has the status of fait accompli but that also has no provenance in the evolution of research thinking. This genre has no visible history but does have a powerful institutional grip. It might be worth briefly exploring some of its assumptions about what research in education essentially is – although to do so it will be necessary to read these assumptions off from the form of the genre and the various articulations of its component parts that prevail. Contemporary arguments about the 'proper' direction of educational research have sought to recover a perhaps mythical past mode that privileges relevance and that operates in the ethic of improvement. Commentators have expressed nostalgia for a time when educational research was directed not only towards the elucidation of educational concepts but also, and more importantly, towards the resolution of problems within educational provision – real-life problems (Carr, 2006, 2007; Pring, 2000). While this attitude may be understandable, it is only from the point of view of a very specific way of thinking about what education is and a very specific way of thinking about what research essentially is that it is possible to think along these lines. This is the kind of attitude that eschews excessive theorizing and that wants to retain a kind of homeliness to the very language of educational research or alternatively that wants to use properly scientific methods to reach decisive conclusions about what we must do next and that wants to influence and even direct educational policy (Gorard, 2013; Thomas, 2007). These are limiting views and views that must foreclose whole worlds of possible practice – often without ever intending to or even knowing what they are doing.

Here is a characteristic outline for a research project:

- Deciding your topic and your research question
- Project management and study skills
- Doing a literature review
- Revising your question and theorizing
- Deciding on an approach: methodology and research design
- Design frames
- Ethics and access
- The right tools for the job: data gathering
- How to analyse the information you gather
- Discussing findings, concluding and writing up (Thomas, 2013)

Not only does such an outline marginalize questions of subjectivity, it reduces the research process to a set of predetermined categories that have little relation to one another except as automatic elements of a genre. That is, the various parts of the thesis as conceived here do not grow from a process of thinking, reading and redefining, but belong to a set format. Hence the idea of a 'literature review' that implies a determinate literature for the topic or object, unaware that placing the object in a context and asking questions about perspective entirely complicate and compromise such a determinate view of what needs to be read and accounted for. According to this model, the question concerning subjectivity has never entered the research equation. Similarly, theorizing is set as a special, discrete task implying that the kind of thinking that belongs to the research process can be contained and explored separately from questions concerning what it refers to as 'methodology' and 'ethics' that seems here to be conceived of as related to 'access'. While this looks like a neat formula, it reveals an ethic, a specific model of what research is. It turns out in this case to be a model that has become ensconced as the model for educational research at doctoral level, even though there is no theoretical or practical justification for it.

Researchers are often advised by handbooks to begin with a research question. The idea informing this advice is of a ready-to-hand process that can be predicted and staged in advance. The stages are then set out into the now familiar formula. Not only is this approach dully predictable and depressingly uniform. In its certitude of form, it drains the research enterprise of its potential originality. The handbook merchant no doubt will argue that this is necessary, that the would-be researcher needs structure and guidance, that the research process is trying enough as it is; but it must be conceded that this approach will always lack an important dimension, a dimension in fact that is deemed to be essential to any research worthy of the name.

Genre questions are fundamental here. The assumption that research theses in social science should follow a particular formula derives provably from the perceived need (often of course leaders in research methods) to provide materials and to offer a secure template for completion to the aspiring researcher. The genre accumulates a certain solidity through practice and repetition. It becomes recognized through practice as what is required and then takes on the character of an established component of the order of things: 'This is how it is'. The form of the thesis becomes 'reified', to use an old Marxist cultural studies term (Petrovic, 1983). It takes on the weight and form of an object that simply exists – naturally, as it were.

Where do I begin? Formula or phenomenology?

In fact, most research do not begin with a specific and formulable question. They begin with a situation, a phenomenon, a researcher. Where does the impulse to do research come from? For the researching subject? This question activates productive lines of thinking that can provide a way out of the formulaic dead end. Entering an open space of possibility, the researcher can immediately lay claim to originality – as well as constructing a rigorous account of the conditions giving rise to the research in question. A good deal of research – almost all the formula-driven genre – neglects this dimension. This question though provides a starting orientation that, without decreeing in advance the point where one must begin, enables the forces involved to be articulated and to be seen in relation to one another.

Few researches begin with a clearly articulated question leading directly into a logical progression of processes. There are good reasons why that is the case. And these reasons belong to the way of understanding things that is frequently sidestepped or foreclosed when engaging with those features of research method courses that want clear plans and that adjure researchers to construct research design according to their own prefabricated model of research procedure.

Here it may be useful to present a difference that is relevant to the whole of this book and what it is attempting. It is a difference that arises from the recognition that a great deal of social science research, particularly educational research, is destined to operate within a particular paradigm of knowledge. As I will hope to demonstrate throughout the book, this strongly institutionalized paradigm is not only out of time, but it is seriously limiting for the researcher.

An important consideration here is the fact that it is deeply traditional in Western thinking to represent knowledge in terms of sight. Much of the familiar vocabulary of knowledge in everyday talk as well as in more formal academic or knowledge specific discourses follow this tendency. We talk about 'insight', about being perceptive, about having vision or having a view, for example. To think of knowledge as belonging to a visual field may offer some useful terms and terminology but it also may, provisionally at least, provide some powerful descriptive schema for giving an account of critical dimensions of knowledge and critical issues at stake in claims to know. At the same time, it is as well to recall that the visual metaphor is a metaphor and that knowledge may be conceptualized differently with different consequences for our understanding of what knowledge fundamentally is.

The visual metaphor will serve here to offer an account of some of the fundamental relations that are at work in any subject and object encounter. Here we are assuming a lot, of course; although we may claim that it is reasonable to do so, we must remember that always when our assumptions seem to be most natural and obvious, they are most likely to be freighted with our unrevealed beliefs and values – Zizek's 'unknown knowns' again (Zizek, 2004). This is true of us as subjects – individuals with our take on the world arising from our experience, education, culture, beliefs, theories about the world. But it is also true of ourselves in a more collective way. One of the interesting consequences, I think, of rethinking knowledge relations in a phenomenological way is that by the end of the process we are likely to have to shift some of favourite ways of thinking about the fundamental categories that are in play. The word 'subject' is used to indicate a sentient, positioned, ideated being – an entity that necessarily brings their own understanding of things to bear upon any 'object' of knowledge. This is an inescapable truth. Knowledge inheres in subjects and so there is always an element of subjectivity in any knowledge, no matter how rarefied or scientific or how much verified by the elaborate techniques and ruses of research method. Even the most meticulously conducted and scrupulously impartial random control trials require a subject – usually several subjects actually – to organize them, to make sense of them and to convey their relevance and significance to the world at large, not to mention to believe in their efficacy. Any formal process of knowledge production requires the engagement – including the animation and 'insight' – of a subject for its existence. Its origins will have been activated by some energized subject's desire, not through some automatic impersonal process of necessity.

That desire belongs to what Heidegger refers to in *Being and Time* as 'being-in-the-world' (Heidegger, 1962). This carefully chosen element of Heidegger's sometimes strange, sometimes estranging, vocabulary is an attempt to think differently about the nature of subjectivity. Heidegger's attempt to give an account of 'fundamental ontology' focuses extensively on that entity that asks the question of Being. But Heidegger wants to shed the inherited vocabulary of subjectivity, because it is loaded with a historical metaphysics. In other words, someone writing philosophy in the 1920s in middle Europe would have a ready-to-hand array of ideas and ways of thinking and ways of writing as part of their historical discursive inheritance. And Heidegger wants to find a new way of thinking. An important move Heidegger makes in this effort is to talk not about a human subject – with all the weight of inherited notions that might carry – but rather to talk about 'dasein', a German portmanteau word that simply means 'being there'. The significance of using this odd word is varied and multiple, but one important effect that Heidegger clearly wanted to achieve through it was to remind us that 'being-in-the-world' is a kind of being-there. The human subject, or 'dasein', is not a transcendental being separated from the world, able to occupy a distant vantage point to view the nature of things dispassionately. Rather, the human subject invariably occupies a specific time, place and range of attributes and ideas arising out of that very specificity. What's more, 'being-there' is also always being there with others ('mitwelt') in a collective form of life that shapes 'dasein'.

Contingent subjectivity: A case study

Perhaps, it isn't strange to claim that this way of thinking, with its emphasis on 'the subject', or on subjectivity, serves to remind us that for all our specificity, for all the partial particularity of our situated apprehension of things and our situated way of experiencing the world, the shape form and even quality of our subjectivity is not an entirely or even predominantly individual matter. What is crucial here is the realization that 'dasein' or human subjectivity always exists within determinate and specific conditions. If we can identify these conditions and give an account of them, then we may have gone some way towards objectifying them, depending of course on the manner we do that in. It is always impossible to step outside of oneself. As Bob Dylan once put it: 'As great as you are a man, you'll never be greater than yourself' (Dylan, 2001). The self then constitutes a limit to our being and a horizon of our knowledge and understanding. But it is worth acknowledging that these last two dimensions of our being are not really – surely – of our own making, certainly not entirely of our own making. While we are individuals, for sure, it is also clear that our very individuality is the product of a process that we might refer to as individuation (Elias, 2000). That process, as many commentators and theorists of identity have noted, is very much the outcome of our interaction with a 'world' ('our world') that is not of our own making but that is very much involved in the making of us. We understand ourselves differently when we understand that self and world relation.

Our existence is contingent in this sense. We belong to what Catherine Malabou has characterized as the 'ontology of the accident' (Malabou, 2012). We do not choose when to enter the world nor in what time, or circumstances to make our entrance. Personally, I often think of the difference between my father and me– as products of quite different very specific histories. I sometimes joke to students that my father made poor choices concerning his natality. To be born in eastern Europe of uncertain nationality in 1916 showed very poor foresight. That was a costly mistake. It meant that he was caught up in some of the most cataclysmic events of the twentieth century and bore witness to and suffered under its most vehement horrors. More sensibly, on the other hand, I entered the world in London in 1952 having waited for the war and its immediate aftermath to pass. Maybe I should have chosen wealthier parents but even so the new welfare state and changing access to education meant that I was able, relatively speaking, to prosper. In making this choice, I avoided, unlike my father, arrest and beating by the SS and two-and-a-half years as a starving haftling in some of the world's most historically notorious places, including Majdanek, Auschwitz-Birkenau, Dautmergen and Allach-Dachau.

The point here, of course, is to emphasize that whatever agency we do have – and we do have agency in even the most restrictive conditions, as Alexander Solzhenitsyn extensively recorded – is always already predicated on material, cultural, historical, discursive factors that make us what we are but that also enable us to be what we are. Our very specificity is both limitation and affordance.

Let me give an example that, forgive me, draws on my own experience. My professional life began in 1975 when I trained to be an English teacher. In 1976, I took up a post in what I then thought (I still do) was a remarkable English department in a newly built comprehensive school. I took a particular route into teaching, having earned an English degree that placed a high value on literature understood as a complex mode of thought that gave access to significant trends in human thinking and that put one in touch with significant ideas, cultures, historical moods and prescient minds. I then did a PGCE at a time when new ideas (it seemed) about language were being imported into English from the then relatively new form of knowledge that was sociolinguistics and what some claimed were new ideas about pedagogy that were associated with the relatively recently discovered Vygotskian mode of thought (Wilkinson, 1971). *The Bullock Report* had recently been published (Bullock, 1975). Circular 10/65 had been issued a while ago, and it seemed that the process of transforming state-sponsored education from the tripartite system, with its inbuilt social divisiveness, to the comprehensive school with its new vision of equality of access and provision, was well under way. It was only a matter of time and of the commitment of new teachers such as myself entering the profession that would see the dawning of a new educational age. After all, I had myself attended an early example of the comprehensive school. I had been enabled to go on to enjoy an extraordinary higher education experience in an ancient, elite university. Things, educationally speaking, could only get better.

That first English department I taught in was a very large London overspill school. It was peopled by some experienced English teachers who shared my interests in and orientation towards literature and language and by some new teachers like myself who expressed a practical excitement in and commitment to what we thought of as the comprehensive ideal and that we also thought was the coming new world order. Department meetings were frequent and supportive. Ideas were freely shared. The curriculum was open – and teachers at that time were enabled to produce their own syllabuses at all levels. It seemed that as teachers of English in that context at that time we had a licence to change the world and that the ideas and practices we lived by would necessarily sweep away what was left of an old and divisive order and usher in a golden age of engagement and equality (Peim, 1993).

When Sir Keith Joseph, a conservative education minister, announced the reform of 16 plus exams, it was only to liberalize provision so that teachers were given more autonomy in a system that integrated examinations across the so-called ability range and that allowed for 100 per cent coursework schemes. In higher education, a new wind was blowing its transformative way across subject English. Questions arose about the provenance of literature, about cultural differences and orientations, about language and identity, and about the politics of race and the politics of gender in education. New forms of knowledge were being brought to bear on subject identity and subject practices. Philosophy, social theory, psychoanalysis, the new insights of cultural studies – loosely integrated into a new force for rethinking things referred to as 'theory'. Basil Bernstein's challenging work on the relations between social class, language and scholastic success was amplified by the newly imported work of Pierre Bourdieu and Pierre Macherey in France (Bernstein, 1971; Bourdieu and Passeron, 1970; Macherey, 1978). With new potential for the transformation of subject identity and new awareness of social class, gender and race, new practices could be conceptualized and delivered in relation to literacy and language in the name of a revolutionized, visionary and progressive model of English – a model that had been demonstrated to work (albeit on a small scale) (Peim, 1993).

The anticipated revolution in English teaching towards a culturally sensitive, theory-informed practice no longer modelled on outdated understandings of literature, and language competence didn't materialize. In England, the 1988 Education Reform Act withdrew teacher control from curriculum matters. The carefully crafted model of reformed English that had been at the centre of my English teaching career would no longer be possible. Things had changed, but not in the expected direction. The assumption of a new comprehensive world order that I – and many colleagues and contemporaries – had made had not materialized but had been displaced now with a more centrally controlled curriculum and more locally managed schools accompanied by a new era of competition and inspection. To cut a complex and not very edifying story short, my own idea of the trajectory of English teaching, schooling and education in general had been exposed as illusory. Perhaps education just wasn't like that – wasn't like that model I had in mind when I entered the profession and when I took up my first teaching post.

This isn't the story of gradual disillusionment in the face of the corroding intrusion of experience. It is rather a demonstration that we must understand the nature of things differently according to how and where we are positioned in relation to them. It is also a demonstration that the divide between the subjective and the objective in terms of our knowledge and understanding of the world is not as strict as we may be commonly encouraged to think by the tenets of common sense. I can now review my own subjective experience in the light of history. I can now appreciate that the moment of 1975 couldn't have been the dawn of a new era in the way that I wanted it to be when I was living it. I now have access to knowledge that I didn't then have. I am now not at all surprised that English teachers across the nation didn't rally to the cause of the new vision of subject identity that I had thought was essential for its legitimate continuation as a comprehensive school practice. I can now see, for example, that the moment of the comprehensive ideal was just that – a moment, and not a new world order in schooling destined by the progressively equalizing force of education as the proper vehicle for the continuation of the European enlightenment's legacy.

What's more, I can also now understand, I claim, the nature of the school and of state-sponsored education in modernity. I now also must take into consideration, in any thinking I do about the history of the school or the history of curriculum politics, what some of the classic sociologies of education have claimed about the persistence of class inequalities and race inequalities as enacted by the school. Now it is possible for me not merely to reject my former belief system concerning the role of the English teacher, the destiny of education and the function of the school. It has become possible or, rather, necessary – through encounters with various kinds of knowledge and through a living experience of history – to see myself, my experiences and my ideas differently. I would now claim that I have gained some objective purchase on my subjective lived experience in education. I wouldn't claim though that I have been able to completely displace my own subjectivity through the application of various forms of knowledge. The forms of knowledge themselves do not come ready-made into an objective story. In fact, they too can only be accessed by a kind of subjective engagement. I can only apprehend them in specific ways from some specific perspectives. For all that I might claim that I have laboured to acquire certain modes of reading designed to reduce the subjective dimension of interpretation, even the most sophisticated hermeneutist or semiotician would have to admit that the subjective dimension cannot be suspended nor erased.

There is a certain irreducibility in the subjective–objective divide and its role in knowledge. A historical account of the story I told above about my engagements with English teaching might at first seem to require an elimination of the subjective story of my own minority beliefs. Yet we can imagine another kind of historical study of the same story that would deliberately seek to include an account of the subjective dimension precisely to render it more truthful, more empirical and, in a significant way, more objective. We could imagine similar tales of professional life – in many different spheres – that might seek to objectify the personal experience of the subject. In fact, I often advise researchers to begin their research journey by giving an account of themselves, by contextualizing their own understandings and belief systems by writing about them while including alternative or additional perspectives from those they might automatically reach for or that might belong to the realm of practice they inhabit. While this adjuration may contain the threat of disenchantment, it may also hold out the promise of renewed engagement, although these alternatives don't have to remain strictly opposed to one another. It does seem to me though to behove any research ethic worthy of the name that transformation of one's perspective or orientation be a possible consequence of engaging anew with the object in question.

The subject and the archive

The researcher's relation to the research object inhabits structurally complex network of factors, but also varies in terms of what we might provisionally refer to as orientation. The identity of the researcher as researcher will always already have been significantly formed by a relation to a domain of knowledge as well as to the object in question. To be a researcher requires a certain inwardness with the domain of knowledge, and often a strong affiliation. The domain of knowledge is often represented as 'my subject'; and it is mine in the sense that I have taken possession of it, if not in its – always elusive – entirety, then in terms of some of its most iconic elements. In the process of becoming a member of the domain of knowledge, there is always a process of initiation and frequently a demand to demonstrate affiliation, in terms of rituals of belonging, a demand to demonstrate credentials and to demonstrate that one is strongly interpellated by its privileged forms. At the same time, the domain of knowledge takes possession of the subject. In the first instance, one's engagement requires a certain submission, an acknowledgement of the authority of the domain of knowledge, its established protocols and its iconic findings. One must submit to what is held in the store of the domain of knowledge's 'treasure-house' or archive.

An interesting feature of this archive is that it requires constant reiteration and constant replenishment. We might say that for all its authority, it is constantly under review. An important, perhaps the most important, dimension of science in modernity, for example, is this relation between the researcher and the archive. Differently from the initiate, the researcher is under obligation to approach the archive with both reverence *and* critical vision: the archive is not a static storeroom, but demands renewal. A domain of knowledge without research cannot survive. The researcher takes on a responsibility to modify, transform and develop the archive: this in effect is, even if in a small and modest way, to undertake a revision and transformation of the domain.

My own career as researcher began with an interest in the very identity of the subject that was 'mine' and that had shaped my own academic identity and probably other dimensions of my being. My subject was English, but, of course, as indicated, the subject is not mine. It is not mine to define nor to determine in terms of what it consists of, what its defining objects are or what its prevailing modes of knowledge are. English constitutes a space I can move within, let's say, but it is a space that is already significantly defined and bordered and, to put it strongly, policed before my own entry into it. We could say that my entry into the space of English – and this is particularly true of my entry into this space as researcher – depends on my having proven credentials. I must demonstrate that I can operate effectively within the norms it promotes. I must submit my individual will to the authority of those norms. I must bend my language to meet the acceptable forms of expression. I must demonstrate familiarity with the range of texts that fall within the subject's domain, and must engage with these texts in the already-defined way that custom and practice determines. I may, should I become a qualified researcher within the subject, shift the language, the interpretations and enter argument and even dispute about what is proper to the domain's being, but to do so I will have had to already have demonstrated not only a familiarity with but an active competence in its norms of expression.

The spatial metaphor is strange here, however. Subject English does not have a strictly policed border in the sense that a geographic area may. In that sense, it is like any subject area, any curriculum 'domain'. The borders of the subject may be contentious, may be disputed. In some cases, as became true of English in the early 1980s for instance, the borders of subject identity may be quite different according to where you stand. At that time in the history of the subject, what might be termed the 'politics of subject identity' was becoming explicitly evident. Factions understood the very purposes and objects of the subject quite differently. Factional conflicts arose that became matters of public interest. A great deal of effort and energy was exerted by those who believed that the subject stood in need of redefinition. There were those who were ready, including myself, to provide a new constitution for the subject, to reset its mission and to announce a new world order of subject being (Peim, 1993).

These kinds of eruptions of difference in relation to subject identity certainly occur in all subject areas. We can characterize them as essentially ontological:

they touch on fundamental questions of what the subject, ultimately, is: what is proper to the domain of knowledge. And even in cases where domains of knowledge undergo a more or less constant growth and change in boundaries, as is the case with mathematics, for example, the ontological question of what, essentially, constitutes the subject, of what makes it what it is, are at least implicitly in play constantly. For the researcher, reflecting on one's relation to the domain of knowledge and to its shifting ontological status can be a highly productive way of articulating and coming to a position, perhaps more productive than reviewing the worn-out categories that research manuals represent as options for an epistemological stance (Crotty, 1998; Howell, 2012; Thomas, 2013).

What, though, might provide the occasion for this will to transformation to be realized in a research endeavour? How can the domain of knowledge, established, specified, secure, allow for its lacunae to be exposed by a relative neophyte? What's more, how can the established, defined subject allow for the element of the new, for what has hitherto not been included within its established parameters? These are critical questions for the researcher working within a subject domain, whose very subjectivity as researcher is defined by a relation to that domain, often expressed as a relation of equivalence or identity: 'I am a … (historian, psychologist, mathematician …).'

Horizons of identity

Well, it could be said that the very existence of the domain of knowledge depends on its having this openness to the new, depends, in fact, on being of uncertain definition, having an area of uncertainty at its edges above and beyond what is established and central. This area – or, to borrow a phrase from Vygotskian thinking – this 'zone of proximal development' (ZPD) exists as a threat to the essence of subject identity (Chaiklin, 2003). Its very uncertainty and openness means that it is possible that what gets engendered in its matrix redefines the established and apparently determinate profile. This is certainly what happens on a grand scale when paradigm transformations occur that demand a rethinking of fundamentals. It is also the condition of being of the subject. The ZPD introduces an ineradicable element of uncertainty into being.

Not all research, of course, has this paradigm shifting effect or impinges seriously on the identity of the subject. More modest, workaday endeavours may seek to modify, expand an already-existing element of subject knowledge in a more modest and small-scale way. Even these small shifts have implications for subject boundaries and have some transformative effect on subject boundaries. The borders may be shifted only slightly, but they are being moved.

Hitherto unincluded elements are now included and the profile is changed. This dimension of transformation cannot be avoided: in PhD research, a universal requirement is for the work undertaken to offer 'an original contribution to knowledge'. That demand has come to serve as a very definition of research. This process must necessarily involve the confrontation with oneself, as it were, as the agent of new knowledge.

Exploring one's subjectivity doesn't have to mean relaxing rigour or indulging one's own sensations, impressions and feelings, taking these for the essential timbre of reality. In the work of Hans Georg Gadamer, a decisive perspective is offered in relation to Heidegger's emphasis on the situatedness of 'dasein'. While Gadamer, who was nothing short of intellectually besotted with Heidegger, followed Heidegger's fundamental ontology and accorded a limit to the possibilities of being for the subject based on material, social and cultural conditions, he used the idea of 'horizon' in an interesting and productive way that is particularly germane to the business of articulating one's research orientation and the formation of one's position. This 'way of thinking', as Gadamer might put it, seems to me to be much more useful than toying with fictitious oppositions such as 'positivism' and 'interpretivism' – positions that make no sense at all in relation to any real research endeavour.

Gadamer acknowledges that we are 'thrown', not transcendental, creatures and that our being is specific to our world including forms of understanding and tools of knowledge available to us. In this specificity, Gadamer also acknowledges that we are frequently confronted with the Other that may appear in many guises and that indicates something alternative to our world. Belonging to a specific world, we come to things with an already-elaborated – through language, through culture, through activity – set of fore-understandings, or ways of grasping, knowing, thinking. We can easily think how elements of our own heritage (including language, culture, education, knowledge) frame our thinking and frame the nature of our encounters with those things we may seek to understand. As we develop, we may accrue variations within these large categories of being: we may cultivate political, cultural, personal orientations towards a host of things and dimensions of our world. This is the complex process of the formation of identity that is never something entirely of our own making either: others intrude upon us and shape our sense of what we are and determine aspects of our being-in-the-world as we go along. We live within the world but we also read the world, make sense of it and ourselves with and among others with whom we share language that carries with it meanings that are not of our own making. Language mediates the world, but this is not 'the' world pure and singular, nor is it all the 'World'. We can't claim that language gives us direct access to the Real of the World. We therefore come to things in a positioned and partial way, shaped by the many factors of our contingency. What's more, as with Heidegger, we are in relation to things that are characterized by 'care': one way or another. This being-attached is expressed by Gadamer as a hermeneutic problem: what enables the knower to know is at the same time a self-limiting condition. According to Gadamer, the enlightenment goal of eliminating all prejudice or prejudgement by suspending or bracketing this limited self somehow is itself a prejudice (Gadamer, 1989).

And yet our 'ready-to-hand' ways of knowing and understanding the world may on occasions be disturbed or interrupted and may be rendered strange (Willett, 1964). We cannot see through other eyes but we can see sometimes that there are other eyes that look at us and at our world and important things in it differently. This too can happen it seems from within ourselves, that we get a sense, an uncanny sense, in dreams for instance, of dimensions of our self that is Other or at least different and unexpected. We may be forced, by circumstances, by history, to see ourselves and our world anew. And this is the significance of the concept of the 'horizon' that plays a big part in Gadamer's hermeneutics. The horizon is a limit on our perfection and knowledge: but we may, always from within our own horizon, encounter other horizons and experience otherness as a disturbance to the stability and security of our own horizon. Gadamer ends up, in his big book on the matter, proclaiming that there is no stable method for the acquisition of knowledge of any kind social scientific or just scientific (Gadamer, 1989). Knowledge is existential – bounded by specificity, contingency, partiality – and the meanings generated by existential knowledge are also circumscribed. But we may be or become aware of the differences that pertain between horizons of being that are also horizons of knowledge.

There now follow some accounts of subjectivity that have a bearing on how, as a researcher, one might give an informed account of oneself in a theoretically informed, objectifying sense.

Lacan: Between imaginary, symbolic and real

Lacan's account of subjectivity places the subject within an interesting and unique ontology that has been influential in rethinking the basis of identity. Lacan's description of the subject – scattered through elliptical statement in numerous texts – follows Freud's enunciation of the division of the subject into conscious and unconscious, a move that disturbs the notion of self-identity and undermines the enlightenment ideal of the purely rational self. For Lacan, the subject inhabits different orders of being (Imaginary, Symbolic, Real) – all at the same time. The subject is constituted out of difference: the difference between these orders and the difference that is introduced into the subject through the acquisition of language (the difference between Symbolic and Real). For Lacan, then, the subject is structurally unstable: subjectivity is dynamic, not a singular and coherent integrated whole. The subject is both incomplete and constantly haunted by this lack that defines its very being. Hence the restless 'hunger of imagination that preys incessantly on life' (Johnson, S., 1985). Language is central to Lacan's model of subjectivity: and it is the division between the 'signifier', or the material component of the sign, and the 'signified' or what the material component points towards that is crucial to this model. The relation between language and the world is structured by an absence, the elusive signified that always fails to anchor the movement of the signifier. This is also the logic of desire, the quest, as it were, by the subject for the lost originary object, 'the obscure object of desire'.

The early inklings of identity in the subject occur in the visual field. Self-consciousness is a matter of recognition. The infant identifies itself in its own specular image. This event occurs within the order of the Imaginary, as the child sees itself and *mis*recognizes itself, in fact, as a complete and distinct entity. With the later acquisition of language, the child both enters and engages with the symbolic order that gives identity to self ('I'), things, relations and experiences and imposes its authority on the child. Entry into and acceptance of the Symbolic Order offers the child a place as a being with a name, a distinct identity and a relation to the Other. The Imaginary order remains in operation as a parallel order of being. But the Symbolic Order gives access to social reality and grants a position within it – so long as we submit to its determinations. At the same time, the Symbolic Order represents the Other within, the uncanny dimension of identity that lies within subjectivity. In accord with the logic of the signifier in its slippery relation with the signified the subject cannot access the other Other that lies beyond the Symbolic Order. The subject is in some important sense then excluded from direct access to unmediated reality beyond the self, even though we know that it is always there. For the subject, experience is always mediated through the Symbolic Order that organizes the Real – the third of Lacan's orders of being – according to its semantic determinations. The realm of meaning for the subject is cut off from the pure realm of being. For Lacan, the Real lies beyond symbolization. It is the brute reality that does not depend on any idea of it. We do collide with it in our everyday commerce with the world. In our dealings with the world, the Real may 'answer back'. To get to grips with this dimension, we can consider the dead 'who' remain within the Symbolic but disappear from the Real.

In Lacanian theory, the ego is formed out of an act of misrecognition. The specular image of the self provides an illusion of unity and remains always outside of the self. It is ideal – the ideal-ego: the image of our self as complete and whole, the image of our narcissism. At the same time, we know that we fall short of this unified, ideal self: we experience ourselves differently, as partial and incomplete and beset by desire, including desire for the realization of this ideal Other specular self and anxiety that we fall short of this integrated whole. At the same time, if that were not complication enough, the ideal-ego operates on the subject along with the ego-ideal: the kernel of the ego-ideal being formed by our tendency to identify with the idealized version of ourselves that we project onto others. My mother wants me to be in such a way; my teacher wants me to be an ideal pupil. I in turn want to see myself as this ideal child, pupil. While the ideal-ego tends to belong to the Imaginary Order, the ego-ideal tends to belong to the Symbolic Order. The ego-ideal relates strongly to our social self, although it occupies a position outside of ourself, as it were, looking at and judging our actual lived experience.

A definition of the distinction between ideal-ego and ego-ideal is provided by Slavoj Zizek:

> The relation between imaginary and symbolic identification – between the ideal ego [Idealich] and the ego-ideal [Ich-Ideal] – is – to use the distinction made by Jacques-Alain Miller (in his unpublished Seminar) – that between 'constituted' and 'constitutive' identification: to put it simply, imaginary identification is identification with the image in which we appear likeable to ourselves, with image representing 'what we would like to be', and symbolic identification, identification with the very place from where we are being observed, from where we look at ourselves so that we appear to ourselves likeable, worthy of love. (Zizek, 1989, 105)

Imaginary identification through the ego-ideal seeks to fulfil an ideal on behalf of a perception of the gaze or desire of the other. Every attempt to realign the self or the ego to a symbolic ideal is structured by a sense of enacting that ideal role or mode of being on behalf of another. The relevance of this way of rethinking identity is particularly strong for education where the ego-ideal may reside in the gaze of the teacher for pupils, of the head teacher for teachers, of the inspection regime for schools, or an external examiner for a PhD candidate. In education, of course, there is a structural order of normativity and surveillance that acts to shape and to aggravate the ego-ideal mechanism in the consciousness of those who fall within the system.

Althusser and interpellation

Althusser's thinking has been influential in an originary sense bringing together legal/political and economic domains with the personal. With Althusser's ideas – among others – the personal becomes the political, or at least a significant part of it. Althusser drew on Lacanian ideas to re-examine the formation of subjectivity. Althusser's initial concern is to explain the grip of ideology even when such ideology may apparently work against the interests of those who espouse it. For Althusser, interpellation is the key mechanism through which we can explain the formation of the subject as an ideologically freighted being. According to Althusser, government depends on state-repressive apparatuses (SRAs) but more pervasively and powerfully on ideological state apparatuses (ISAs). The latter are essential for the cohesion of capitalist societies. ISAs operate through and include the family, religious organizations and, most importantly, the education system. ISAs are crucial in the formation and maintenance of identities being fundamental to the process of identification that identity production and maintenance requires. As powerful public institutions, education contexts produce and maintain received ideas, normative ways of being and project a certain metaphysics onto the social world.

For Althusser, no one ISA produces in us the belief that we can act as self-conscious and free agents. Acquiring and developing this belief is essential to learning what it is to be a daughter, a schoolchild, black British, a steelworker, a head teacher. Our identity is constituted by this background belief that we have a hand in becoming what we are and that that process may express something about our essential nature. Ideologies infuse our sense of how things are in the world and our sense of our place in the world including the reasons why we occupy such a place. Wherever we may stand in the social order – and we invariably occupy more than one place or position in that order – it is through ideology according to Althusser that we are constituted as a subject. A key term in Althusser's consideration of the role of ideology in identity formation and maintenance is 'interpellation'. Interpellation begins to form our subjectivity from a very early age, from the time in fact when we are 'called' to be what we are. We are called to be the name we have been given, a name that places us in a family and social relation of some sort or other. We respond to this appellation and, in doing so, we accept the identity that has been granted to us, or thrust upon us, depending on how you want to look at it. I am 'hailed' as something; when I respond to that hailing, I accept the designation accorded to me. We can think of occasions when we feel the force of interpellation strongly. As children, we must be made accustomed to our own name: we learn to read it, we see it on stickers in school and we gradually internalize it as signifying who we are. A teacher in training might be surprised or discomforted by being referred to as 'Miss' or 'Sir', a name not chosen but conferred and may gradually have to learn to accept that form of hailing, may gradually respond it with a naturalized ease. An extreme and distressing example of interpellation might be the numbers given to prisoners in concentration camps. In that case, responding to your number, using your number to refer to yourself in a roll-call, say, confirms your status as a creature without a name, as a 'haftling'.

Interpellations happen to us all the time and become ingrained in our sense of ourselves and our place in the order of things in our world. The process requires not just that we are recognized as such by others; but equally that we recognize ourselves as such. According to Althusser, this act of recognition, even in the most positive cases ('Your highness', for example), is a *mis*recognition ('meconnaissance'). Our conferred identity belongs to a process of creation that must be without any foundation expect in the ritualized practices of naming within a specific cultural ethos. But this process has 'disappeared'. Our identity has become inscribed in a naturalized order of things that occupies material space in the practices of social action. As Althusser puts it:

> Ideas have disappeared as such (insofar as they are endowed with an ideal or spiritual existence), to the precise extent that it has emerged that their existence is inscribed in the actions of practices governed by rituals defined in the last instance by an ideological apparatus. It therefore appears that the subject acts insofar as he is acted by the following system (set out in the order of its real determination): ideology existing in a material ideological apparatus, describing material practices governed by a material ritual, which practices exist in the material actions of a subject acting in all consciousness according to his belief. (Althusser, 1984a, 169–170)

Althusser's articulation of ISA indicates something of the far-reaching extent of symbolic governance. We become what we are through processes that shape the most intimate relations and that occupy the most everyday practices and spaces. The subject's formative relations with key ideas, institutions and practices in the social realm offered the possibility of vastly extending the critique of ideology. It was possible to extend this critique into the very detailed operations of everyday life, seen as saturated with symbolic meaning relating to cultural differences as expressions of class identity, for instance. Even if the original term, 'misrecognition', with its connotations of a duped mass, had to be modified, it was easy to apply this line of thinking to the functioning of the school where subjects were invited to recognize (or misrecognize) themselves in relation to the institution's definition of them: 'good pupil', 'poor pupil', 'more able', 'less able', and so on.

According to Anthony Easthope,

> The work of Althusser imported into Britain at least three lines of thought, three conceptualisations ... the account of the historical formation as decentred; the assertion that knowledge as proceeding from theoretical practice is discursively constructed; the account of the subject as effect rather than cause. (Easthope, 1988, 17)

The argument that key 'ideological' apparatuses are equally significant as economic conditions enabled the then-emerging field of cultural studies to claim a relative autonomy from economics and more empirically oriented sociologies. Within a reconfiguring of superstructural relations, subjectivity is seen in terms of a complex amalgam of determining forces, and is conceptualized in a new way by Althusser (via Lacan). The relations between the subject and ideology are crucial for Althusser: ideology isn't a force external to the subject and imposed from without; it is the very mechanism by which the subject recognizes its own identity and partakes of social life. According to Richard Harland, Althusser provides 'a vision that inverts our ordinary base-and-superstructure models and sees what we used to think of as superstructural as having priority over what we used to think of as basic (1987, 9)'. Ideology is the necessary condition for organizing ideas about the world, for perception and knowledge. The subject is always a decentred subject: 'the human subject is de-centred, constituted by a structure which has no "centre" ... except in the imaginary misrecognition of the "ego", i.e. in the ideological formations in which it "recognizes" itself' (Althusser, 1984a, 149). The integrity of the self is a function of ideology. But there can be no 'unmasking' of ideology that can give direct access for the subject to 'the real' self or the real anything. The knowing subject must always operate within frameworks that organize and interpret perceptions.

Althusser's reconceptualization of ideology and subjectivity clearly has implications for the role of education in general. After Althusser, it seemed clear, for example, that the distinction between politics and culture cannot be sustained and that the institutions of education are saturated with both. For the researcher, the Althusserian perspective demands that the subject of research, the researcher, acknowledge their positioned, interpellated being within an order of identities and implies perhaps that that is perhaps the essential starting point for thinking in research.

Butler's performative subject

The Althusserian account of subjectivity is developed by Judith Butler specifically concerning gender – understood to be quite distinct from sex. Beginning with a basic phenomenology of gender as the cultural signification of sex, for Butler, gender must be learnt. Taking on a gendered identity must involve, above all, the element of performance. There is an analogy here with the idea of script and audience. The script is the established norms of conduct and modes of being that gendering requires. The 'audience' is the social pact that accords such performances recognition. Gender is not chosen but neither is it entirely imposed or inscribed from without. It belongs with the Althusserian idea of interpellation, as a relational process. Gender is certainly not, therefore, an internal, intrinsic, stable quality (Butler, 1988).

Borrowing a Freudian-Lacanian perspective, Butler explores gendered identity in terms of performances that are deemed to signify 'normality' as a privileged mode of being. The subject comes to see herself as she is recognized and affirmed by others within a norm-saturated environment. In *Gender Trouble*, Butler argues that the natural seeming coherence of gender is culturally constructed through stylized body acts and discourse. These accrue the status of naturalness over time and become norms. Borrowing Foucault's notion of 'regulative discourses' and 'disciplinary' regimes, Butler enables us to explain both the changing and persistent forms of gendered identities, seen not only as imposed categories but also as performed with a modicum of self-fashioning involved. Butler challenges biological accounts of binary sex, strongly embedded though they are in Western metaphysics. The apparent obviousness of sex is simply a function of its deeply embedded status: its production in discourse and cultural practice is foreclosed. So, Butler challenges the history of both gender and sex including the history of earlier feminisms – agreeing in effect with the Lacanian assertion that those fixed categories of identity – 'men'–'women' – are not given by the Real but are the productions of the Symbolic Order and enter our awareness through the Imaginary (Butler, 1990).

Butler's reading of identity is far-reaching. It has entered significantly into gender studies and into awareness of gender and identity issues more generally. If we think of the world of education, identity issues arise in many forms. We might consider, even, that education in our world is the space where identity is most strongly, and perhaps most decisively, played out. After Butler, we may consider how the repetition of educational practices, as with gender, secures their ontological status and naturalizes them. In answer to some big but mostly unasked questions – concerning, for example, age stratification, the role of testing, the arbitrary structure of the curriculum, to mention only a few – we might reach for Butlerian ideas to inform our sense that these things that impose constantly on the identities of subjects have become naturalized in our world and enjoy the privileged status of necessity. At the same time, if we look at how education works to produce ideal identities – ideal student, ideal teacher, ideal school and so on – we can see the same processes at work to induce the sense of a natural and proper order of things from the very contingent and arbitrary elements of that world. The importance of Butler's emphasis on a regularized and constrained repetition of norms in the determination of identities in the field of education can hardly be overemphasized. In this sense, performance is not singular but is ritualized – ritually reiterated under strongly controlled surveillance and supervision, including ultimately, self-supervision. We hardly need to be reminded of the highly ritualized practices that are embedded in educational institutions, and that frame everything that goes on in schools. We cannot escape from these ritualized and interpellated forms of identity that constitute significantly what we are. But we can become aware of them and negotiate our relation to them. This is both true and significant for educational researchers.

Foucault's care of the self

Butler also draws on Foucault's far-reaching and varied concerns with subjectivity that propose some very original and still-to-be-thought-through (especially in the field of education) ways of thinking. Foucault wrote about the 'great transformation' of modernity, noting how Western nation states, initially, became governmentally concerned with ordering the life and environment of the mass populations that arose in the period (see Chapter 5). This huge change involved the invention and proliferation of modern institutions. The school is a paradigm case: an apparatus applied the whole population: to train, to inculcate literacy and numeracy and to cultivate citizenly dispositions. Later, Foucault coined the term 'technologies of the self' to indicate the ways that institutions sought to render subjects self-managing, enabling subjects to shape and fashion themselves-within limits, of course. Education is as such a technology of the self *par excellence* with its emphasis on self-direction, self-discipline and self-improvement.

Foucault extended his reflections on subjectivity by looking back to consider ancient practices of care of the self as a moral enterprise in relation to modern and contemporary practices. Foucault considered how ancient ethics regarded caring for oneself as a social matter. To care for oneself involved inward reflection aimed at thorough self-control, an ideal state of individual and social being.

The injunction 'Know thyself!' attributed to Socrates was directed at attending to one's own inward being to care also for the souls of others. Socrates's inner dialectic involved the intense examination of the truth of his own thought and conduct as well as those he interrogated. Truth here is pursued as a way of ensuring the ethical probity of the self: philosophy and ethics, in the figure of Socrates, are united. Truth here is not substantive, not a matter or correlating propositions with world. Truth involves a pursuit that must always trouble one's present standing.

Foucault claims a change in Western metaphysics with the 'Cartesian moment' (1637). For Descartes, self-knowledge is concerned with clearing the mind for the determination of truth understood as a function of propositions. In other words, Descartes self-consciousness is without ethical import. It seeks rational clarity to test propositional truth. As touched on elsewhere, this shift is expanded and takes stronger hold in the moment of Kant's *Critique of Pure Reason* (1783) when it is established that the subject's own thinking is constitutive of the very possibility of knowledge. In the legacy of modernity, claims Foucault, philosophy engages in truth questions without reference to ethical development. That's not to say that modernity eschews moral rationality. Rather, moral reasoning gets separated from philosophy and philosophy becomes a more academic, professional pursuit detached, mostly, from questions of conduct (Foucault, 1997).

For Foucault, a reflexive orientation towards truth is a vital element of freedom connected to a politics of self. This desired kind of critical self-consciousness requires the cultivation of flexibility of mind that can be mobilized in the face of more rigid and determinate relations to truth questions. This means that freedom is possible for the subject capable of challenging any stabilized view of the ever-changing present, and of maintaining a critical awareness of oneself and the place and time one residesin. While this mode of care of the self that we might refer to as 'critique' does not claim to own truth, it evaluates what Foucault calls various 'discourses of truth'. It seeks a subtle orientation to truth (Foucault, 1997).

Objectifying the subject

Giving an account of oneself can be a significant, if not vital and essential, component of research. This is perhaps especially the case for the social sciences and perhaps is more significant in research that speaks of or relates to domains that include professional practices such as education.

One inescapable fact about the relations between the subject and the object becomes very clear if we return to our posited visualization of this fundamental relation. A simple two-dimensional drawing of this relation must separate subject from object in some way (see Chapter 1). They cannot be identical, although it is true to say that the subject – as in any reflective exercise – can become an object for itself. And, of course, it is also and perhaps very obviously the case that any subject can become an object for another subject. A schematization that separates subject from object will necessarily have to put some space between them or indicate that they do not share the same space to the same degree. In their separation, we may instantly note that the subject at any point in time will be in some positioned relation to the object. The subject occupies a specific position and this serves as a useful illustration of some fundamental condition of subject–object relations. This takes us back to the description of professional orientation offered above – where I attempted to give a brief account of my own positioned relation to English teaching, to schooling and ultimately, I suppose, to education in general. That position changed with history – in both a personal historical sense and in the sense of a broad sweep of changes in the public world of educational history.

At any given time, it would be possible to produce an account of one's position in relation to the object that one seeks to know. And let's not forget that, in a research context, seeking to know is often seeking to know differently. Research itself is that process of producing new knowledge, not just about new objects of knowledge but also about what might be already well known in some ways and deeply familiar. It is after all commonplace in research to come across the claim that some familiar object (practice or entity) is now being revealed in some new way for the first time. That's at least partly why research training courses in Universities spend so much time and energy devoted to techniques to produce new as yet unrevealed ways of knowing and understanding existing and known phenomena.

A subject may be positioned in relation to any object by dint of many categories likely to inform our understanding and knowledge. At first glance, the question of what the object is may seem unnecessarily to complicate a simple matter of identity. Things are after all what they are. Much of the time this is exactly how we inhabit and behold the world, of course. It would be tedious and unproductive if we were to constantly interrogate the fundamental nature of the things we encounter in our everyday dealings with the world. As Heidegger noted, we live with objects mostly in a ready-to-hand kind of way. We pay them little heed as we use them. From time to time, however, we encounter even very familiar objects differently. They may thrust themselves forward for our attention: when they break down, for example, or when they change or when we seek to consciously know them differently by subjecting them to some scientific or research scrutiny. At such times, the object in question may appear to us in Heidegger's terms as present-to-hand. What has been taken for granted as known, given and predictable suddenly becomes intractable or out of joint (Heidegger, 1962).

As the subject acknowledges its positioned stance in relation to the object, how – in what terms? – does an account of this being-positioned get articulated? There is no rule book – and no handbook, either – to answer this question. Just as there is no definitive genre for a thesis – or any other kind of research statement – despite the efforts of the research manuals to set one down. The extent and nature of the engagement with the question of the subject will vary according to a range of factors.

Some researchers are wary of suggesting too strongly and too openly that their own subjectivity shapes their engagement with knowledge preferring to suggest that objectivity may be enhanced by the negation or foreclosure of subjective factors. Isn't that after all what authentic research seeks to achieve? An encounter with the object of enquiry that adopts random control trials as its sovereign method is surely designed in its very essence to transcend the subjective.

One of problem with this stance is that implies that purity and rigour require the subjective dimension be eradicated. There is sometimes perceived to be a divide in social sciences such as education between research that is conducted scientifically with procedural rigour and research that is conducted in a more nebulous, less focused and rigorous way. This division has in one form or another haunted educational research for the past many years. It is echoed in a problematic of value that has also characterized debates within education studies as to the ultimate purpose and value of educational research. Perhaps more than, but at least as much as, any area of social science research education has been burdened with the question of use value. It is not very difficult to see in this recurrent insistence that educational value is deemed to inhere in what is purposeful in a functional sense. Allied strongly to this, almost all educational research manuals imply that proper educational research must have an empirical dimension. The empirical dimension, so the implied story goes, secures both truth and practical value. This powerful idea is ideological and belongs to what we might call the specific ethic of educational research. It is a dominant tendency that organizes the field of education studies. That it also has commonsense valence is a tribute to its authority and testifies to the authority granted to the research handbooks that proliferate.

If we take the question I raise about use-value in relation to social science research seriously – as a question – we may be enabled to expand our thinking about the relations between subject and object that generally characterize research within the field. Careful attention to the phenomenological dimension – without needing to take recourse to specialist philosophical vocabulary – can give a more complex and more attentive account of the field it addresses. When the phenomenological dimension gets carefully articulated, explored and expanded, it is inevitable that issues will be raised that go to the heart of the research in hand. In any field of practice, there will be difficult or even intractable issues – and this is where some understanding of the aporetic dimension, as described in Chapter 1, comes into play. Issues, questions and knotty points of difficulty belong to the subject's relations with the object within the field. To give an account of these is surely important, if the knowledge production process is to be 'honest' or 'true'? In this respect, we can see how a procedural matter – how to articulate the role of the subject, in what terms and with what degree of elaboration – touches also upon what we must acknowledge as an ethical dimension that exceeds the requirements of ethical bureaucracy of the kind favoured by contemporary universities to ensure that the student's engagements with subjects and institutions outside of itself are regulated.

In later chapters, questions concerning objectivity will be further explored especially in relation to ideas about science. The question of knowledge that consideration of subjectivity rouses – especially after Descartes and Kant – has significantly been revisited in recent times in the work of Quentin Meillassoux, who has sought to establish firm grounds for acknowledging the independent existence of various phenomena outside of the intrusion of human consciousness. This chapter has sought to affirm the subject as a legitimate, even necessary, element of articulating a research position. This has been done, though, with an awareness that whatever we might refer to as the 'Real', to use Lacan's strange but compelling term for what exists independently of consciousness, our Symbolic Order articulations of it are necessarily caught up with who we are in an expansive sense that includes reference to the subject as a historically, culturally complex specific entity.

Chapter 4

Truth in Question

Questions of truth or truth(s) in question

This chapter takes on questions about truth in research. It will ask, not so much, What is truth? but What is the modern concern over truth? What is the value to research of this question of truth? This position addresses what truth is. It considers the problematization of truth in modernity and the strident efforts of many to reaffirm truth as an essential goal of knowledge. Truth is not so much the elusive object to be discovered nor a category either to deny or to save. Truth appears rather as a phenomenon for analysis or an issue for consideration, perhaps the issue of issues. Truth explorations may reveal much to us about the possibilities for thinking significant issues in knowledge that have interesting implications for the specific research issue or object we are addressing. Ultimately, as researchers, after all, we generally seek to reveal some dimension of the truth concerning some specific entity. At the same time, we need to be aware of issues that surround truth and the resources available for articulating these issues as they relate to our specific quest.

Truth questions commonly relate to questions about validity and reliability but, ultimately, they touch on fundamental concerns about knowledge in social science and in education. Questions about truth may have an element of all of the domains of philosophical thinking that were introduced in Chapter 1. So there is a phenomenological dimension to truth. When we declare even in the most casual way that that is how thing 'seem to me', we are expressing a phenomenological perspective, acknowledging that my position is one among others and that others may 'see' or know or be oriented towards the very same object – or issue or question – differently (Butler, 2005; Habermas, 1984; Lyotard, 1988).

Truth questions are ontological: when we declare something to the effect that 'That's just the way it is', claiming to have a sure purchase on the very 'nature' of reality. Although quite commonplace in everyday parlance, in some quarters – in the field of quantum mechanics, for instance, or in the field of Derridean deconstruction – such ontological certitude would be frowned upon if declared without careful qualification (Derrida, 1978). In fact, one of the effects of the return of ontology in modern thinking has been to revisit questions concerning truth, including efforts to carefully redefine what we might mean by that much-contested term (Heidegger, 2002).

In the domain of hermeneutics, truth takes on a different character, often being suspended in the name of interpretation. It's not so much that truth can be seen and known from different perspectives, and therefore can be formulated differently. For hermeneutics, truth itself is shifting, always subject to movement from the intrusion of another horizon. Truths may be established, but we must, hermeneutically speaking, remain open to the possibility that any stability we grant to what we categorize as truth may change its form, may shift its grounds or may undergo metamorphosis. This idea about truth acknowledges, at least implicitly, the historical dimension of knowledge. We can describe this as a parallax view of truth, one that is not necessarily concerned to settle between different modes of knowing and apprehending (Gadamer, 1989).

A hermeneutic stance we could say takes truth as something not present but as a desired end to be sought, even though that end might not ever be achieved by any one seeker. And this agrees with the general ethos of research, surely. It is a tenet of science, where it is always assumed, as in the field of knowledge more generally, as we shall see later in this chapter, that the whole truth will *not* be revealed all at once and that the goals of research, the direction of truth, as it were, may be subject to change, depending on what we find out in the meantime in our more specific and partial quests for the truth of a portion of reality. At times, science also acknowledges that there may occur revolutionary shifts in thinking and in modes of knowing (Foucault, 2005; Kuhn, 1959, 1970). Change in truth regimes is evident in the history of knowledge.

In the domain of ethics truth becomes both more urgent and cloudier. Truth has an ethical force; truth makes a claim on our conduct as researchers. The ethical dimension of truth is complex, and much more so than is generally recognized and practised in social science. In educational research, ethical problems immediately arise stemming from assumptions about the nature of education and its status as a taken-for-granted 'good'. Ethical problems also inhere surely in all those unthought assumptions concerning improvement and redemption that characterize the field (Peim, 2011).

A commitment is ethical in some simple and direct way, surely. And yet that doesn't guarantee ethical purity. Our interest in the first place in an object, field or practice will usually arise from our 'care' or concern for a form of knowledge that calls forth our ethical being, as it were. Our very interest in truth is motivated by our mode of being-in-the-world and our commitments. Our desire for truth is situated and cannot be free from some element of faith. According to Alain Badiou, truth arises from our commitment to an 'event' conceived of as a transformative upheaval. On this view, truth is a break in mundane reality, a specific occurrence that calls forth our ethical self (Badiou, 2007).

During and after the twentieth century, truth comes increasingly to occupy the domain of the aporia, the space of what is knotty, irresolvable and contested (Derrida, 1993). The twentieth century was a period of intense scientific theory production, scientific knowledge and technological achievement. It was also a period of very intense reflection on the nature of truth in the face of cataclysmic events and realizations. Between the 'death of God' and 'the postmodern condition', there has been a strange amalgam of intensive knowledge production and powerful theory generation *and* an irreversible loss of faith in both religious and secular grand narratives (Lyotard, 1986; Nietzsche, 1892). Recent philosophies have affirmed that knowledge of 'solar death' enforces the radical contingency of life as we have known it, rendering questions concerning truth more knotty and intractable (Brassier, 2007; Lyotard, 1991). Perhaps it is wise to be wary of those who claim to know the truth and align with those who seek it.

In the field of education, the big questions of truth are very much in play at the most minute level of practice. All educational practice implies some sense of 'education as a whole' lurking albeit in the background of its immediate concerns. In fact, much of our world, as educationists, is predicated on a powerful, pervasive ontological assumption: the idea that education is a force for good – in itself, as it were. That assumption carries with it the status of a truth universally acknowledged. In truth, it belongs to the shadowy realm of the 'unknown knowns' those unrevealed forces that shape our most abiding beliefs about the nature of things (Zizek, 2004).

Truth questions are particularly germane, it seems to me to the currently dominant ethic of educational research, particularly so in relation to discourses of improvement and redemption. Both begin by assuming that the truth of education is already known and settled. This is far from being the case (Peim, 2016).

Foucault's strange truth

Foucault addressed questions concerning truth in an interesting and rather provocative spirit. In a late interview, he discussed the relation of his scholarly work to truth:

> I am fully aware that I have never written anything other than fictions. For all that, I would not want to say that they were outside the truth. It seems plausible

> to me to make fictions work within truth ... and in some way to make discourse arouse, 'fabricate', something which does not yet exist, thus to fiction something. One 'fictions' history starting from a political reality that renders it true, one 'fictions' a politics not yet in existence starting from a historical truth. (Dreyfus and Rabinow, 1994)

The first sentence might look like a self-denying mockery of the painstaking, carefully composed, meticulous work of history that characterizes Foucault's writings. Does Foucault seriously aim to compromise the truth of this work? The first sentence seems decisive in its insistence that Foucault has 'never' written 'anything' that is not fiction. This must include, then, the scholarly and voluminously authoritative *History of Madness* as well as the theoretically sharp and decisive *Archaeology of Knowledge* and the whole series of texts that have rewritten our sense of modernity, its invasive politics and its extensive technologies of the self (Foucault, 1977b, 2009). The statement offers an extraordinary assertion, then; but not without an equally extraordinary qualification.

Foucault's statement concerns something essential to the production of knowledge. Even in its brevity, it seems to propose a rethinking of the relations between writing, the production of knowledge and 'political reality'. Maybe this statement is, in its implicit account of the relations between writing and 'the Real', in its assertion of the power of writing to conjure 'something', the expression of a spectral phenomenology that disturbs all theories of knowledge that aspire to a correspondence theory of truth (Lacan 2006). In other words, the correlation asserted between fiction, production, history, truth, political reality – that seem necessarily distinct from one another – appears as a philosophically bold or mad claim. It certainly touches on questions that this book addresses about how philosophy and theory can provide significant ways of thinking relating to key dimensions of the research endeavour.

In Foucault's statement, we can 'hear' a message providing a series of resources for rethinking the temporal relations of history, truth and identity. It is important here to register the knotty complexity of Foucault's modest and calm statement. A summary can hardly do this justice since the statement expands its range of meanings even as it moves. Far from the vulgar perception, Foucault has no interest in dissolving either the category of truth or his own right and even obligation to embrace it as his own. Fiction, it is claimed, might be made to work within truth; but this is no safe recovery of truth as we have known it. This is the very antithesis of certain conceptions of truth. But the relations between truth and fiction become dizzyingly complicated from here on. To write within truth is to partake of the possibility of arousing something in discourse, some not-yet-existing projection. Such a truth of the future *must* take the form of a fiction. On the other hand, history, as a ground of another kind of truth, is the product of an active act of 'fictioning', that is itself grounded in a present 'reality' that is political. Being 'present' no more guarantees authenticity than it affirms temporal specificity. So already, truth, fiction, history, the present, reality, the political and the movement of time are caught in a mobile logic of mutual self-reference where what grounds what is always uncertain. There is no safe point of origin. And yet this does not erase truth. Truth remains a necessary goal, in this account, of Foucault's knowledge seeking quest.

Of course, most research projects don't begin with the kinds of problematizations of fundamental categories that the university-level introductions to social science and educational research often suggest (Perneckky, 2016; Swain, 2017). Most research projects don't have their genesis in the explicit domain of epistemology or the very fundamental business of ontology. Most research projects begin from within an already-positioned position: that is, they begin from within a world of practice or an established truth regime. In a way, surely, that was what Foucault was referring to when he used the word 'fictioning' as a metaphor for knowledge production that might still have some significant relation to truth in spite of its own admission that it is essentially made-up (as, being new, it must be).

In arguments about truth and its role in science and knowledge, it is often the case that truth is conceived of in some absolute but essential way, as already existing and waiting to be revealed. To suggest that truth might be generated by specific worlds or practices, although quite common in everyday parlance, seems somehow to touch on a raw sensitivity, as though one were suggesting that nothing matters because we have no absolute authoritative point to anchor it to or that can hold everything in place. We might turn that kind of anxiety around by suggesting that, as Derrida and Foucault's work both emphasize, it is vital for the pursuit of truth that truth itself be maintained as an unoccupied and, in effect, empty space.

Truth and the rise of epistemology

Through the twentieth century, epistemology was a dominant concern for thinking. This concern remains potent in philosophy and for theorists of science and knowledge. The epistemological irritant – the question hanging over how we know what we know – is the question of correspondence. To what extent do our ideas correspond with what is out there in the world? Is my understanding of education in accord with what happens or with what might happen in actual educational settings? How can we even claim to know an entity as vast and differentiated as education? Such questions can take on a very abstract and difficult to determine – or aporetic – form. So, does mathematics constitute the language of nature? Or, is mathematics the language of our understanding of nature? The question of correspondence has recently returned to philosophy in powerful form (Meillassoux, 2009).

Modern philosophy since Descartes focused on the question concerning the relations between representations and the world outside our consciousness. Descartes's ruthlessly rational doubt about things outside ourselves in space and time was explored further by Hume, who asked with a deep and abiding scepticism how we might know that our experiences of regular associations of ideas correspond to necessary connections in reality? While Hume was content ultimately to rest in uncertainty, Kant thought these questions required an answer and sought to produce one – at great length, in fact (Kant, 2003). Kant's modestly decisive answer was to acknowledge, through rigorous logical exploration, that fundamental categories required to explain the nature of things such as time, space and causal laws, could not be disentangled from our understanding and defined as objective, external phenomena. For us to represent anything – or any 'thing' – at all, the object must be represented as existing in time and space as part of a network of causal laws, according to Kant. The objects of our experience exist in time and space and are governed by necessary causal laws because otherwise they could not be objects of our experience. Ultimately, the categories of our understanding define the very knowledge we can have of things. The upshot of this is that we are limited to knowing the world as we experience it from within the frames of understanding we have so that the 'phenomenal' world cannot be claimed to be the world as it is in itself, the 'noumenal' world. On the other hand, this limitation, this being framed by categories of experience and knowledge, is precisely the condition for us to have any 'objective' knowledge of a world at all.

One consequence of this realization is that, as bearers of knowledge, human beings begin to see themselves as its objects. If human consciousness is part of the necessary ground for any knowledge, then it would be useful to understand and know what that consciousness is. This gradual dawning of radical self-consciousness has massive implications through the eighteenth and nineteenth centuries and beyond. The path from Alexander Pope's buoyant declaration that 'The proper study of mankind is Man' (1733–1734), through Hegel's labyrinthine celebrations and Freud's darker account of the radical disturbance of the unconscious (1900), to Heidegger's account of 'dasein' as fundamentally situated continues into more recent accounts of epigenetics, for example. The way is complex and many faceted. The question of 'the human' is far from closed – nor is the implication it always has for knowledge. In fact, there is a rich, diverse and productive contemporary range of thinking on this topic (Cavarero, 2000, 2005, 2008; Derrida, 2004; Malabou, 2015).

The putting of truth into question, the very suggestion that there may be epistemological issues to address regarding truth has worried many, especially a group of researchers that call themselves 'realist' sociologists of knowledge (Maton, 2013; Moore, 2009; Muller and Young, 2007). This group are especially bothered by what they have assumed to be the relativism of positions that they describe as 'postmodern', although it has to be added that they *never* engage with any of the key texts that introduced the actually complex and rich idea of a postmodern condition, preferring to project the idea that 'the postmodern' simply refers to a belief system that is essentially relativist and that eschews any recognition that there might be a strong relation between knowledge and truth, in spite of the complications of any (legitimate) sociology of knowledge. What these writers fear most is their version of relativism. In reaction, they affirm the authority of knowledge to claim an independent right for its claim to truth. The point here, though, is that questions of knowledge and truth have always been fraught with complications. Even divine truth had to be subject to interpretation and produced its own powerful schisms. The postmodern condition, anyhow, is less a series of bullet point beliefs or creed than a complex series of reflections on contemporary conditions of knowledge and the condition of the world, sometimes handled with great ingenuity (Harvey, 1991; Lyotard, 1986). That it can be reduced to a simple and not well-thought series of affirmations is the product of negligent reading. It is advisable to beware of any who refer in general to 'postmodernism' or 'poststructuralism' as bodies of thought. They are almost invariably the projections of those who seek to reject ideas – less commonly to embrace them – that they have not meaningfully engaged with. Several examples of this dismissive non-thinking can be found in the annals of mainstream philosophy of education (Carr, 1998; Pring, 2005).

One of the problems with the automatic dismissal of 'postmodernism' – and its relation to truth – is that it is hard to identify who is being accused of abandoning truth. Most of the usual suspects, including philosophers and thinkers or theorists, once grouped together under the heading of 'poststructuralists' do have a great deal to say about truth. None claims that truth is not of interest or concern and that we should abandon the idea altogether. I've heard prominent 'philosophers' of education proudly declare in public gatherings that they have not and will not read certain modern and contemporary philosophers because they know in advance that they are not worth reading. What orientation to truth is expressed in such a declaration? Such reductive thinking is almost invariably a sign of pure ignorance and failure to engage seriously with serious ideas.

One significant point of entry for an engagement with the question of truth is in Nietzsche's thought, much of it reaching back to rethink the legacy of Kant's interrogation of the possibility of human understanding accessing the object-in-itself. Nietzsche considered the idea of an 'eye' or a knowledge that was detached from the body of the knower as an absurdity. This image carried with it the implication that all knowledge, all claims to truth are grounded in some specific life form. The value of truth was not so much its correspondence with the world 'as it really is' but how that truth enables a vigorous life-affirming spirit for a certain way of life. A constant strain in Nietzsche's thinking was his rejection of the platonic idea that the 'really real', the domain of truth, is somehow beyond this manifest world. This didn't necessarily endear Nietzsche to the idea that we can engage with 'the truth' of this world – a truth that would have to exist neutrally beyond the bounds of any life world. Nietzsche would rather reject any claim to have a secure purchase on such an ideal world on the grounds that no one would recognize it. What's more, the projection of an ideal world implies a rejection of this world. Much of Nietzsche's effort as a philosopher was to promote an active love of this life in the form of an 'amor fati' (Nietzsche, 1990).

Nietzsche's approach to knowledge then is not so much to ask if it is true against some universal standard but rather to ask if it is helpful to realizing the aim of living a meaningful, impassioned life (Nietzsche, 1990). Life as it is the dominant principle for Nietzsche – and insofar as this stands in for some kind of orientation towards truth, it can be said to hold a supreme value (a kind of truth) (Heidegger, 1991).

To put it all too briefly, Nietzsche rejects the quest for 'truth' in the conventional sense, at least. Not that truth doesn't exist, nor that truth is not important: truth rather is always a projection onto the world. Sometimes truth is 'a mobile army of metaphors', to be diagnosed. Sometimes truth is another name for error, albeit essential and necessary error and sometimes merely the expression of the 'Will to Power'. Nietzsche asserts that the very multiplicity of truth means there is no sense in seeking truth as some pre-existing, absolute, palpable thing to be settled upon. Nietzsche often wants to affirm the truth of 'life'. For Nietzsche, what is worth believing in is what enhances life. Hence Nietzsche's preference in *The Birth of Tragedy* for the world of Attic tragedy with its strange myths and attunement to contradiction over and above a platonic or Christian view of a fallen or unideal reality. That there is any truth at all is a function of the difference between and collision of the Apollonian with the Dionysian. Truth on this view is dynamic, mobile and is the expression of the affirmation of a way of life, a way of being in the world. The truth of Attic tragedy, for Nietzsche, is not a truth of correspondence (Nietzsche, 1956).

Nietzsche rejects dogmatism: there are many kinds of eyes in Nietzsche's thought and many ways of seeing. Nietzsche's 'perspectivism' implies that philosophy needs to liberate itself from its systematic ambitions, borne out in Nietzsche's practice of philosophy, most of it written in aphorism, while his one big statement is written in the form of a myth (Nietzsche, 1892). Nietzsche's approach is experimental, inviting us to consider things in a more conditional spirit. This means that serious thinking can draw on a range of examples for its articulation, development, refinement. In *The Birth of Tragedy*, Nietzsche affirms Greek tragedy as the most potent form of thinking (Carson, 2009; Peim, 2016). The thinking in tragedy does not belong to the order of systematic rationality, but represents a more powerful way of knowing the world.

Perhaps, no one would expect the truths of tragedy to be consistent with the truths of science. They belong to different orders of knowledge, different ways of understanding the nature of things. Sciences have their own world view, as do religion and morality. In this Nietzsche goes beyond Kant's 'two standpoints' idea, suggesting that different domains of thought might proliferate and produce an endless series of 'truths' or modes of truth. This does not dissolve truth nor does it seek to do away with it in the name of some endless relativism, but shifts the grounds we think questions concerning truth on.

Ideas concerning truth, its identity and its value abound. There is a vulgar misapprehension that modern continental philosophy and or 'postmodernism' (see above) have abandoned truth and merely affirm that truth is purely relational or relative. In fact, modern philosophy, including modern continental philosophy, has a great deal that is subtle, complex and useful to say about truth. Such thinking, I believe, is particularly relevant to questions concerning education in our time including the less-frequently posed question of 'the truth of education'. And truth is a particularly sensitive issue in the field of education, surely. In education, as I have argued, there is a strong ethic that forecloses certain questions concerning the nature of educational truth (Peim, 2016).

The truth of the matter is that truth has many guises, many modes. We can think of different forms of truth. Axiomatic truths, for example, are self-evident – although some axiomatic truths are more self-evident than others. The twentieth century witnessed a whole series of philosophies based on the attempt to render axiomatic propositions safe to sustain a clear distinction between facts and values, science and metaphysics, to safeguard the realm of truth – or rather to safeguard the special status accorded to certain modes of truth (Ayer, 1971). Logicians for generations have struggled to establish how matters of truth might be logically expressed. 'Axiomatic theories of truth' seek to define the relations between sets, properties and predicates in a way that might avoid the ambiguities, uncertainties and slippages of the so-called ordinary language. This craving for clarity, precision and regulation in the production of statements of truth is very much the concern of a certain ethic, a certain way of regarding the foundations and significance of knowledge, its varieties and their 'proper' place in the world. This is the terrain of the logical positivists (*c*. 1930) and those who follow them (although it remains a strong assumption embedded even now in much everyday educational thinking). The logical–positivist ethic expresses an overriding desire is to purge knowledge of 'metaphysics'. Language is meaningful insofar as its statements are verifiable. There is a desire among logical positivists to render philosophy like natural science – or rather one narrow view of natural science.

Later developments in the twentieth century, as we shall see, will declare that natural science is by no means unambiguous in either its methods or its modes of expression. What's more, it seems much harder to banish metaphysics totally from the practices and ways of being that animate science. As Derrida noted in the mid-1960s, language itself is always already freighted with metaphysics. And Wittgenstein, much earlier in the twentieth century, realized that the desire to perfect a purely logical form of expression was both impossible and futile:

> The more narrowly we examine actual language, the sharper becomes the conflict between it and our requirement. (For the crystalline purity of logic was, of course, not a *result of investigation:* it was a requirement.) The conflict becomes intolerable; the requirement is now in danger of becoming empty. – We have got on to slippery ice where there is no friction and so in a certain sense the conditions are ideal, but also, just because of that, we are unable to walk. We want to walk: so we need *friction.* Back to the rough ground! (Wittgenstein, 1968, #107)

Here Wittgenstein has awoken from the logical positivist dream of a pure logic that can express the nature of things and can clear up unnecessary philosophical mystifications. Yet we can see in the history of science quite different attitudes towards the necessary acceptance of a dimension of uncertainty. Even in the most apparently hard-headed of natural sciences, quantum mechanics, 'the uncertainty' principle operates as the most fundamental principle regulating the constitution of matter (Heisenberg, 1930). The uncertainty principle is not that there is a bit of uncertainty about out judgements or measurements, nor even so much that measuring something interferes with the very thing you're measuring. It is more fundamental and far-reaching. It concerns rather an ontological uncertainty about the very nature of things – including very fundamental things. And seems to imply an irresolvable ambiguity. Quantum physicists are now happy to live with this principle just as high-status cosmologists are happy to concede that central aspects of their thinking belong to the order of speculation.

Science as truth

Science provides a useful context for the exploration of truth questions. This is partly because of the status of science as a type of knowledge that is different from prosaic or mundane knowledge. Science, it is claimed, has put knowledge on a different footing from assumptions, perceptions, insights and intuitions. Science asks for evidence, so the story often goes, and will not rest content with mere theory without the truth test of empirical data to verify. A classic example of this would be the case of the theory of relativity. General relativity produced in 1915 was generally regarded as a brilliant theory but lacking in empirical verification until Eddington tested its validity by a complex observation that could only take place during an eclipse. The data had to be careful scrutinized but it was eventually decided that it was sufficient to clinch the general theory of relativity. What is interesting about this case perhaps is that the theory precedes the production of the data. Without the theory, the data gathered would have been either meaningless or uninterpreted – perhaps amounting to the same thing.

The relation between theory and data is in this case is illustrative of the fact that theory does not necessarily derive from data in any absolutely founding sense within the operations of science. While science retains a commitment to the examination of evidence and to finding ever more cogent ways of engaging with the real material stuff of being, there is in fact no hard and fast scientific method for gathering, sifting and interpreting the meaning of data. One of the interesting things about this insight is that science must concede – and during the twentieth century itself becomes happy in some significant instances to concede – that its relation to the real is provisional. The principle of falsifiability (see below) decrees that scientific theories or knowledge can only be deemed to be scientific if they are falsifiable, that is, if in the structure of their being they have the potential to be disproved.

Major theories of science have examined the question about what makes science scientific and have in the process been concerned all the time with questions about the status of scientific knowledge in relation to truth. In truth, none of the various theories of science has taken an authoritative and dominant position, although several different theories have been regarded as significant and worthy of consideration. The point here is partly to affirm that science has no final, definitive character or series of indispensable qualities that make it different in some decisive and radical way from other forms of knowledge. And this absence of a definition or final truth of science and what it is brings home the fact that science is not a unified and entirely consistent, logically coherent entity. We might be better advised to think of science as a series of interrelated but different activities, practices and modes of engaging with specific aspects or elements of the material world. What tends to determine the scientific status of a theory of a body of knowledge or of a discovery, say, is that it meets that approval of a scientific community that have agreed a set of applicable criteria. In other words, whatever else it is, science is a social practice and relies on a degree of social cohesion for its continuation. As such, it relies on an authority system that can finally arbitrate between differences of position and that can determine whether or not the truth of a theory, of a discovery or of a piece or a body of knowledge can be accepted into the domain of the scientific. In this sense, science exercises a kind of police function to exclude what it deems to be the unscientific. In this science also perhaps acknowledges its own provisionality and fallibility.

This indeterminacy is characteristic of what happens when we ask ontological questions such as What is science? It isn't as though science disappears under the weight or the insouciance of the question, but rather that issues arise from it that mean that the foundations of the entity under question, if indeed we can speak in terms of foundations, are not straightforwardly present to us. We have begun to problematize the 'thing', and in the process we have opened the possibility of rethinking its premises. This in a way exemplifies the kind of argument and position that this book seeks to advance. It involves the privileging of the question and involves accepting or affirming the productive value of ontological thinking. Rather than putting us into a daze about the nature of things, ontological thinking – although it might have that dazing effect at first – opens the possibility of exploring the grounds on which we know something and determine its nature. Ontological thinking, we might say, gives us access to a mode of knowledge that is properly exploratory, that is a research ethic. Such an ethic demands that we consider questions concerning modes of knowing and their provenance.

With science, it is easy to see quite quickly how this problematization of essence must be the case. We can also see perhaps how pursuing the problem of essence in relation to science can reveal some of its ontological distribution, as it were, some of the ways that it appears to us as a phenomenon in our world. In addition, if we pursue this process, we can also see how examining aspects of science can put us into a different relation to its conventionally held identity and status. We can think what is anew, in effect. We are, in doing this, surely grappling with the truth of science and finding for ourselves some version of its status a privileged and powerful knowledge in our world and seeing it in relation also, perhaps, to issues that beset our times. We can formulate that this is we want to as a method of interrogation, a way of putting something we already know perhaps mostly in an inexplicit and habitual way in order to reconfigure our understanding of what it is. We might ask ourselves to investigate the role science has played in our own lives.

For definitions of science, one issue is that science isn't a unified entity in the first place. So that a total idea of what it is already seems to be difficult: mathematical physics, cosmology, geology and biology are different not just in the characteristic objects, but also in their procedures and primary methods. And, of course, the names of disciplinary fields like 'social sciences' or 'political science' further complicate the determination of the field under any unifying idea or principle. While all may lay claim to a certain rigour in their determination of the eligibility of knowledge within their domains, all vary in the procedures and criteria they apply to ensure the validity of the sifting process. None are entirely internally consistent (Feyerabend, 1975a,b; Kuhn, 1959, 1970). We might say, for example, that there is a distinction to be made between the moral sciences and the natural sciences. Nevertheless, all of the academic practices that come under the heading of the non-natural sciences, if we can put it that way, seek to claim their own kinds of rigour in order to secure that their particular system or space for the production of knowledge stands in some positive relation to truth. We can extend out exploration of what science is – and what is its essential characteristic way of being – by considering mathematics as neither natural science nor social science. We can further ask: Where does philosophy stand? And once we do, of course, we run into the ontological kind of question again: What kind of philosophy do you mean? Some kinds of philosophy will be deemed – positively and negatively – depending on where you stand, to aspire more to borrow the rigour of the natural sciences.

For Heidegger, physics is the most representative of modern sciences. For Heidegger, science in modernity begins with Galileo and continues in the European tradition with the enactment of the mathematical projection of nature. The function of such projection, according to Heidegger, is not so much the revealing of the fundamental nature of the world as a projection onto the world of a way of understanding where its essence lies. For Heidegger, the idea of objectivity obscures the fact that science activity, institutions, beliefs and world picture belongs to a specific understanding of things and a specific way of being in the world. Science is always a situated project. As such, it cannot but reflect in some significant degree a specific perspective, an orientation to Being. The value and meaning of science, its remit in the world, cannot be determined by science itself objectively using the so-called scientific procedure or method.

Heidegger engaged in a lifelong critique of science that perhaps remains significant. And it is essentially the metaphysical dimension of science that Heidegger takes exception to, its mathematical projection onto what it determines as 'nature' and the epistemological ideal of objectivity that masks the determination of science to represent the world in its own way (Heidegger, 1993a).

For Heidegger, the Cartesian-Newtonian heritage is the basis of the world order he refers to as 'technological enframing' (1993b). Here we see science and technology hand-in-hand as kind of powerful, perhaps indomitable, forces that dominate social practices and institutional thinking. We can link this strongly ingrained ontology with Weber's 'instrumental rationality' a force that clearly effects much educational practice. All the emphasis on measuring achievement and success, all the charted norms of development and attainment targets, all the benchmarks and national curricula, all the regimes of inspection and all the emphasis on all the apparatuses of examination seek to put things into order, to identify their quality and to maximize their use value in what are deemed to be appropriate spheres of existence. We could say that the whole ethic of the performative now dominates education and has become essential to its public existence. Tied in with national economic proficiency but also associated now with personal fulfilment, the norms and values of education seem like a powerful grid through which we must see, understand and experience the world and ourselves (Wolf, 2002). If that grid also appears at times like a cage, it is because of the remorseless logic of improvement that dominates and that is the expression of the history of rationalization that education has come to represent. All of this enframing' confirms the diagnosis offered by Heidegger in the face of 'the question concerning technology' back in the early 1950s (Heidegger, 1993b).

But that's by no means the end of the story. As indicated above, science has never been a unified field working consistently under one theory. Science changes, varies, is fraught with differences and conflicts and includes many false projects. Science is not only not consistently successful, but it operates with a range of ideas in a range of contexts that means that its procedures and its methods vary as well as its dominant ideas and ethics. There are significantly different ways of thinking involved in different forms of science – ways of thinking that may challenge received or dominant ideas about what science is or should be and about what its role in our individual and collective lives might be. Heidegger's vision of modern science as linked to an essentially limiting and potentially exploitative 'technological enframing' might be significantly challenged by some of its different modalities. Quantum mechanics has interesting ontological implications that led Niels Bohr to become fascinated by questions concerning being and that also led Werner Heisenberg to seek out Heidegger's thinking (Heisenberg, 1990; Lindley, 2008). The uncertainty principle and other anti-common-sense features of quantum physics make it more difficult to present as an ontology of domination. It certainly problematizes the will to knowledge in any simple sense. The history of twentieth-century physics can be seen as a struggle between different ways of understanding fundamental features of the physical world. Classical Newtonian physics was in some ways displaced as the key paradigm by Einstein's general theory of relativity. And then along came quantum theory to complicate matters further. No one has been able to resolve certain fundamental differences between relativity and quantum theory – meaning that the much sought-after 'theory of everything' has never been attained and seems to recede further with each new proclamation of its immanent revelation (Greene, 2011). In addition, cosmology has to, at some point, admit that it must move into the realms of speculation in order to advance plausible theories of the origin – and without such a theory much of what follows in terms of giving an historically reliable account of the development of the universe is conjectural. String theory develops mathematical models that define extra dimensions that there is no empirical evidence for (Susskind, 2005). In recent times, a great deal has been made in cosmology of the proposed existence of both dark matter and dark energy. Both phenomena are not in any way directly accessible to instruments of measurement or even to any apparatus that can confirm their existence. They are assumed to exist because of what else physicist claim to know about the universe and its 'laws of nature'. This knowledge and the picture it projects, for all its potency, its astonishing technological apparatuses, its immensely sophisticated calculations and its powerful theoretical frames, remain inconsistent and incomplete. Although there are scientists who look forward to the day when a complete unified theory of everything will be revealed, there are many who accept that our cosmological knowledge must always necessarily be partial and limited. For all our ingenuity, and for all the power of our languages of knowledge, the final truth of things is not accessible (Nicolson, 2007).

And this is only for the physicality of the universe. There is also a great deal of other stuff happening. Heidegger would say that the very desire to produce an authentic, scientific theory of everything is a symptom of technological enframing (Heidegger, 1993b). It represents an overweening will to knowledge that not only is doomed to fail in terms of its avowed purposes but also is based on a sheer misunderstanding of the nature of human existence.

Bill Bryson's populist account of science

Bill Bryson's *A Short History of Nearly Everything* has become a popular classic, available on station bookstalls and in motorway service stations. The book seeks to make the wonder of science available to a popular audience. Its history of the current state of science is also a self-proclaimed reflection on the nature of things. It is ontological, if not ontotheological, from the outset. From within the 'community' of science, the book received contradictory reviews: one referring to its 'sparkling wit' in 'embracing the whole of science', lauding Bryson's writing as 'consummate'; another claims Bryson is 'hopelessly out of his depth', concluding, 'There is almost no attempt to explain anything that could be called a scientific principle or to show what follows from it'. This difference in reception is itself significant. Here, Bryson serves to typify what I take to be an influential and often-held attitude. A parallel can be found in public accounts of the significance of science offered in the media by notable scientists (Nurse, 2016).

Bryson gives an awestruck account of science in modernity, with one or two, relatively minor, but telling, misgivings. The text confidently presents science as a progressive, teleological narrative, even though the end of the book considers the fragility of life and worries (on behalf of the human species) about its capacity to withstand possible ecological and cosmological futures. For Bryson, science holds out the best hope for any kind of future. It doesn't seem excessive to claim of *A Short History …* is representative of a dominant strand of Western metaphysics that takes science as knowledge itself and that sees science as being concerned with *everything*.

A Short History of Nearly Everything enacts what Lyotard affirms as science's dependence on the mode of knowledge it seeks to transcend to secure objectivity and freedom from any taint of the metaphysical that might compromise its truth. In Lyotard's account of science, narrative operates as supplement, as both other and necessary to its ontological status (Lyotard, 1986). Science must – in order to be science – differentiate itself from narrative, its necessary, but necessarily obviated, other. But in order to present itself as a unified entity, science must construct a narrative concerning its significance, its progressive nature, its beneficial role in history, in the future of the world, life itself and humanity, as exemplified in Bryson's conclusions (Bryson, 2004, 563–574). This ontotheological dimension of *A Short History …* reaffirms a series linking notions of being and truth with ideas about verification, veracity, the domain of the empirical, the role of logic, notions of data and analysis: in other words, the whole hermeneutic and epistemological apparatus of contemporary knowledge systems and their institutions. At the same time, across and against this apparently blithe narrative, we can detect several troubling Derridean motifs that disrupt this apparatus.

Bryson's book undertakes the role of defender of the faith. As a middlebrow author, Bryson – a non-scientist – is appropriate to fulfil this function. Bryson writes from a position outside science, as an interested but impartial spokesperson. Accounting for the genesis of the book, Bryson explains how a moment of anxiety concerning his ignorance of various 'things' – 'oceanic salinity', 'a quark', 'a quasar', 'a proton', 'a layer of rock' – triggers panic concerning his general ignorance of science and therefore of the nature of things. This revelation through anxiety is expressed as an 'insistent urge' to engage with 'the greatest of all amazements … how scientists work things out' (Bryson, 2004, 23). Interestingly, there appears a shadow question concerning the recognition, for Bryson, that scientists 'often seem to know nearly everything' and yet 'cannot predict an earthquake' and cannot foretell the weather (Bryson, 2004, 24).

Bryson explains the present order of things in key areas of science, presenting a survey of knowledge and charting various histories of scientific development. The word "survey" doesn't do justice to the enthusiasm of Bryson's wonder at the achievements of science, at the features of 'nature' science reveals and at the persistence of scientists in producing breakthrough theories, in their sudden leaps of insight and in the great paradigm shifts.

And yet, the book doesn't only naively celebrate the triumphs of science. In darker moments, the book ponders the parlous contemporary state of taxonomy, for example, and is shocked at the severe limits of direct empirical knowledge of the composition of the earth. Such anxiety, however, is always a concern *for* science. Any darkness attending the perilous future of the scientific quest, or identifying some radically underdeveloped aspects of science, serves only to indicate the importance of retaining faith in the project of science.

Two apparently contradictory strains characterize Bryson's account of science. The dominant tone of the enthusiast celebrates the triumphs. An undertone acknowledges the failures, gaps and blanks, but always expressed as problematic remainders and unfulfilled quests: the implication being that with more resource the gaps might be filled and the project of total knowledge be restored to its proper teleology. Any disappointment in science is never expressed in terms of failures of science as a way of knowledge, a way of life. In Heideggerian terms we might say that the book's darker moments are ontic; its wonder and faith are ontotheological. To anticipate, we might also add that the difference, in *A Short History …* between the ontic and the ontotheological has the effect of a deconstruction.

Exploring what it takes to be key domains of science, the book informs us of the developments of its great disclosures. The book implies that science holds the key to everything worth asking about 'everything'. Or rather, '*nearly* everything'. But the significance of the remainder is not articulated in the book. Does this 'nearly' signify the spacing between what is known by science and what is yet to be known? Does it anticipate, then, a time when the 'everything' will be fulfilled? Or does the 'nearly' indicate that while science may encompass just about everything that is or might be, there is still some small matter to be considered? In this title and in the discourse it announces we encounter themes that are unmistakeably Heideggerian. Wonder at the triumphs of cosmology is supplemented by anxiety over its lacunae. Only more science can fill the gap?

Having celebrated the triumphs of twentieth century theoretical physics, the book pauses soberly: 'The upshot of all this is that we live in a universe whose age we can't quite compute, surrounded by stars whose distances from us and each other we don't altogether know, filled with matter we can't identify, operating in conformance with physical laws whose properties we don't truly understand'. Bryson admits to finding this state of affairs 'unsettling' (Bryson, 2004, 219). Is the unsettling thought that some of the questions concerning fundamental 'matter' are as yet unresolved? That cosmology is a relatively young but nonetheless maturing science? That one day the progress of science will ensure that these things that we don't yet know will be known? 'That the deficiencies of the present day will be supplied by the morrow'? There is no expression of doubt concerning the project of science.

Science, metaphysics, truth

Near the beginning of 'What Is Metaphysics?' Heidegger acknowledges the determining role of science in 'in the community of researchers, teachers, and students' and asks: 'What happens to us ... when science becomes our passion?' Noting the diversity of the scientific field, held together by 'the technical organization of the universities' and the determination of 'the practical establishment of goals by each discipline' as a discrete discipline (Heidegger, 1993a, 94), Heidegger seems to question any unity for science.

And yet, in a swift reversal, the essay affirms an essential feature of science: 'in all the sciences we relate ourselves to beings themselves': it is the peculiarity of science to be concerned with 'beings themselves', with the determination of 'their grounds', an approach or attitude that 'gives the matter itself explicitly and solely the first and last word' (Heidegger, 1993a, 94). But the category of beings is complicated. Science is characterized as 'the irruption by one being called "man" into the whole of beings' with the effect that 'beings break open and show what they are and how they are' (Heidegger, 1993a, 95). Heidegger refers then to 'scientific man' as concerned above all with 'beings only'. And beyond that? Heidegger introduces the resounding 'nothing' – the 'nothing' that is raised, as it were, by the specific concern of 'scientific man'. Concerned only with 'beings', science 'wants to know nothing of the nothing' (Heidegger, 1993a, 96).

Subjected to further interrogation, the 'nothing' turns out to be both elusive and troubling at the same time. On the one hand, it cannot form the 'object' of scientific enquiry. According to the 'rule of logic' (Heidegger, 1993a, 97) the nothing is inadmissible. But Heidegger's argument finds a necessary connection between the act of negation and the nothing, as a manifestation of 'the intellect'. Doggedly pursuing the question, Heidegger asks in what manner the 'nothing itself' may be approached. This nothing, it turns out, is closely related to our sense of 'things as a whole', albeit rather oddly: 'The nothing is the complete negation of the totality of beings' (Heidegger, 1993a, 98). Further on, Heidegger articulates this association between our experience of 'things as a whole' and the 'nothing' as 'the fundamental mood of anxiety'. This is no ordinary anxiety arising from a specific issue – 'fearfulness', as Heidegger puts it. The 'impossibility of determining' this anxiety is essential to its nature. It is an anxiety that arises in the face of the impossibility of grasping 'beings as a whole' and an anxiety that reveals to 'us', as 'dasein', the nothing. Without reference to this nothing, experienced as the nihilation of beings, there can be no appreciation or grasping of 'beings as a whole': what's more, without the 'original revelation of the nothing' there can be 'no selfhood and no freedom'(Heidegger, 1993a, 103). For Heidegger, selfhood and freedom, both essential to dasein, are products of a carefully defined dimension that arises from the encounter with 'the original revelation of the nothing'. Dasein can never comprehend absolutely the whole of beings in themselves, yet dasein finds itself 'stationed' so that it can be aware of 'beings as a whole' – 'if only in a shadowy way' (Heidegger, 1993a, 103). Heidegger refers to this sense of things, never a permanent condition, but always a possibility, as 'being attuned'. This is the condition that enables us to 'find ourselves among beings as a whole'. In fact, this 'revealing' is fundamental to dasein's very existence. But so is this attunement to the nothing that is anxiety. Even though the 'original anxiety occurs only in rare moments', all our detailed and specific engagements with beings are predicated on a necessary 'turn away from the nothing':

> This implies that that the original anxiety in existence is usually repressed. Anxiety is there. It is only sleeping. (Heidegger, 1993a, 106)

This anxiety has essential consequences for Dasein. Its relation to the nothing is the condition for dasein's engagement with 'metaphysics itself' where metaphysics is defined as 'inquiry beyond or over beings'. Bryson's anxieties in *A Short History* … can be interpreted as shadowy engagements with 'the nothing'. As Heidegger indicates, any attunement to 'beings themselves' as exemplified in science must be attended by the spectral supplement defined as 'inquiry beyond or over beings' – or metaphysics.

Science and deconstruction

Derrida's supplement and the series of terms that attend it – trace, spacing, difference, graft, for instance – can be considered as a refinement of Heidegger's dramatic 'science, nothing, metaphysics' series. Convention frequently takes 'Structure, Sign and Play' as the seminal articulation of the terms of deconstruction and of themes that remain consistently at play in Derrida's work. 'Structure Sign and Play' might be read as a statement on the very possibility of the human sciences as *science*. It can be read implicitly as an articulation of what science *is*. In the second paragraph, we read:

> It would be easy enough to show that the concept of structure and even the word 'structure' itself are as old as the *episteme* – that is to say, as old as western science and western philosophy – and that their roots thrust deep into the soil of ordinary language. (Derrida, 1978, 278)

We may note here a dramatic, scandalous series: structure, episteme, science, philosophy. We may note, no less scandalously, a further correspondence between these entities and 'ordinary language'. Derrida's thinking, from the 'outset', is concerned with 'science' with its deconstruction – just as it is 'always already' concerned with 'the episteme', with metaphysics and, therefore, also, necessarily, with everyday language. In the 'affirmation' of the absence of a centre, Derrida identifies a strangely dislocated, decentred unity for science and knowledge with a 'necessity' that 'is irreducible' with 'roots' in 'the soil of everyday language'. The correlation between the elements of this series is continued in the far-reaching aside that 'ethnology – like any science – comes about within the element of discourse'.

The spectre of science, then, and the implication of science as spectral, is evoked early in 'Structure Sign and Play'. It is hardly surprising, given that Derrida *affirms* that identity is predicated on a certain kind of absence – the absence, in general, of anything that might correspond to a centre, or a self-contained, intrinsic organizing and stabilizing feature or force. This absence, we take to be, consciously or otherwise, a development of Heidegger's affirmation of the nothing as what problematizes the identity of science – or anything else.

The moments of aporetic bewilderment in Byson's texts appear as encounters with what lies beyond the borders of present science, as encounters with various kinds of nothing. For all its breezy cheer, Bryson's text is littered with anxious questions concerning the breakdown, absence or negation of what is proper to science. Bryson's narrative goes a long way towards combating the 'nothing' but is itself an attempt to provide a structure, a coherence and a totality that ultimately proves elusive. We can interpret Bryson's cheerful anxiety as an expression of desire for the always elusive, centred structure of necessity for science. And we can understand Bryson's book as a whole as an implicit, unintended deconstruction of the very centred structure it craves.

Derrida's anti-structuralist position that emphasizes differences and 'play' at work in discourse provides an explicit articulation of the condition that fractures Bryson's discourse:

> the moment when, in the absence of a centre or origin, everything became discourse – provided we can agree on this word – that is to say, a system in which the central signified, the original or transcendental signified, is never absolutely present outside a system of differences. The absence of the transcendental signified extends the domain and the play of signification infinitely. (Derrida, 1978, 280)

Derrida's insistence on the infinite extension of the 'domain' of signification and its endless 'play' indicates the exclusion of the possibility of totalization:

> If totalization no longer has any meaning, it is not because the infiniteness of a field cannot be covered by a finite glance or a finite discourse, but because the nature of the field – that is, language and a finite language – excludes totalization. This field is in effect that of *play*, that is to say a field of infinite substitutions only because it is finite, that is to say, because instead of being an inexhaustible field, as in the classical hypothesis, instead of being too large, there is something missing from it: a center which arrests and grounds the play of substitutions. One could say ... that this movement of play, permitted by the lack or absence of a center of origin, is the movement of *supplementarity*. (Derrida, 1978, 289)

Supplementarity disables intrinsic identity. Identity is subject to endless play and endless deferment, always dependent on something *else*, something extra, an additional not-present move or element. Here Derrida articulates play and supplementarity as expressive of deconstruction, understood as dependence on supplementary meaning that is, in turn, dependent for any affirmation of identity on institutional frameworks. Deconstruction is what puts 'play' into play:

> The *overabundance* of the signifier, it *supplementary* character, is thus the result of a finitude, that is to say, the result of a lack which must be *supplemented*. (Derrida, 1978, 280)

A key series of terms in Derrida – 'play', 'supplementarity', 'the trace', 'différance' – articulates the deconstruction of being-as-presence in terms of the necessity of the 'non-' in the non-present elements that come to force through deferral and that enable the 'play' that deconstruction activates:

> Play is the disruption of presence. The presence of an element is always a signifying and substitutive reference inscribed in a system of differences and the movement of a chain. Play is always play of absence and presence, but if it is to be thought radically, play must be conceived of before the alternative of presence and absence. Being must be conceived as presence or absence on the basis of the possibility of play and not the other way around. (Derrida, 1978, 292)

And we must, surely, given the explicit reference to 'Being' here, interpret this affirmation as the expression of an ontology that is remapping the field of subject–object relations that must be more than tangentially relevant to the question of science, its subjects, its objects and its general ontological condition. On this view, the interpretation and organization of phenomena must always come from outside, imposed, as it were, partially and provisionally, by contexts, discourses and social practices.

For both Derrida and Heidegger, then, 'nothing' is more interesting than at first might appear. Nothing is both a condition of the being of any being or entity; but nothing is also, in some inescapable sense, generative: furthermore, nothing stands in a special relation to meaning, for Heidegger for the question of questions, and for Derrida for an engaged deconstruction. Deconstruction is what opens the relation between 'everything' or 'nearly everything' and the nothing, elaborates this, through a series of related terms – trace, supplement, graft – and articulates this into a 'principle', différance, that enables us to articulate fundamental ontology again, and above all, to resist ontotheology, or the affirmation of a centre that might hold together a totality (Derrida, 1978). At one level, this series of terms articulates an account of the condition of language; at another, it is implicitly presented as an account of writing in a metonymic relation to Being. It is possible to consider Derrida's extended statement concerning the science of grammatology not only as a deconstructive account of that science, but also, implicitly always, as a deconstruction of science 'itself'. Hence, perhaps, the teasing ambiguities in the title of that book that signifies Derrida's appropriation of grammatology: 'De la ...' – 'concerning', 'what belongs to', 'what is proper to' but also 'a bit of', 'some', ... and so on.

Just as Derrida's work implies that the dream of a science of writing – a grammatology is impossible – so too we may reflect on the relations between science, truth and metaphysics, not at all with the intention of denying scientific truth, but rather of understanding the complexities that attend it. As Heidegger dramatically explains the scientific view is not exclusive and there is an argument for calling into question some aspects of modern science – especially in its relations with technology, and especially in terms of the privilege science sometimes enjoys as the essential form of knowledge itself. Bryson's case illustrates the problematic nature of science in its relation to truth – and there are some very significant cases of science itself asking about its own foundations and its own claims to be grounded in a neutral form of reality through some direct access to truth, as we may see in what follows here.

Paradigms and the provenance of metaphysics

What is particular to science that makes it science and that also makes it a different kind of knowledge from other knowledge? Heidegger's answer proclaims that science operates in a particular relation to beings. It also claims that modern science gives rise to a mode of technology that is thoroughly characteristic of a vision of the world. For Heidegger science distinguishes itself from metaphysics. Heidegger has no argument with science but does suggest that the specific modern technological-scientific outlook has strongly destructive potential especially in terms of its fundamental relation to Being.

Heidegger's thoughtful approach to what science is, is relevant today. Science itself includes some famous thinking about its own nature, above and beyond the mere celebratory. On the one hand, science is still held to hold out the promise of the ultimate resolution of some persistent problems that beset human life: how to sustain a burgeoning population, how to provide energy sources that will replace depleting and dangerous carbon-based fuels. On the other hand, beyond these questions are others that science and science-based technology may have contributed to but seem to have no way of addressing: the gradual erosion of wilderness areas, loss of non-human ecosystems and forms of life and others that are the direct consequence of scientific development, including: massively destructive nuclear weapons, biotechnologies that may interfere negatively with the reproduction of species.

Earlier in the twentieth century, scientific advances – especially in physics – prompted a group of philosophers who came to be known as logical positivists that philosophy might model itself on science and draw from the triumphs of science a more solid foundation for its own advancement particularly in the direction of objectivity. After all, scientific questions could be settled objectively. Experimental testing enabled facts to test out theories – and for theories to be verifiable therefore. The subjective component of scientific discovery – intuitions, insights, unprompted leaps of thought – was offset by the objective systems of justification that came into play to verify scientific knowledge. As a fundamentally rationalist activity with proven and provable results, science could provide a paradigm for softer, less certain forms of knowledge that were increasingly making claims for their right to occupy the organized field of knowledge. In science competing theories could be checked against the observable facts of a matter – reference to material that could not be disputed and that clearly belonged unproblematically to the state of affairs (Uebel, 2016).

One of the problems with this view was that it foreclosed the historical dimension. It needed to forget that science had a history and that it was a history characterized by scientific *revolutions* – large-scale changes in the understanding of things: the Copernican revolution in astronomy, the Darwinian revolution in biology and the Einsteinian revolution in physics are key examples where science undergoes a great upheaval. Most of the time we may imagine science continues in a state of normal activity without upheaval and without demanding the production of new sets of ideas to replace the set of ideas overthrown by revolution in thinking. This normal condition though is historical and belongs to what Thomas Kuhn came to define as a 'paradigm' – a set of fundamental theoretical assumptions that all members of a scientific community would accept, a set of exemplary scientific problems or findings that occupy a central series of illustrations of the agreed methods within the field. The paradigm not only defines established knowledge and procedures but also determines what are the key directions for thinking what are the essential problems of the discipline. A paradigm is really an implicit outlook made up of shared assumptions, beliefs and values that becomes taken for normal and proper and that exerts powerful, normative influence on practices but also on the attitudes and behaviours of the constituency of the discipline. Results that challenge the paradigm will be taken as evidence of faulty technique or incorrect application. The supervention of the normal is the product of the inviolability of the paradigm (Kuhn, 1959, 1970).

The norms of science, of any particular mode of science, are not fixed forever, however. And this is where things get interesting. Science produces 'breakthroughs' that are hailed as having great significance. Such breakthroughs involve challenging the established norms of science. Anomalies, if not resolved, may generate crisis. According to Kuhn, whose ideas I paraphrase here, a period of revolutionary consciousness may prevail that is not within the bounds of science – as hitherto understood anyhow. Thus, a revolutionary science prevails, challenging the ancient regime. Science is not consistent with itself. Quite fundamental ideas may be subject to scrutiny even redefinition. Through the force of generational change, a big shift may take place witnessing the emergence of a new paradigm. Members of the science collective must be won over to the values and precepts of the scientific revolution (Kuhn, 1959, 1970). There are matters of faith and commitment at stake in all this.

Kuhn's thesis appeared reasonable when set against the history of science. Big paradigm shifts had occurred between Ptolemaic and Copernican astronomy and from Newtonian to Einsteinium physics, although some more recent examples don't fit the Kuhnian model so readily (molecular biology, for example).

Kuhn's position was not without controversy especially in relation to the question concerning motivating force of the paradigm shift. To imply that the change in allegiance was more likely to be an act of faith than a simply and purely rational choice was contentious. What's more, rapid collective acceptance of paradigm shift within a community was likely to occur under pressure from prominent members of the field suggesting in effect that scientific change might be driven by the internal politics of research collectives. In both above respects, it seemed that Kuhn was suggesting that major changes in science were not essentially rationally motivated, deflating the positivist image of science (Kuhn, 1959, 1970).

The overall direction of scientific change – according to Kuhn's position – also challenged the idea of a linear progression for science. It could be, for example, that Einstein's theory of relativity was more Aristotelean than Newtonian theory, since another key idea of Kuhn was the theory-laden nature of data itself. Essentially this idea affirms that data belongs with paradigms and that there is not an appeal to data that could resolve differences between paradigms. There is no neutral vantage point and objective truth, ultimately, is called into question. Theory neutrality is illusory. While logical positivists believed in the existence of pure data independent of theory Kuhn's affirmation of the prevalence of theory challenged that apparently fundamental assumption. Scientific truth is relative to paradigm. For Kuhn the scientist's very perception of what is must be heavily conditioned by more or less implicit beliefs: seeing and believing are intricated. The very idea of paradigms and paradigm shifts, surely, throws objective truth into question. Was this not scandalous for science? What constitutes even a basic unit of truth – a fact, for example – might vary according to the dominant paradigm. If the very facts about the world are subject to change, it makes no sense to ask if any theory corresponds to the facts as they *are* since the theory determines what the facts might be at all in the first place. Everything is relative to the paradigm. And paradigms are 'incommensurable' with one another (Kuhn, 1959, 1970).

A scientist's paradigm determines the scientist's world-view and acts like an unsurpassable lens. Kuhn refers to scientists within different paradigms as living in different worlds. Such worlds share no common language. Common terms will have quite different import or meaning within different paradigms. In a quite radical and challenging sense, incommensurability of paradigms implies that scientific change is directionless and not progressive (Kuhn, 1959, 1970).

The above account is a simplification of the position that Kuhn finally arrived at that revised the pure incommensurability thesis; but Kuhn continued to maintain that any fully objective choice between the truths of different paradigms was impossible. In some ways, this whole problematic that Kuhn addresses and his revelations appear to be a version of Kant's phenomenology applied to science.

Kuhn's ideas are still debated. A second edition of his book *The Structure of Scientific Revolutions* affirmed that he had not denied the rationality of science but had reminded the world of its historicity. Neglecting historicity had led to a simplistic positivism that was not only idealistic but was also misleading. In addition, Kuhn reiterated in the later preface that there was no algorithm to determine theory choice in science. In other words, there are no rules that can strictly guide the decision that one theory is superior to another, although positivism in science had been predicated on just such an idea. In fact, no algorithm for theory choice has ever appeared. Many scientific decisions concerning theory choice are made by appealing to common sense, but common sense is notoriously value laden and ultimately ideological. This basic insight recalls the idea that the adoption of a new paradigm demands acts of faith. Kuhn was to insist that his work was not an assault on the rationality of science, although it rejects a certain conception of that rationality Ultimately, it had to be conceded that scientific thought cannot be simply defined in terms of logic but that it must also carry the 'taint' of psychology (belief!), albeit social psychology.

Kuhn's work had implications: one was that science was subject to philosophical analysis and questioning. Another was that science belongs to a social context, but more importantly perhaps, as later thinkers were inclined to develop and demonstrate, that science belonged to a particular *episteme* – a whole way of seeing and understanding the nature of things that was historically, socially and culturally specific. Heidegger had already made a strong case for calling into question what he saw as the unholy alliance of science and technology in framing a destructive attitude to the world and to the creatures inhabiting it (Heidegger, 1993c).

Whatever objectivity science might want to claim for itself would then have to be weighed against powerful contextual considerations. There would even be those who would claim that in privileging science human thinking had taken a wrong turn. Kuhn's work certainly does seem to raise, for modernity, questions about the faith expressed in knowledge, and this questioning extends beyond science, for science had become the paradigm case for the very possibility of objective knowledge.

Kuhn, it should be borne in mind, is informed about the history of science; he can therefore focus on real, empirical cases and is not therefore obliged to essentialize the scientific. Paul Feyerabend takes these insights further to look at science as a form of social practice, re-examining its authority through its institutional being. For Feyerabend, it is the processes of institutionalization that occur in science that render science more than and different from the disinterested pursuit of knowledge (Feyerabend, 1975a, b).

Feyerabend's work is radical and opens decisive questions concerning the provenance of science that remain highly cogent. This is a complex matter, but it is easy to see how powerful investments get tied up with the practice of science and that these investments will often have powerfully conservative effect, in the sense that they will tend to organize the life world of the scientist and of scientific practice in particular ways. Investment here refers to the emotional, affective dimension as well as to the financial. If we think of science within the context of a university, we can see immediately how the social and social psychological dimensions come into play. The division of spheres of knowledge and the attendant identities they support and demand are strongly derived from the hierarchical order of the field of practice with its tightly organized distributions of identity. The setting up of criteria of excellence based on what has become taken for 'normal science' in Kuhn's terms ensures that paradigm cases exemplify excellence and come also to direct and even perhaps to dominate further enquiry. All of these factors amount to a delimitation of practice as the conditions of practice become enframed within an institutional order that claims the allegiances of its practitioners. As Heidegger would have it, such organizations are world forming: they demand investment in terms of commitment and faith; they interpellate identities strongly (Althusser, 1984a, b; Heidegger, 1993a). 'Normal' science is then contained and we might say constrained by the norms that determine what it is (Feyerabend, 1975a).

We can see how this works very vividly in aspects of social science where whole fields are dominated by certain norms that provide a whole way of understanding knowledge within the field but also that provide a whole way of conducting and understanding what research is. More than that, normative thinking decrees what counts as meaningful in terms of the pursuit of knowledge in the field. The topics of research, the modes of research and the ethics of research must all be strongly enframed by the normative. The dimension of meaning – the metaphysical, in effect – cannot be eradicated from science or from any other field of knowledge.

It often seems as though science is separated from metaphysics – and this is exactly the point the Heidegger makes in that stunning and revealing paper

'What is metaphysics?' When Heidegger asks, 'What does science know that is not science?' the answer is simple: nothing. But this nothing turns out to be not so simple as its automatic utterance might suggest. It becomes clear that the nothing science knows is actually the very grounds of the very existence of science itself! This idea concerning the essentially metaphysical nature of science, which Heidegger posits but does not develop in his essay, returns in the twenty-first century in powerful form in the work of Catherine Malabou, as we shall later see.

That there is an essential metaphysical component to science should not really surprise us even if it does perhaps conflict with our everyday understanding of what science is. After all, science must, in certain inescapable ways, lay claim to express something concerning 'the nature of things'. Both of those elements, 'expression' and 'nature', carry with them the necessity of the metaphysical. For, as we must recall, language – the mode of expression (including mathematical language) – belongs to the order of metaphysics. We recall that even the most humble everyday language is implicated in metaphysics even if it doesn't know it (Derrida, 1978). And to express something of the nature of things – as science is compelled to – is to affirm our grasp of reality, or things-in-themselves, or the noumenal.

One of the scandalous features of quantum mechanics has been its famous readiness to own up to its metaphysical pretensions. When Einstein wanted to refute the centrality of the uncertainty principle, he was happy to declare that 'God does not play dice', and by 'God' we assume he refers to the very order of things or 'nature'. The invocation of 'God' surely betrays the ontotheological aspirations of certain forms of modern science. The kind of physics Einstein and the pioneers of quantum mechanics study often claim the epithet 'fundamental' for their focus and findings. It often claims to be getting at the essential nature of reality. More recently, the hitherto elusive Higgs bosun was popularly, but also among scientists, referred to as 'the God particle'. In the search for the very fundamental, we can detect a powerful strain of the theological.

On the other hand, Heisenberg's great uncertainty principle declares itself to be inescapably in the register of phenomenology. It declares that there are no absolute terms about what it is possible to claim to know at any one given time, from any one given perspective, and what it is not given to know (Heisenberg, 1930, 1990). Niels Bohr, a leading star of quantum mechanics, was famously obsessed with questions concerning 'being' and when contemplating the ontological status of certain particles became decidedly deconstructionist in his problematization of the usual, automatic correlation of being with presence (Murdoch, 1989). Schrodinger's famous cat experiment involving a poison capsule in a box – the theme of many trendy and witty T-shirts – was a 'thought experiment'. These examples all signify significant elements or events in the evolution of quantum theory. They constitute essential components – along with other more conventionally scientific elements – of quantum theory's scientificity. These cases, were we to examine them in detail, reveal the important principle that it is not possible strictly to delimit the border between metaphysics and physics. In contemporary cosmology, particularly in its more adventurous and advanced branches, the role of speculation is vital and plays a significant role in organizing the kind of data that is sought and revealed but also in determining the interpretations of the possible significances of data (Susskind, 2005).

A similar line of thinking, one that disturbs the idea of traditional boundary between 'hard' forms of knowledge and speculative thought, haunts the various uses that mathematics gets put to in science and concerns the very status of mathematics as an enterprise. From ancient times there has been a curious correspondence between mathematical concepts and our understanding of nature and the patterning of natural phenomena. When mathematicians discovered a relation for example between the Fibonacci sequence and the number of petals on various different kinds of daisies, or the spiral organization of the seeds in sunflowers, it gave rise to a curious uncertainty about the very nature of mathematics. Essentially, it is possible to see – as both mathematician and philosophers have – mathematics as essential ontology. Being, it is claimed, is fundamentally mathematical (Badiou, 2007). On the other hand, as hinted above, more deconstructive approaches to the philosophy of mathematics problematize the essential qualities of mathematical thinking, without doing any violence to their power to both describe the world and to create new possibilities for understanding 'the real' (Wittgenstein, 1967).

Falsifiability as validity: Truth and relativism?

Both Kuhn and Feyerabend rethought the very status of science as an enterprise. They put into questions the possibility of claiming an essential rationality for scientific method. We can easily comprehend this if we consider the extent that our culture – our age and our place in history – have determined that science is a major mode of practice and thought and has in significant ways dominated our horizon in terms of knowledge, especially given the awe-inspiring achievements of science in modernity and its relations with everyday technologies. For us, we might say, this very puissance carries with it a magical, mythic aura.

The serious philosophy of science has had to wrestle with key features of its practice and being in modernity, while also belonging to the very order of a world where science occupies that mythical and culturally central, if not theological, role. Theorists have also had to wrestle with problems concerning the certain ossification of scientific ideas – or ideas about science – and practices within powerfully established traditions (that have often achieved remarkable successes) with the tendency for science to make drastic quantum, paradigm shifting leaps that often problematize the very conditions that allowed those big changes to occur. In many famous cases, the role of contingency cannot be excluded, but it hardly seems compatible with strictly scientific view of the progress of scientific knowledge to allow that accident may play a significant role in the movement of science. Another key dimension of course that may problematize any mythic status accorded to science as necessarily attached to and a vehicle of progress is the fact that science in some fundamental way, according to Karl Popper, especially must always be predicated on its own failure (falsifiability) to even count as science at all the principle of falsifiability is rather like the interminable in deconstruction: it involves the recognition that nothing, even our most secure knowledge, is ever complete – and therefore is never secure. In fact, this is the very condition of its claim to scientificity.

While Richard Feynman claimed that philosophy of science is as useful to scientists as ornithology is to birds, Feynman rather missed the point about the point of metascience. The point is to understand the nature of such a form of knowledge and to consider its history and its place in our world and in our understanding of things. As we have seen, some figures in recent times, Heidegger, or Feyerabend, for instance, have wanted to critically delimit the potentially overweening ambitions of science or at least to come to an understanding of the limitations of science in answering significant questions and particularly in relation to giving an account of the 'nature' of things.

This is not a mere trivial pursuit of a certain logic following on the idea of falsifiability but can be dramatically illustrated, as Catherine Malabou has done, in relation to some of our most important inherited modes of thinking that science in modernity has embodied (Malabou, 2015). If we accept that falsifiability is an ontological predicate of science in general, then we have to accept that science is, in some never-ending sense, subject to a Kuhnian law of revolution. In this condition, a key term appears – incommensurability. This is perhaps the most radical of all Kuhn's key terms: as it indicates that our present science must always be superseded by some science to come that will be incommensurable with the science we presently express faith in and that seems to correspond so effectively with the very nature of things. This means that even as one paradigm, in Kuhn's account, gives way to another, the newly dominant paradigm in turn must await its own displacement by yet another. There are then no conclusive, ultimate grounds for the holding sway of one paradigm or another. Although this doesn't mean that the paradigms of science are ungrounded or groundless, of course, it makes us think ontologically differently about what science is and about the history of its progress – that latter word perhaps now needing the safeguard of scare quotes.

Important consequences flow from the philosophically protean implications of the idea of the 'paradigm' or paradigm theory and falsifiability. One key implication is that there are many ways of doing science and at the same time these many ways negate the possibility of defining securely and delimiting what constitutes legitimate method. Even more significant perhaps, though in some ways perhaps a harder point to grasp, is the realization that the existence or at least the possibility of there being many ways of doing science indicates that there is no secure way of determining what problems, questions or issues are important. In other words, the field of science is not automatically governed by any principle that will suggest what needs to be studied, what new knowledge needs to be produced, what established knowledge needs to be rethought. Even so fundamental an idea to research as observation has had to undergo serious rethinking that can only finally be characterized as leading towards the aporetic. It's not just that what counts as observation may be enormously or perhaps even infinitely variable; it is the recognition that the very act of observation plays a significant role in determining the very nature of the thing observed, its status, its condition being interfered with in that very process.

Languages of description, what's more, cannot be neutral and innocent. Malabou has recently shown very powerfully how the language of biology has been dominated by a more or less explicit affirmation of the principle of sovereignty, even at the level of the cell, and much of her recent thinking has been to show that this is not an appropriate way of conceiving of certain essential biological phenomena and functions, drawing as she does on recent insights from neuroscience (Malabou, 2015). And it is not only Malabou who has identified this 'ideological' dimension in biological language of description: biology itself has undergone its own internal 'paradigm shift' in relation to key findings of genetics in epigenetics that it has had to rethink and is still in the process of rethinking its understanding of many fundamental entities and processes. One noteworthy consequence of this has been that Malabou has deployed this paradigm shift in biology analogically to conduct her own far-reaching re-examination of political sovereignty (Malabou, 2015).

But doesn't all this shifting leave us rootless and relativist? Thomas Kuhn himself was concerned at the charge of relativism that was levelled against him. And this is a feature that frequently recurs in relation to thinking that tends to disturb settled understandings of the order of things. 'Relativism' has frequently been used as a term to discredit or undermine any position that seeks to problematize any system of thinking or any way of thinking that lays claim to having the right to declare a determinate or absolute truth, as though this were an offence against science, or the honest pursuit of knowledge, or worse a denial of the very possibility for ethical being. Relativism is often charged as being dangerous. In fact, science itself utterly resists the idea of determinate or absolute truth – even in relation to its most fundamental principles. It's worth remembering that the opposite of relativism is absolutism – and that is far from a scientific cast of mind. There are ways and ways of being relativist.

Foucault: 'Episteme' and the order of things

For Foucault, every mode of thinking involves implicit rules that restrain its possibilities within a certain range: our own thinking is of course governed by such rules that mostly we cannot get outside of to examine or to change. We are hardly aware of their existence. The history of ideas therefore is not only about the explicit thinking of influential individuals that appear to epitomise the spirit of the age; more important, but also more difficult to pin down, is the structure of ideas that underlies such thinking and that determines its limits. This is the notion of the 'episteme' or larger regime of knowledge and thought that underpins the world view and the detailed forms of understanding that constitute an era, a culture or a movement. The thinking of any individual or any system must derive from and stand in relation to the 'episteme' that in some significant way it both belongs to and derives from. This idea is useful in limiting the claims of knowledge to universality and to timelessly and accords, if by quite a long shot, with all those understandings of science that suggest that even what might be taken as the fundamental grounds for knowledge is subject to seismic historical shift. The idea of the 'episteme' can be construed as a kind of geological metaphor whereby epochs may produce radically different ways of thinking that are difficult to reconcile (Foucault, 1977b). Anyone who has read Aeschylus, for instance, or looked at the cave paintings from Lascaux must experience something of that difference.

Foucault's reflections on the provenance of knowledge are in many ways parallel with modern and contemporary accounts of the theory of scientific knowledge. Foucault's own work – in *The History of Madness* and in *Discipline and Punish*, for instance – seeks to delineate the thinking that both constrains and enables possibilities for the existence of certain practices, institutions and the beliefs that attend them (Foucault, 1977, 2009). Foucault claims in this sense that his work is not hermeneutic: it doesn't seek to recover an underlying meaning in textual historical material, still less to reveal something of the individual insight of an individual. The archaeological approach to knowledge is more monumental. The significance of a text, for example, emerges from its relation to a series of texts so that what is revealed concerns the scattered ordering and structuring of thinking in its time, rather than from uncovering the meaning latent in its content and internal structure (Foucault, 1977b).

This method and its theoretical basis can be opposed to the standard history of ideas that sees a progressive trajectory at work in texts that belong to quite different epochs. Foucault's 'history of systems of thought' eschews subject-centred accounts of the development of ideas but also seeks to challenge the kind of retrospective narratives that such histories give rise to with their assumption of continuity, transcendence and teleology. Foucault's archaeology suggests that factors outside of consciousness belie continuity and explicit purposes. On this view, the history of human thinking is not necessarily the logical outcome of the circumstances of its production and its place in a line of development: it is much more contingent than that. It develops its own internal logic. If being determines consciousness, then it does so in ways that are not necessarily predictable or schematic (Foucault, 1977b). And for those who are seeking to understand the relations between their own specific being in terms of the knowledge it relates to, it can be difficult to discern or delineate its conditions of possibility. Such conditions – referred to by Kant as 'transcendental' – are not empirically available even while they are absolutely necessary for there to be experience at all, including knowledge. For Kant, the conditions of possibility for knowledge were universal: time, space, causality, for instance. For Foucault, they could be seen as varied across specific historical conditions and domains of knowledge and being. This makes Foucault something of a radical thinker in terms of the history of science, especially in relation to the history of received ideas. Should we be tempted to declare that modern science presents universal truths in a way that no previously existing form of knowledge has we might, in Foucauldian mood, be tempted to think 'Well, we would say that, wouldn't we?'

At the beginning of *The Order of Things* Foucault cites a mythic ancient Chinese taxonomy from a short story by Borges. According to this ancient document:

> animals are divided into: (a) belonging to the Emperor, (b) embalmed, (c) tame, (d) sucking pigs, (e) sirens, (f) fabulous, (g) stray dogs, (h) included in the present classification, (i) frenzied, (j) innumerable, (k) drawn with a very fine camelhair brush, (l) *et cetera*, (m) having just broken the water pitcher, (n) that from a long way off look like flies. (Foucault, 2005, xvi)

The point of the joke is to introduce this idea of the episteme as a horizon for knowledge. Here it is evident that the form of knowledge that produces these categories is not available to us, as products of modernity and what follows. The episteme operates as a kind of unconscious organization of rules and things that might be referred to as an 'historical a priori' again indicating conditions of possibility. The medieval, renaissance, classical, enlightenment and modern epistemes differ in significant respects. And at the end of *The Order of Things*, Foucault, rather darkly perhaps, predicts the end of the world order of knowledge as we know it, foreseeing the inevitable shift to some other as yet unimaginable episteme.

Time and again, Foucault's work indicates an essential idea that derives from directing a critical intent towards the order of things in terms of a society's self-understanding. *Discipline and Punish* goes to great lengths to describe the change that occurs in the organization of social practices between two different types of power: sovereign power and biopower. In doing so, the text retraces the emergence of modern institutions – such as hospitals, prisons and schools – from various practices that arose in response to contingent needs to organize otherwise dangerous, unhealthy and growing populations. In the meticulous history that is laid out before us, we can see education developing not so much as force for enlightenment, social justice or redemption of the self as it now is often represented as being. The school arrives as an indispensable but contingent outcome of a new form of government dominated in its arrival by practical concerns of population management. Its habitual practices are dedicated towards the production of useful 'bodies' that would in the end internalize the discipline that sought to shape them. In the process, such bodies would become self-managing within a form of government that reached into hitherto unreachable aspects of life itself: hence 'biopower' (Foucault, 1977a). This account potentially problematizes a great deal of what passes for knowledge and insight in the field of education and offers, by focusing on the coming together of the episteme of modernity and the social practices of its key institution, a drastically alternative vision. We can speculate on the meaning of this fact. For the dominant, university discourses of education in our time, such a perspective would be potentially terminal. And it is the case that there are those who read and discuss Foucault in the context of education without ever taking on this potentially fatal effect (Ball, 2013).

Are we enlightened?

Perhaps because of the apparent scepticism of Foucault's version of the history of ideas, later in his thinking career Foucault revisited the very idea of enlightenment. After all, the theory outlined above would tend to argue against the idea of a 'breakthrough' movement in consciousness implied in the very idea of enlightenment. Foucault didn't want to dismiss the idea of enlightenment out of hand but wanted to interrogate it following Kant's affirmation but with a distance of almost two centuries of seismic shifts in thinking and of history (Foucault, 1984).

Foucault picks up on Kant's affirmation that enlightenment is overcoming our immaturity by daring to think for ourselves rather than accepting the authority of others church, state, social hierarchies. For Kant, reason itself must come into question to qualify for enlightenment. The critique of reason, according to him, is the absolutely necessary precondition of enlightenment. The function of critique is to define the conditions for the legitimate use of reason. This includes the conditions that *limit* the proper use of reason, and that determine the range and scope of reason: so that, for example, theoretical reason could not be applied to 'limit-questions' such as the origin of the universe or the immortality of the soul. For Foucault, what is significant here is the fact that Kant is reflecting on the contemporary status of his own enterprise. Kant is articulating a response to the question concerning what it is that makes the contemporary way of doing philosophy different from what was done previously? According to Foucault, this move heralds a new development: the focus on philosophy – or our resources for thinking – to put into question what is decisive about our current situation. I don't think that it's hubristic to suggest that the spirit of Foucault's return to the question of enlightenment is exactly what motivates much of this book: to rethink precisely the conditions of knowledge and thinking that may inform our conduct of research in the field of education, a field that has relied heavily, too heavily by far, on formulaic approaches to research and on thinly authoritative accounts of what education is and what the study of education is for.

Foucault, contrary to some accounts, explores the idea of the modern in terms of self-invention, in rather subtle Nietzschean manner. In modernity, Foucault sees a general ethos that promotes a critical attitude towards our historical era, one that seeks transformation – of both self and conditions. There is a politics of the self that shares a logic with the desire to transform the historically established conditions that shape our world. Not to accept oneself as one is doesn't have to mean self-negation; rather, it is the condition of freedom. We may address the fact that we take to be our 'self' is as much the product of historical forces as our world. Foucault effects a reversal of Kant insofar as criticism is to be directed towards analysis and reflection of limits. This critical project means interrogating whatever is taken for universal, necessary and obligatory and finding the necessary contingencies and the arbitrary foundations of the constraints imposed by those powerful categories. This is the meaning of Foucault's will to displace the 'transcendental' with the genealogical through the application of 'archaeology of knowledge'. Foucault is interested in revealing the historical contingency of what we take for necessity, for what is inscribed in our order of things as given. Foucault's challenge is an invitation to rethink where we stand in relation to the world of education and the world of knowledge it has constructed. This is an attitude that will seek to interrogate truth as is in the name of truth to come. What more spirited challenge could be offered to the current state of research and knowledge in the field of education (Foucault, 1997b, 2005)?

Chapter 5

Time, Place, World

The question of world: 'Being-in-the-world'

This chapter will explore context. In this dimension, the humblest research project becomes ontological. It touches on far-reaching question of meaning. It invites us to ask about the very nature of 'our' world in its relations to 'the' world. This question does not take a form that can be answered, nor is it singular. The question of world is far from simple: its significance takes the form of a productive questioning. The 'world' question can never fall clearly within our rational grasp (Heidegger, 1962). Attending to it may expand our research thinking. It calls us to give an account of our understanding of meaning and purposes that are more than local.

The word 'world' always has interesting ontological resonance. It is a meeting point for everyday language and metaphysics. We all use the word 'World' habitually without necessarily ruminating on its implications. Our use implies that we know what we are talking about: that we have a metaphysical grasp of the world. Pausing to explore this dimension of our thinking, to make explicit the implicit, is both theoretically important and practically beneficial to the researcher. Dwelling on our sense of 'world' will contribute towards an articulation of questions concerning the significance we attribute to a research project, a research orientation and a research ethic.

The relations between the world of the researcher and the world at large are inescapable. This means that much as we may want to insist our orientation is practical, as much as we may want to avoid the apparent futility of abstract thinking, our practical being-in-the-world is always already in a relation to questions of meaning and Being. Every instance of specificity stands in a significantly determining relation to the world at large (Heidegger, 1962). That world at large can only be available through some theorizing of what it is. Practice is always already freighted with theory.

Heidegger's *Being and Time* claims the question of *Being* as the most important question: as it is the question most likely to give rise to questioning (Heidegger, 1962). For Heidegger, questioning holds a special place in 'thinking' to be distinguished from mere philosophy (Heidegger, 1993c). The history of philosophy and metaphysics has been a forgetting of the question of Being (Heidegger, 1993d). Systematic thinking, including much of the heritage of modern Western philosophy, has dedicated itself to providing ways of understanding the limits of reason, the nature of aesthetic thought, the pure grounds of certainty, the essential driving force of history – all seeking to articulate the grounds upon which we can strive to reach for and articulate the truth of things.

While the question of Being, the question of questions, may largely have been unaddressed, the question of Being, somehow, can't be entirely suppressed. It appears as a symptom of its explicit absence; it returns as revenant when the question is displaced by an answer. What's more, it connects philosophy with everyday thinking, despite its apparent strangeness. The question of Being is implicit in many everyday expressions. It is there sometimes in our most everyday moods, especially in our existential anxiety, the motive force that drives us to pursue world-making activities, including the activity of the researcher (Heidegger, 1993d). The question of Being is like a spectre haunting our everyday understanding of things. Parallel with anxiety, it is always lurking.

On this view, the dimension of thinking can never be reduced to philosophy as an abstracted minority academic pursuit. The lines of thought which philosophy proposes are reflections of and projections into activity-based thinking available in myriad contexts and epochs. As Derrida insists, everyday language is freighted with 'metaphysics' (Derrida, 1978). Everyday discourse carries meanings that claim a purchase on the nature of things (Heidegger, 1962). Mostly, we are only semi-conscious, at best, of our strongest and most abiding convictions. We unintentionally perhaps suspend the question of Being to engage with practical being. We tend not to ponder so much the question concerning the kind of being that we are ourselves and the premises we live by (Heidegger, 1962, 1993b).

That doesn't mean we don't carry an implicit understanding of what we are. The enlightenment period witnesses the emergence of the idea of the human as we know it now. The idea of humanity emerges in its modern and recognizable form. This is also the period when this idea takes on some of its subtly powerful but also highly questionable resonances. The medieval world order, whereby human existence knew its place more securely, gets disturbed and displaced in Western culture by new forms of thinking arising in the renaissance and through 'the new science' (Belsey, 2005). In this complex and subtle process, Western metaphysics experiences a pressures and torsions. The triumphs of accelerating scientific knowledge, and the confidence of enlightenment faith in rationality, are met with various disturbances to the centrality of the human, especially to the idea that the human has been deliberately forged in the image of God (Foucault, 1984). Later, the nineteenth century witnessed powerful lines of thinking – from Darwin, Marx, Nietzsche, Freud and others – that problematized the idea of human sovereignty (Darwin, 1860; Freud, 1900, 1901, 1921; Marx & Engels, 1848; Nietzsche, 1892). Even reason, central to the enlightenment, was no longer a guarantee of securing an authoritative sense of the meaning of human existence and its place in the order of things. Cosmology had already asserted that human being was not even topographically at the centre, a troubling idea that continues to cause insecurity and speculation, even among the most sophisticated cosmologists. Latterly, the question concerning human–animal relations has been troubling for species identity: with serious ethical issues being raised over the quality and ethics of the distinction (Derrida, 2004; Singer, 1985). Epigenetics has problematized familiar ideas about the relations between environment – or in the wider sense, culture – and the once-popular idea of a genetic blueprint (Malabou, 2015). Recent questions have been raised concerning the origin of the human species causing uncertainty about the genealogy of human descent. Do we really know who we are and what kind of being (Simonti, 2016; Stringer, 2012;)?

These tendencies suggest both caution and radical uncertainty concerning what we are and our place in the order or things. Surely, caution is equally advisable when making claims about the meaning and value of our everyday practices? If the very identity of the human is in question, a certain interrogative approach seems appropriate to the questions that arise in the everyday practices of education, as well as in its big, theological ideas. Isn't this caution a necessary condition for all educational research?

The upshot of this perspective is the realization that the world of practice, 'my world', the mundane world, the 'ordinary', the 'everyday' (that is sometimes felt or thought to be free from metaphysical complications) stands in a relation to the world in the larger sense. In one way or another, the researcher has to negotiate this relation. The world of the classroom cannot be entirely separate from the 'World of Education', the globalized force field that enframes the most mundane arena of practice. Another side of this realization is that the very identity of the researcher may also need to be put into question, in order to articulate what sense of its foundations, functions and purposes might be articulated in the name of the production of new knowledge (Peim, 2009).

Specific being, field and world

For the research project situated in a field of practice, in a specific institutional setting, within a specific historical period, in education, fundamental ontology might begin with locating itself. A research project in education may address the particularities of its setting, its history, its practices as part of the process to define what the object is, what the position(s) of the subject(s) might be and what the research seeks to reveal that is new to knowledge. I have argued that this gives the researcher plenty to go on with. Careful detailing of the specific conditions in which a research question or inkling arises, the personal history and orientation of the researcher, including a specific orientation to knowledge and some sense of the larger social purpose of the practice or field they are addressing, are necessary or at least highly significant elements in establishing a 'fundamental ontology' for the project. This potentially – or perhaps essentially? – narrative dimension sets the scene for the possibility of making an original research contribution – and can be regarded as defining the staging of that knowledge that it will claim to have generated. The first stages of reflection on these elemental things are essential to the final product. The significant preliminaries cannot be subtracted from the meaning that may attach to the final research outcome that will take up its place in the catalogue of knowledge as an 'original contribution'.

These specificities in one important sense have no limit. Where do we stop giving an account of ourselves, our object, our world, its world? How does this account relate to what we might only be aware of faintly – and yet what is powerfully, significantly determining our understanding? That perhaps vague awareness of something beyond has been given various names. It relates to the idea, particularly strong in our times, perhaps, that the world in the larger sense, the world understood as the configuration of history, culture, social organization, material conditions is not a merely abstract space. The world in this larger sense is perhaps more present to us, through globalization, than in previous epochs. That larger world contributes to the shaping of who we are and of significant components of our existence. If this sounds at all grandiose, or inflated, it is perhaps because we are rarely prompted or invited to think ontologically, that is to think about the larger forces that shape our specificity. Nevertheless, it is demonstrably the case that we are products of our world in several senses and dimensions.

But hasn't recent thinking encouraged us to think that the world as a totality is a kind of mythological construct, anyway, that according to the postmodern condition – the 'real', demythologized condition of our time – there is no vantage point from which we could apprehend the world as totality, that we are always condemned to see the world from a specific position and that every effort to think beyond that horizon anyhow will be reinterpreted by the overriding way of thinking that is 'Western metaphysics' (Derrida, 1978; Lyotard, 1986)? And haven't we also been encouraged to think that we had better be modest in our research goals – and that to take on the world as a whole is really beyond our limited capacities and that – after Bruno Latour – ordinarily every system is quite complex enough to tax our most intricate knowledge generating resources (Latour, 2011). In addition, there are other philosophical tendencies that suggest that the world itself – as a totality – is only an aggregation of discrete spheres of action, operation and being. This is the general thesis, in vastly simplified terms, of Peter Sloterdijk's 'bubbles' ontology. No doubt this way of understanding the world, while relieving thought of its larger ontological obligation, can account for some features of our actual experience of modernity. The problem is that once we characterize the world as this agglomeration of discrete 'bubbles' or spheres of operation, we have committed ourselves to this view as an ontological condition, a way of understanding something fundamental about the nature of the world (Sloterdijk, 2011). Much the same can be said when we consider the world as a series of discrete activities, as with Activity Theory. At some point, we may want to consider that the activities of the world, for all their differences, share common conditions of being but also bump up against one another and that we still hold onto the idea of a larger organization of things – the social, say – that transcends the local and specific while also being part of it (Peim, 2009).

The Marxist legacy with its emphasis on the politics of distribution and its powerful desire for social transformation in the direction of equity retains a strong value for 'world'. For Marxism, the world is decisively a unified totality, albeit organized in complex ways according to specific histories and conditions. One world uniting condition in Marxism concerns the relation between 'base' and 'superstructure', between 'being' and 'consciousness'. Economic relations determine how we are and how we think. This essentially unified, or at least interrelated world, is politically important, of course. It is likely to foster collective consciousness and to encourage the idea that the world can be transformed by collective action. Neither of these are ideas that have been erased by more fragmenting accounts of the structure of things. In relatively recent times, Jurgen Habermas has affirmed the public sphere as a space for rationalist purchase on what Habermas sees as 'the human project' (Habermas, 1984, 1990). Habermas is in no doubt that it makes sense to think and act in terms of a unified world, given that the forces of history are global and integrated. An interesting variation of this idea is expressed by Michael Hardt and Antonio Negri in their vision of *Empire* (1990) that reinterprets 'the postmodern condition' in terms of new modes of connectivity that enhance the range and power of hegemonic forces of domination but that also, and potentially at least equally, enhance the range and power of forces of resistance.

Both the above positions, and many others, accord with global education. The global dimension of education in our time is immensely important. It should be evident that global education includes, of course, the humblest and most practically oriented practice in the most mundane institution. Such contexts are not free from the metaphysical and institutional forces at work through globalization. If not addressed, in educational research projects this global, ontological dimension is likely to be furtively lurking in the background and will betray itself in key assumptions and ways of articulating the nature of things and their significance.

Consider the case of the university: What is a university?

Educational research necessarily addresses institutions that have both a specific and a general form. Giving an account of institutional context for educational research can be both important and complex. Consider for the case of institutions of the university. Anyone who has been involved in university life knows that these institutions are powerfully configured with their own internal logic. There are specific rules and regulations of conduct, determinate spaces, protocols, procedures and an array of identities that belong to the university. At the same time, we might also refer to a university culture, a more nebulous, complex but highly significant dimension of the institution. Even more important than the explicit rules and regulations is that the culture constitutes a symbolic order that ascribes nuances of identity and circumscribes behaviours. This culture may vary in some respects from institution to institution but, overall, it would be possible to identify certain general tendencies that will be recognizable as feature of 'a' university, any university. Across the world, universities tend to partake of this general form and structure and culture. That's partly what makes them universities. In addition, universities themselves will have their own internal ways of understanding themselves, their own corporate identity that they will ask their members to subscribe to. A way of being-in-the-world is characteristic of the university sustaining a repertoire of ways of being in the world for students, university academic staff, administrative staff.

Universities compete in a strange market of knowledge. Universities are required not only to have but also to generate knowledge in the form of research. Today, university research is under pressure to demonstrate its impact and is formally assessed with significant status and financial rewards at stake. Research is now required not only to demonstrate rigour, but that its impact, its use-value is visible, palpable. This demand instrumentalizes research and the university. By demonstrating research impact, the university provides public notice of its value and so justifies its existence and the resources it expends. It also justifies the various positive forms of social status it confers on its members and the kinds of credentials it provides that frequently have positive exchange value in the employment market. We can say that there is a large investment in the university in its members. Those agencies that fund the university, perhaps even those larger populations that support them, believe in its efficacy. The university itself promotes the idea that it performs essential functions that contribute to social well-being and that the advancement of knowledge and progress is designed to secure a more fulfilled, more enlightened future for all.

From some perspectives within the institution, the above affirmations of function and purpose will perhaps seem obvious, without question – truthful and faithful to what the university is. That doesn't necessarily mean that each university is a happy and positive place working merrily towards its explicitly stated goals. But even in times of relative discontent – like the present when academics bemoan the instrumentalization of education and the bureaucratization of university life – they will probably affirm the enlightenment version of the university function referred to above. This ongoing affirmation, even in the face of evidence to the contrary, seems to be a necessary belief for the institution's continuation. Students equally have a similar investment to academics. In the main, they likely to do so with an idea about the value of university education that is likely to exceed its use value to them in the employment market.

I don't think you have to be an iconoclast or a hopeless cynic to suggest that the university might be understood differently. Looked at from outside the university's own self-proclaimed and publicly affirmed identity, the university may appear strangely unfunctional. From a critical point of view – one that doesn't automatically associate formal institutions of education with progress and the pursuit of enlightenment – several alternative descriptions and ultimately definitions may be plausible.

For some, the university may be a symptom of a global knowledge system that privileges certain ways of knowing and certain perspectives above others. It is perfectly possible to see strong connections between what has been referred to as cultural imperialism and the role of university hierarchy in global cultural politics (Tomlinson, 1991). Dominated by the West, especially by the United States and by the United Kingdom, global education seems organized to promote and sustain world view that is exclusive and excluding. Elite institutions dominate global education, where a particular vision of knowledge – and of the knower or knowing subject – is pervasive and powerful and where, increasingly, more local forms of knowledge are excluded from the official canons of knowledge, curricula and institutional organizational structures. Prestigious English schools replicate themselves in China. English and American universities are likewise cloned. Curricula from California, promoted by private Californian consultancy companies, displace and replace curricula for school systems in the Middle East (Peim, 2011). From this point of view, the university system partakes of and is associated with a world dominating projection of knowledge and accreditation. It projects its vision of knowledge and its hierarchical modes of engaging with its subjects onto the world. Within a discourse of progress and modernization, it attracts human and financial resources and seeks to mould the world of knowledge in its own image. The global university will claim that it performs its sovereign operation of power in the name of disinterested enlightenment.

Yet another perspective on universities and their contemporary role might suggest that, while universities claim to have essential social functions, in fact they exist for quite different reasons. Rather like medieval monasteries, they operate to sustain a world order more about maintaining social distinctions, sustaining myths about knowledge and, above all, projecting the idea of their contribution to the general well-being of the world. Universities represent themselves as working tirelessly towards improvement and progress, and claim an essential economic function, providing an elite with transferable skills or highly technical knowledge, both necessary for economic competitiveness within national contexts. None of these claims stand up to close scrutiny, according to some (Wolf, 2002).

The question of what a university is, essentially, remains. A historical informed ontology may seek to affirm that the university needs to return to its essential function, to its true ideals, but then again, can we be sure about what those are? Post-enlightenment thinking produced an idea of the university according to Humboldt's model: a centre for the pursuit of knowledge in a spirit of intellectual freedom detached from the control of the state where teaching and research went hand-in-hand to realize goals of growth and the internationalization of knowledge. Newman's nineteenth-century idea of the university was as a place where knowledge might be pursued without the demand for 'impact' or the imposition of use-value – a very different ethic from the dominant ethic of today, but also a very different world wherein the university was accepted as an elite and minority institution. The context changed radically. In 1963, in the United Kingdom the Robbins report ruminated on the nature of the university and on the requirement, under the pressure of a democratic ethic, to expand the reach of the university and to enhance its inclusivity. Robbins regarded the university as a centre for both personal and social development, important in the development of skills and general powers of mind but also important for 'cultivation' – proposing a 'civilizing' role. Subsequent expansions of the university have led to increasing access, in the United Kingdom, for example. But they have also led to an increasingly differentiated, hierarchical university system (Anderson, 2006; Nybom, 2003; Rothblatt, 1997; Scott, 1993; Tight, 2009).

We soon run into incompatible claims for the actual and proper identity of the institution, claims that belong to quite different horizons of understanding that can't be reconciled. Different and conflicting positions arise from a number of causal factors: they might be ontological in the sense that they arise from the investments made by those whose existence depends in some powerful way on sustaining a certain order of belief and subscribing to a certain order of things a certain form of social organization. The commitment to a model might express self-interest but might derive at the same time from ideology or from an explicitly held epistemological stance. Both positions are likely in turn to be informed by an implicit social theory, perhaps, again implicitly, linked to an understanding of history and to ideas about the role of knowledge, and knowledge institutions in the destiny of human progress.

While these latter, more grandiose conceptions may only be tacitly or unconsciously held, they are nevertheless significant for the chain of belief they belong to. In the end, they appeal to an anchoring idea that holds the belief system in place, to an ontotheology. In modernity and beyond, justifications for practices or policies appeal to 'realities of the world'. Politicians, for example, appeal to 'modernization' as the essential grounds for their reforms or changes to be justified. The implicit message is that the realities of the contemporary world demand these changes and that to resist is to be caught in an outmoded understanding of 'the real world'. Pragmatic thinking is never purely pragmatic, of course, and always appeals to some ontotheological principle.

All appeals to an 'ultimate reality' or to a 'really real' are ontological affirmations. And because they derive, necessarily, from ideas about the nature of things, they are, ultimately, also ideological: they are expressions of a faith in an assumed order of things. This logic applies to education as much as it does to anything else. For as much as education may seek to represent its concerns in purely educational terms – being about personal growth, being about the cultivation of the people, being about the promotion of essential new and socially improving knowledge or being simply just about the cultivation of knowledge in general – it cannot help but be entrammelled in an ontology (conscious or unconscious) that goes beyond the borders of what we might conventionally accept as belonging to education. The world is more interesting and complex than 'real world' appeals suggest.

'World': Specificity, belonging and investment

Such ontological positions are mostly inexplicit, rarely entirely consistent and coherent systematic creeds. For the researcher, though, awareness of such ontological belief systems and orientations in the world of practice or the sphere of knowledge under scrutiny can be significant. Engaging with these systems, networks or 'rhizomes' provides a useful, perhaps necessary, line of enquiry. Identities, dominant modes of practices, alternative models of practice and all decision-making processes within a specific sphere of practice may relate to them in a strong, motivated sense.

The dimension of world invites an existential account of identity attachment. Heidegger's 'What is metaphysics?', outlined briefly in Chapter 4, suggests an ontological approach to professional attachment and identity. This analysis seems pertinent to education where identities are strongly interpellated according to differing institutional spaces and practices. Briefly, to reiterate, in 'What is metaphysics?' the relation of care that we experience in our attachments to the things of our world is predicated on a kind of primordial 'nothing'. Anxiety generated from the possibility of this nothing is metonymically related to death. This deep-seated ontological dread in the face of primordial nothing also engenders the positive relation of 'care' – care for others, for things, for significant aspects of our world.

In Heidegger metaphysics, ordinary, everyday experiences of belonging and belief are critical. The being of 'dasein' is predicated on key features: 'thrownness', 'mitsein' and anxiety-towards-death and care. They are fundamental and are relevant to whomever wherever. The last two – anxiety and care – are most significant in understanding our commitments to social practices. They give us strong clues to explain the emotional and ideological structure of professional practices. They also indicate that our most apparently rational choices and commitments are freighted with metaphysical intent: that our 'knowledge' – be it professional or otherwise – and engagement with the world is always accompanied by metaphysical commitment. Even if we may feel relatively uncommitted.

Being-in-the world might seem a kind of obvious way of referring to the condition of existence of conscious beings – and for unconscious beings, also. In *Being and Time*, this phrase is indicative of the radical specificity of finite human existence. Heidegger's existential semantics reminds us that we do not and cannot rise above the specific conditions that we live within and see the world as a whole from a detached, Archimedean perspective. We are not transcendental beings. Our life is set within a particular time. We are born to a particular place. Both time and place have far-reaching implications for what we are, what we may be or become. Heidegger seeks to remind us that a radical contingency inaugurates and accompanies our time. If we are ever tempted to think of our lives as having an ordered and ordained structure, we are mistaken. The ontology of the accident supervenes (Malabou, 2012).

My world is individual to me. Only I experience it as such. It is perhaps a common idea perhaps even a cliché that a single life encompasses a unique world of knowledge, experience, that the death of an individual is the death of a world. One can map out the dimensions of one's own world, the places, events, encounters and so on that constitute its topography as well as its particular experiential quality. The significant components often have a generally experienced timbre and will be framed in culturally common ways. Their specific configuration is unique and legitimately suggests that an individual life constitutes a world. In a mundane sense, at least, that must be true. Anyone can lay claim to an experience of 'my world'. But that world, on reflection, has some important features that are not encompassed merely in terms of a bald account of where I was born, into what social class fragment, within what family history and cultural circumstances, to experience what type of education, upbringing, unpredicted disasters, unpredicted strokes of fortune and so on. My world also includes some element of agency. I have made certain choices, taken certain actions and given myself perhaps to certain projects that have determined the nature of my world. My world is a function, in this personalized sense, at least, of the intersection of determinations of time and place, the accident of my birth, the circumstances of my formative experiences and context and of the actions and decisions I have taken. This is neither an entirely social nor an individualistic view of subjectivity. It considers the coming together of social, cultural and historical factors with the personal and the 'agentic'. In the professional context, it is immediately obvious how this nexus might give rise to a specific way of being that is constitutive of 'my world' in that more delimited sense. This is, of course, an important line of enquiry to follow. For the researcher, to look back upon their own specific engagement with a topic of interest, with a domain of practice, with a commitment to a professional ideal, perhaps, in a systematic way offers the opportunity to objectify the subjective and to begin at least the often difficult but liberating process of understanding one's own embedded nature.

My world is part of the story. My world represents the world as is with my experience of it. It acknowledges the intrication of the subjective with the historical, social and cultural. Neither can exist independently of the other.

I may be the focus of an experience, a world on my own, as it were. There is no 'me', though, without the social, cultural, historical nexus. That dimension of the world exists independently of my being. While I might dream of the idea that education will never be the same without me, I know for sure that education, its apparatuses and its practices will continue with or without me. Education has a material or concrete reality independent of my perception or experience or understanding of it. That is not to say that the independent, objectively existing world of education, for example, does not depend for its existence and its continuity on the subjective engagement of individuals. It always does. It does mean that education is shaped by forces, processes, materialities that exist at another, non-individual level. In fact, those forces, processes and materialities are always concerned to shape the individuality of the individual into an image of their own projection: say, ideal teacher, ideal administrator, student.

How can I as a subject of education, as a researcher, get hold of the objective realities of the world I occupy? There is no sure answer to this question. There is no certain procedure whereby the researcher can apprehend what Husserl might have referred to as the-object-of-education-in-itself-as-it-really-is. The attempt to produce an account of such a 'thing' is fraught with difficulties that are at the heart of the story of Western thinking.

And yet the world of education exists. Its existence impinges itself on any portion of that world that concerns me. As a practitioner or as a researcher, I cannot easily claim to have a purchase on the totality of things that constitute education, can I? And yet I must acknowledge that there is something out there, in existence, occupying significant space in social reality, as it were, that constitutes education as a whole. The problem that this issue poses is a significant problem for any research occurring within a field – and that really means that it is a problem facing any research at all. What's worse, though, is that it is a problem that gets magnified and accelerated the more we ponder its implications.

The state of the world?

Let's consider the question about the world of education as a whole. Educationists know that education as a sphere of knowledge and practice exists within a 'wider world' – a world 'at large'. And educationists also know – whether or not they acknowledge it in their thinking, their practice, and their knowledge production efforts – that, dialectically speaking, the world of education has an essential relation to the larger world. How can we make sense of the world of education without also at the same time taking into account essential features of this 'world-at-large', the condition of which will inevitably have a strong bearing on the possibilities of education for being one way or another? Or put it another way, is not the power of education a shaping force in the world at large, a significant dimension of its very being?

Theories of the world have been powerful and significant in the era strangely perhaps known as globalization. Such theories articulate the shrinking of the world, Western imperialism, the mingling of different modes of life, the homogenization and hybridization of culture, the end of indigeneity, global-scale conflicts, global industrial projects, the rise and prominence of multinational corporations, and the rapid increase in power and range of communications technologies.

Global theory represents the huge shift in collective awareness of the world as a unitary, if complex, entity. This shift has a deep history, stretching back perhaps to the global expansion of European power and influence signified by the first forays of Henry the Navigator from 1415 from Portugal to the West African coast, the 'moment' that initiates what the age of global exploration or global conquest. And increasingly, the nature of the world-at-large has been intricated with education (Peim, 2011).

In contemporary discourses, the condition of the world becomes an urgent topic in several fields of knowledge. In relation to ecology, scientific knowledge entwines with political practice. The condition of the world as ecosystem has become the defining issue of our times, while ideas about cultural imperialism, the postmodern condition and even the anthropocene have entered the small change of everyday discourse. The legacy of the enlightenment – wherein 'the proper study of mankind is man' – projected the idea of 'the human condition' and gave rise to discourses concerning the human–world relation. Who is included within the human may have been in question, but the sense of a collective entity, the human, as a proper subject or topic for understanding, knowledge and research takes on increasing force in the late nineteenth and early twentieth centuries. The parallel idea that the destiny of the world resides with the human also becomes entrenched. The rise of humanism reflects a self-consciousness about the species producing the academic study of anthropology, as well as an anthropological 'turn', the formal study of cultural differences, the formal study of language and the philosophical wrestling with the meaning of language. Sociology conjoined with cultural studies and various forms of critical cultural theory during the 1970s and 1980s particularly drew on re-readings of Hegel combined with Marxist self-consciousness about history and questions concerning the ultimate destiny of the species. Scientific concerns with species-being had their parallel in the human sciences.

Various blows had occurred to trouble the relatively brief period of enlightenment confidence: the origin of species, including the role of contingency in Darwinian evolution, served as a reminder of the animal provenance of the human. Urbanization heightened awareness of what came to seem intractable problems for human social life. Civic consciousness and civic technological projects that in the nineteenth century held out so much hope for transforming the conditions of mass collective living, had to deal with the burgeoning population growth of the late twentieth century. Bureaucratic systems, designed for the rational management of highly organized social life, detached from their intended functions. Decentred, self-proliferating and unmoored from functional or ethical drivers, they could take on a totalitarian will-to-power. Freud's revelations had already cast doubt on rationality as the social mode. Driven by libido, dominated by repression, the divided collective at times appeared to be characterized by a blind drive towards self-annihilation, a death instinct enabled by new technologies of mass destruction and a rabid plundering of earth's resources.

While science made giant strides and enabled new, immensely powerful technologies available it turned out that the new powers harnessed by human knowledge were not straightforwardly beneficent. The new forms of social organization that arose during the nineteenth century established mass education systems across the so-called developed world. Public hygiene improved and, according to Norbert Elias, 'civilised' behaviours became established as norms for significant portions of the world's populations. These apparent gains were not unambiguous, however: the population management systems that appeared along with and through public education meant that whole populations were to be subjected to a normative regime that would ensure the development of not just accomplishments but ways of thinking and modes of deportment. It is possible, in darker moments, to see this form of social training as the necessary prelude to the mobilization of populations across Europe for war between 1914 and 1918.

The realization that rationalization itself – the triumph of enlightenment applied to social life as Max Weber put it – became oppressive. Rationality applied became 'instrumental rationality', a bureaucratic force that took on a life of its own. Bureaucracy became an end in itself and claiming its rights independently of the purposes it purported to serve. More disturbing came the later realization that instrumental rationality could be put to quite dangerous, destructive purposes. The Second World War required huge efforts of organization only possible because the societies involved had developed invasive, far-reaching systems for tracking their populations, managing their dispositions and categorizing them into its own – sometimes deadly – definitions of identity. It was a well-developed bureaucratic system across Europe that enabled the mass deportations and exterminations of the Second World War in two senses: (1) logistically and (2) emotionally. A bureaucratized language of identity and purposes enabled officials to make mortal decisions without troubling their conscience: as 'units' were assigned for 'special treatment' and so on. Sitting in an office signing papers is quite different from delivering death face-to-face. The mechanization of the death process was an important part of the logic of mass murder, but also essential was the bureaucratic machinery that enabled horrific decisions to be made coolly and deadly processes to be calculated without visceral emotion (Bauman, 1991).

Rationality then was troubled by the realization that the human organism's form of consciousness is itself divided and cannot understand itself fully.

Consciousness cannot fully access the unconscious energies that both motivate and inform it. At the same time, rationality applied to social life carried extreme dangers: populations becoming subject to logics of biopower, the new form of vastly intrusive government that concerns itself with the life of the people. A 'great transformation' of the way of life occurred that enabled the rise of modernity with its scientific-technological industrial apparatuses and their requirements (Foucault, 1977a). Education and educational research are caught up in this world 'order' (Peim, 2011).

Heidegger's technological enframing

The ethics of improvement, reform or redemption that dominate so much educational research thinking fail to seriously engage with the ontological implications of long-established lines of critique of the role of schooling in modern and contemporary societies. The following perspectives, to begin with, problematize both improvement and reform and redemption: the sociology of education (Bernstein, 1997; Bourdieu and Passeron, 1970; Bowles and Gintis, 1976; Willis, 1979) that challenges the foundational assumptions of improvement; the troubling discourse of 'governmentality' that represents education, alternatively to improvement, as a means to a more disciplinary, surveillance-directed end; the postmodern condition, as defined by Lyotard (1986), wherein the condition of incredulity towards meta-narratives calls into question the overriding dominance of performativity as the essentially empty motivation of scholastic and related activity. We may ask: How do the logic of improvement and the discourse of redemption remain impervious to these critiques? They are well known; but they don't themselves explain their own failure to open the question of education and its dominance in our times. Has educational research foreclosed certain unpalatable ways of thinking?

The rationality of improvement and critique can be understood in terms of 'technological enframing' defined most prominently in Heidegger's (1993c) 'The Question Concerning Technology'. This is a serious statement about knowledge in modernity that seeks to explore the relation of the contemporary world with the question of Being and develops an attempt to open a space for thinking outside the most familiar enclosures of Western metaphysics. Modernity is characterized as the era of 'technological enframing', the world-dominating adaptation of Being. It is manifest in world of education in emphases on performance, improvement and the remorseless logic of productivity (maximizing human resources). We can see this 'enframing' most clearly in the endless logic of assessment. The simplest mundane act of assessment – determining a piece of work or defining a student as being at 'grade C', for instance – is clearly working within 'technological enframing' insofar as the action expresses a relation to Being. The 'enframing' in this case seeks to determine and shape the existence of entities that fall within its power according to its own grid of identity (Heidegger, 1998, 82). Education ranks and orders.

'Technological enframing' has become the dominant mode of 'revealing' of the modern world. In Heidegger's terms, this means technology that always has a strong relation to Being and to the possibilities of beings has taken on a particular character. The delimiting of both Being and possibilities and limits to (the Being of) beings is expressed in the term that Heidegger coins to express the essence of modern, science-based technology: 'das Ge-stell' or the enframing. The current hegemony of the principle of assessment in education can be seen precisely as determined from 'das Ge-stell' (Heidegger, 1998, 82). This 'state of affairs' refers to the defining power of 'science' – where science, as a technology of knowledge, seeks to determine the 'real' in terms of determinate objects. In education, targets, grades, criteria, measures of performance, tables, for example, all constitute such objects of the enframing. All are generated objects within a specific technology of knowledge. Subjects on the curriculum – with their detailed specifications, attainment targets, normative levels – also come to constitute powerful, complex objects of the enframing. The professional institutions and their hierarchies that provide legitimacy for assessment and that enable its processes are similarly expressions of the enframing. In Heidegger's terms, the enframing is the adaptation of Being that generates all these things, 'naturalises' them, gives them the authority of unquestionable categories.

Heidegger's account of the domination of modernity by technology is not a simple anti-technological position and differs significantly, from, say, F. R. Leavis's (1969) diagnosis of a 'technologico-Benthamite' cultural crisis. Heidegger is seeking to re-examine the relations between technology, human being (or 'dasein') and Being as configured in modernity. Heidegger is no luddite: there is no demonizing of technology and no call for a return to a more simple, imaginary relation with 'earth'. In fact, in addressing the 'question concerning technology' Heidegger typically puts the emphasis on the 'question' and promotes a mode of thinking that challenges all our assumptions in this area, defying anything that appears self-evident and unproblematic. It turns out in this analysis that technology is the world-forming predisposition of 'dasein' and that the essence of technology is nothing technological.

To regard technology as neutral, as a means–end-oriented phenomenon, independent of the mode of being it inhabits, is mistaken. This delusion can arise when technology is understood as a tool at our disposal. There is no doubt that there is an instrumental dimension to technology, to expedite what are assumed to be 'our' objectives, just as technology also may rightly signify the network of tools, equipment and practices that inform human activities in the broadest sense. But that's not all: the question is not exhausted. There remains something in technology beyond these common-sense definitions (Heidegger, 1993c).

Heidegger's redefinition of technology engages with Aristotle's account of the metaphysics of production. Heidegger proposes that production is a kind of 'bringing forth', or *poeisis*, in the sense that things are made; but, equally, insofar as things manifest possibilities of Being, production is also a kind of revealing – and therefore stands in a relation to truth. Means–ends technology is a way of revealing, and in its global reach has become the dominant way of revealing the world. For Heidegger, the upshot of this line of thought is that the essence of technology, as a mode of revealing, is the realm of truth.

In this guise, as a form of revealing, technology determines or brings to light something that has the potential to be there but is not already there: for example, when a student's work is designated through the procedures of assessment as being within a particular category, say, Level 2 or Level 3. Considered in this way, Heidegger's account of technology is looking to preserve a more original sense of 'techne' as first and foremost a way of revealing. Revealing is conceived of as a bringing-to-presence of particular beings within a horizon of Being, showing them to be in a certain way.

Taking this idea – of technology as revealing – we can see how technology opens the Real to us in a certain way. Using the example of grading, the technology of assessment reveals a kind of truth about the student's work, and by implication about the student, but at the same time conceals other kinds of truth about the student's work and, by implication, about the student.

The desire of modern technology has been significantly to manipulate or manage Being, to impose upon it a symbolic order. Modern technology marshals the knowledge of science to interrogate, dissect, expose and organize every aspect of the world. There is the danger that in thinking of modern technology as a means to an end we are seduced into the false assumption that technology is something that we control, that we can 'master'. It may seem obvious that modern technology's revelatory directives are created and controlled by human purposes and human will; but, Heidegger's position indicates to the contrary. Human beings do not control technological activity and development. And we can easily see this when we look around and see our lives organized in relation to technologies we have not had a hand in making.

For Heidegger, technology constitutes a framing for human activity and knowledge, certainly not the only one, but in modernity the dominant one. We do not govern or control the mode of 'unconcealment' of 'the Real' that belongs to modern technology. This idea of a limit to human knowledge and control is a recurring theme in Heidegger's work. It concerns the manner of our access to truth and raises fundamental questions about how we relate to the world around us, and the status of knowledge. The idea that truth is always to be understood as a way of revealing what is belongs to Heidegger's (1962, 1991, 1993a 1998, 2000) attempt to think differently from Western metaphysics – where the exalted human subject is the epistemological centre of the world.

In its claims to exactitude and certitude, and in attachment to the detached, free-floating certitude of self-confident, enshrined knowledge, Western metaphysics would seem oblivious to the temporal and spatial finitude of 'dasein'. Against this excessive, inflated subjectivity, Heidegger reminds us – in *Being and Time* – of the limits of our command when it comes to the unfolding of truth and the revelation of what we take to be the Real at any time.

Schooling has become a highly organized system of difference, framed by the technology of assessment. Who or what, though, manages and controls this system that determines and delimits what counts as the Real in the vast apparatuses of education today? In 'The Question Concerning Technology', the question of the extent that human beings are responsible as active agents for the ordering of the real is urgent. After all, our institutions, in the field of education, are technological in character and enact a powerful form of technological enframing. This is a vital insight towards understanding the world of education.

Foucault and the great transformation

Drawing strongly from Heidegger's technological enframing it, Foucault produced an elaborated account of what he referred to as 'the great transformation', the historical change that occurred in the organization and management of societies in Western Europe during the eighteenth and nineteenth centuries. Foucault's often highly detailed but equally carefully staged account offers a meticulous elaboration of the main features of education today, even though Foucault rarely addresses educational questions explicitly (Foucault, 1977a).

Foucault's 'biopower' perspective, although long available, rarely organizes thinking concerning mainstream educational studies. For Foucault 'the great transformation' signifies a new form of governance, a new kind of power. Concerned with governing 'life' the new form of power is capillary: it reaches into the most minute sectors of the life of the population. It is decentred and pervasive and works through an array of forces, institutions and apparatuses. Its first task is to enact a regime of discipline.

The radical edge of the concept of 'discipline' and its implications for a politics of identity is dangerous for contemporary accounts of schooling, especially for school reform advocates and the improvement discourses they espouse, but also for reformers with more lofty aspirations to liberate education from its fallen institutionalized self (Foucault 1977a). This includes so-called 'critical education studies' (Apple, 2014). Foucault meticulously demonstrates features of the 'great transformation' that shape the founding topography of the school as government, suggesting that it is vain to seek to reform this deeply embedded apparatus of discipline in the direction of freedom. Discipline involves the enclosure, separation and coding of spaces, the production of choreographed 'tableaux vivants', the 'microphysics' of 'cellular power' dedicated to transforming time itself reconstituted as a moral, economic, governmental dimension of being. Thus, 'dangerous multitudes' and 'unregulated time' get transformed under disciplinary time in managed spaces dedicated to carefully articulated actions. Increasingly subtle mechanisms of self-government are enabled within the more or less subtle 'technologies of the self' developed by the institution (195–222). So, discipline becomes self-regulation. Discipline gets internalized.

In the field of education, we can see how this apparatus works hand-in-hand with systematic social differentiation. Age-stratification goes along with an organized social stratification that gradually comes to be based on the dangerous idea of meritocracy. Norms of development that become increasingly refined and specific justify distinctions of attainment that in turn become predictions of social economic status (Bowles and Gintis, 1976; Willis, 1979).

Within highly codified institutional contexts, a thoroughly normative model of knowledge prevails. What's more, the remit of education expands. Life itself is increasingly seen as an educational project. In the latter half of the twentieth century, this tendency continues to accrue momentum. Under the logic of 'lifelong learning', the self always stands in deficit, subject to the remorseless logic of inspection and improvement. Self-critical consciousness and 'the examined life' are celebrated as opening the possibility of endless education. The school becomes the paradigm institution of modernity. Its logic reaches beyond the specific age of schooling. This enfolding of life can be seen in relation to Giorgio Agamben's analogy (see Chapter 8) of the contemporary political order with the paradigm space of 'the camp' (Agamben, 1997). Education is entwined with the questionable juridical structure of the modern state.

After all, schooling and much of education in general operates under the compulsion of the law. In Europe (and in most of the world, in fact), schooling is obligatory. In many countries, 'home-schooling' is illegal and non-schooling in all countries is under absolute prohibition. There is an interesting and sometimes dark history here. The school is highly exceptional space – juridically speaking – and yet is utterly mundane, normal and dispersed. Much of its internal practice is immune to the law. Decisive decisions that the institution makes in terms of identity and social trajectory are beyond law. There is no recourse to extra-institutional authority to challenge life-changing determinations and distribution of social identities. Schools operate that is a crucial form of symbolic violence as well as depending, ultimately, for their authority on the machinery of state violence, albeit restrained and refined.

The constituency of the school is not free to determine its own relation to time and space: and is far from free in several ways. Schooling operates in contexts of confinement, the restriction of association and the strict organization time and space. Perhaps one of the most interesting features of the school 'dislocating localization' is its reterritorialized ubiquity, its non-special enclosure of space as a series of 'zones of indistinction' or as 'hybrid space of exception' (Agamben, 1997, 113).

Schooling is now essential to government; indeed, it is the very essence of contemporary government. In the nation state of modernity, schools/schooling has been configured typically as an agent for national belonging and national cohesion, from Empire Day to more recent and more subtle attempts to organize collective culture and the ongoing governance of language (Peim, 2009). This cultural governance parallels the 'government of the soul', the dimension of schooling concerned with inculcating deep-seated modes of conduct and orientations towards the self as self-managed project. And, of course, in their usually strict hierarchy of authority schools model a specific organization of power in the name of institutionalized authority.

The deterritorialized governmental force of the school operates also as a dimension of security: in Hannah Arendt's striking if strange phrase 'to protect the child from society and to protect society from the child'. The school can also be related analogically to the camp insofar as its inmates have a special, non-citizen (not-yet citizen) legal status conferred upon them. This circular logic of identity pertains to childhood in modernity (Agamben, 1997).

The analogy with the camp that Agamben's thinking prompts is an analogy. No one is claiming to draw a direct parallel between the experience of schooling and the experience of the camp. Some of the parallels are important, though, in opening the ontology of the paradigm institution of modernity to serious, critical rethinking – thinking beyond the confines of the so-called critical education studies. The camp, like the modern school, is a European invention, has colonial origins and has been concerned with displaced national security. According to Agamben the camp constitutes the 'fundamental biopolitical paradigm of the west' (HS: 181). The same claim can be made for the school. The school as fundamental institution of governance has been exported increasingly, often in more explicitly violent form (Harber, 2004). Agamben claims, as I will now claim for the school, that the camp is 'an event which decisively signals the political space of modernity itself' (1997, 113). The camp according to Agamben is 'the hidden matrix and nomos of the political space in which we are still living' (1997. 106). The school is not hidden except in terms of enjoying a mythical identity and status essentially at odds with its governmental instantiation.

While it is often – and often all too simply, naively – claimed that education is an essential component of democracy, it is obvious that the paradigm institution (and virtually all the other known examples) of modern education, the school, is far from democratic in structure, practices and effects. Insofar as the school constitutes the key instrument of government – the production of citizenry, the management of population, the essential technology of the myth of meritocracy – then its form and characteristic modality expresses the essential quality of the political order of our time. The contemporary form of schooling, then, can be seen as fundamental to a political order that is constitutionally, genetically at odds with any democratic modes of order. Its mode of pastoral discipline works within a more feudal hierarchy of being. This analysis is rarely taken seriously by advocates for reform and redemption. It threatens the very existence of academic discourses of education that remain strongly predicated on a misplaced ethic of improvement or an unaccountable faith in reform (Peim and Flint 2011).

Two significant social theories

During the 1970s, two parallel social theories emerged that challenged dominant, contemporary understandings of education. Both Pierre Bourdieu's 'reflexive' sociology and Basil Bernstein's code theory, related to classification and framing, confronted liberal notions of education as essentially a domain for the free cultivation of the self and of knowledge independently of strong socially stratifying forces.

Bernstein's code theory developed from an interest in how class differences translate into cultural differences and how class cultural differences relate to power in certain institutional contexts. This work began by identifying different patterns of linguistic usage according to different social class of users. These differences were found to correlate strongly with different family types that arising from the different modes of interaction that in turn derive from different positions within the social division of labour. The language differences that emerge are not therefore simply surface differences of expression. They are expressions of identity and operate according to different principles of organization, different grammars, even.

Code theory explains how class differences get manifested at the level of speech above and beyond individual differences and dialect. Code theory is an explanation of symbolic domination through language – where one form of language, 'elaborated code', is favoured above another, 'restricted code', within the formal and official institutional operations of the school. The terms 'restricted' and 'elaborated' refer to different modes of language use that represent different orientations to meaning. These different orientations to meaning arise through social solidarity in the contexts of daily life. Contrary to some accounts, this is not at all a deficit model. Codes represent different orientations to meaning, not different levels of competence. Elaborated code takes symbolic precedence in certain contexts (Bernstein, 1971). Elaborated code is, in fact, the dominant institutionalized language of the school. Code differences get translated as differences in aptitude, intelligence and aptness for academic reward. Users operating predominantly in restricted code are effectively excluded by their primary socialization through the family from the dominant codes of schooling. This does not mean that their language is itself 'restricted' in some absolute way or at all impoverished. It is simply differently coded. Middle-class children, in contrast, tend to have their habits of speaking and thinking reaffirmed by the dominant language of the school. In the case of lower-working children, there is discontinuity between the symbolic order of the school and the symbolic order of the child (Bernstein, 1971; Christie, 1999).

On this view, there cannot be an objective judgement of linguistic performance against a normative standard across code modalities. What's more, code theory relates the symbolic domination achieved by the official discourses of the school to the economic and social division of labour. The theory thus avoids any strict divide between the economic base and the cultural symbolic world of social interaction and avoids making one of these domains either logically or actually prior to the other. Schools and classrooms are linguistic environments infused with social distinction. There is continuity between the social division of labour, orientations towards meaning and institutional practices. In other words, social differences translate into cultural differences manifested in the very texture of the language you speak. Language performances in the school are brought within an ethos of judgement that takes as symptomatic of different competences. This process confers identities on pupils and confirms social identities in different outcomes via assessment procedures that are represented as being neutral in relation to culture and class.

Code theory provides a linguistically based account of the cultural politics of class in the school. Code theory problematizes the very idea of the school as primarily a context for learning, for the simple acquisition of knowledge, skills and competences. The school is, above all and always already, a social environment where class differences are caught up in operations of power. Neither learning nor teaching can be free of this social fact. Social differences, expressed at the level of culture and realized in the symbolic domain via language, must always be in play in the minutest operations of the institution. This fundamental fact about the school cuts across any idea that access to schooling in itself can simply effect opportunity.

Code differences form a fundamental condition of teaching. From this perspective, the very idea of a neutral practice in relation to either language or culture is negated. The dominant liberal position of much teaching that claims to view all as equal and that claims to offer all equally the opportunity for response and for self-expression must suppress this fundamental sociological point. In effect, this means that the apparently open invitation of the subject to participate makes an offer many can neither refuse nor accept.

Knowledge: Systems, borders, identities

While the liberally oriented tradition of English teaching might perhaps balk at the idea of English as being systematic, nonetheless the subject takes up its position in the curriculum system and operates according to principles of definition that are codified and systematic. Whatever English is, whatever form it takes, it belongs within the system of differences – differently coded forms of knowledge – that is the curriculum.

Bernstein defines the connection between power and discourse in schooling thus: '[how] a society selects, classifies, transmits and evaluates the educational knowledge it considers to be public, reflects both the distribution of power and principles of social control' (Bernstein, 1971). Knowledge is selected, classified transmitted and evaluated within the institution. According to this position, school curricula are not identical with knowledge itself. They are recontextualizations of established 'official' discourses in distinct knowledge fields. For Bernstein school curricula are socially organized, institutionalized knowledge. They do not simply express or reflect given knowledge that is already out there (Hirst and Peters, 1970). They constitute that knowledge. Knowledge doesn't stand outside social class relations. Freighted with social symbolic meanings as well invested with the power to confer social identities, knowledge is thus necessarily caught up in social relations of power and control. The process Bernstein refers to as recontextualization means that knowledge in schools cannot liberate itself from the operations of code, for instance.

While no doubt there are things in the world at large that relate to English – reading, writing speaking and listening, for instance – the social fact is that English as a school subject constitutes these things in very specific ways. It is only within the relations of power and control that infuse the school that English as a school subject exists. The upshot of recontextualization is that both curricula and pedagogies are always encodings of power. In other words, the differences in terms of identity and solidarity that are out there in the social world are reflected in the school context through the action of pedagogizing knowledge. In other words, subject content cannot liberate itself from contamination by pedagogic relations – that are always social relations.

There is an extensive institutional machinery sustaining the organization of knowledge. Knowledge systems and fields of knowledge operate according to rules that permit legitimate combinations, legitimate modes of apprehension and legitimate forms of language. Bernstein characterizes the form of their organization as working according to two dominant principles: classification and framing. Classification is the process whereby objects are identified as legitimate objects of knowledge (literature in English, for instance) and set within an ordering system that makes distinctions between objects (literature as against popular culture, for example) and determines appropriate modes of engagement with them (personal response or critical analysis, for example). Classification also sets boundaries between discourses and operations within them. Reading a tabloid newspaper is different from reading a Dickens novel, but both in turn are defined as different from reading documentary evidence in history (Bernstein, 2000. 99–100). These are in effect encodings of power. The codes (not always explicit or visible) determine possible combinations, possible meanings. Furthermore, codes define what counts as a proper way of engaging with knowledge.

Formal curriculum knowledge is organized within co-ordinates defined in Bernstein as integrated code and collection code. The integrated code implies systematic relations between different sectors of the knowledge domain; it implies a hierarchical ordering of concepts. The collection code, on the other hand, implies a more horizontal organization of knowledge and its domains where different discourses may speak according to different contents, structures and rules and where at the same time there may be more intermingling of conceptual material. This might be characterized as a more open system of knowledge than the integrated code. English can be identified with the collection code: hence its apparent liberality (the invisibility, in effect, of its pedagogic work) and its inexplicit relation to coding. 'Liberal' English is an interesting case in point as the subject appears to be loosely classified and fairly loosely framed. At the same time, it retains a cultural orientation to certain textual forms and modes of response. The liberal invitation to respond is always already loaded with linguistic-cultural judgements. In the case of English, the collection code means, among other things, that the rules of the game are not made explicit.

In relation to hierarchical and 'open' discourses of knowledge, Bernstein draws a further organizing principle of difference (Bernstein, 2000, 155–174). In making this distinction, Bernstein refers to Habermas's contrasting discourses – one form of discourse is seen as constructing the 'life-world' of the individual, and the other as the source of collective, instrumental rationality (Bernstein, 2000, 155). The distinction is essentially between informal, 'everyday' discourses dispersed through social life and those that are more formal, institutionalized and systematic. To characterize this difference, Bernstein characterizes knowledge discourses as falling within the distinction between vertical knowledge and horizontal knowledge.

Vertical discourse refers to a coherent, systematic, explicit and principled structure that is hierarchically organized (in the sciences, for instance) or that takes the form of a specialized language with specialized modes of interrogation and specialized criteria for the production and circulation of texts as in academic social sciences and humanities. Vertical discourse can also be differentiated according to its principles of organization (according to the collection code or the integrated code). Horizontal discourse is 'common-sense', everyday knowledge. It tends to be acquired contexts where the affective loading may be considerable and in face-to-face encounters in socially familiar situations. It has its own modes of pedagogy, also, limited to the context of its enactment. Segmental pedagogies of horizontal discourse may well depend strongly on modelling or showing 'how to' and this everyday pedagogy of learning how to tie one's shoelaces or how to use the lavatory (two instances from Bernstein) – is directed towards acquiring a common competence deemed necessary in the context of social solidarity rather than being directed towards a graded performance against publicly defined criteria.

One special (though not exclusive) function of English has been to blur distinctions between knowledge belonging to the domain of social solidarity and the official public domain of knowledge. English requires 'informal' open responses and expression and thus calls upon the expression of its subjects' (pupils) encoded social solidarities. At the same time, there are powerful judgements relating to code modalities being made about the nature and 'quality' of these expressions. English teaching has blurred the distinction between vertical and horizontal discourses. While this may have been acclaimed positively as openness to the personal in terms of expression and response, the downside is that crucial judgements are then made about the encodings of such expression and response. Code theory, again, reminds us that personal expression is always already class coded. The collection code as organizing principle for subject knowledge means that the coding of expression becomes a determining factor in success and failure.

Control: Pedagogy and social power

As students of progressive education know, in pedagogical practice the exertion of power and control can be more or less apparent. Bernstein characterizes invisible pedagogy as where the teacher has implicit rather than explicit control over the child, where the teacher arranges the context, where the child explores and discovers, where the child has power over the context and over the time scale of activities, where the child regulates his or her own movements and social relations, where there is reduced emphasis on the transmission and acquisition of specific skills and where the criteria for evaluation are diffuse and multiple. Bernstein goes on to define invisible pedagogy in terms of its deployment of play as a means to define and act upon the child's identity as learner. The kind of learning processes and the relations and identities these imply relate to and act upon identities that are socially constructed in family types (Bernstein, 1997).

In Bernstein's account of knowledge, then, social differences are vital. The classification of knowledge stands in a dynamic relation to framing. Framing in Bernstein refers to the principle regulating the encounter between teacher and taught. Classification provides the ostensible occasion, as it were, and the symbolic material for the framing encounter. Framing relates to the control over modes of access to and relations with what is classified as knowledge. Framing determines the nature of the mediation of knowledge. In the context of schooling, framing refers to practices determining the mode of transmission of knowledge, the pace of access and acquisition, the style of realization and the type of evaluation. The nature and extent of the options for the learner (or taught) are determined by framing. Framing is the explicit social form of the pedagogic power relation. The ethos of an institution, its deployment of space and the way it organizes and manages time may all be characterized as aspects of framing. Like classification, framing can be defined as varying along a continuum from weak to strong. Strong framing implies more visible control mechanisms, more formal control of learning. Liberal versions of English – particularly those predating the National Curriculum belonging to the post-Bullock hegemony – may frequently have had more open framing, less visible control.

Bernstein's distinction between visible and invisible pedagogies is particularly relevant to the class politics of English teaching, especially in relation to developments that can be traced to Vygotsky's influence via James Britton into 'new' practices that emerged strongly in the 1960s and that became commonplace in the first wave of comprehensivization. The influence of Britton and the Dartmouth conference liberalized the subject, insisted on pupils engaging in 'their own' languages and voicing 'their own' responses. This depoliticized version of English seemed to offer an open invitation to the pupil to participate in and with the pupil's own language, and remained blithely unconcerned with the sociology of language.

Globalization

'Globalization' is perhaps another term for the ongoing condition of modernity, a feature of the world taking on increasing significance since Henry the Navigator began to sponsor forays along the west coast of Africa in 1415 (Parry, 1990). Even before then we can imagine a world to some significant extent as globalized. The cosmopolitan condition of the Roman Empire as a conglomerate of different identities brought together into a pragmatic unity serves as a historical parallel. Globalization can also be seen as a specifically 'postmodern' phenomenon, a product the shift from a 'solid' to a 'liquid' modernity, signifying a more recent and more radical transformation of the world (Bauman, 2000; Lyotard, 1984). On this view globalization is recent, has been rapid and has occurred beyond any controlling power. This version of globalization is often represented as fraught with dangers. The very identity of things is destabilized. Familiar borders shift; time and space are compressed; information flows at the speed of light. Globalization comes to inhabit and define all aspects of life: geo-politics, geo-communications systems, geo-economics and geo-culture, including education. The world takes on a new guise. It is no longer a space for separate, disentangled forms of existence, human, animal or otherwise. In the Anthropocene period, the world has changed irrevocably. Politically, globalization often takes negative implications: the dominance of multinational companies, the Americanization of global culture and the eradication of indigenous modes of being. 'Deterritorialization' has undermined traditional cultures, stable values and forms of conduct, unmooring communities from the stabilities that have historically guided them in the long, slow processes of cultural adaptation. This is the era of neo-liberalism, the domination of the econo-sphere by vast forces that ensure an uneven distribution of the world's goods. What's more, globalization impacts on our inner lives: Zygmunt Bauman claims 'negative globalization' is the driving force behind the intense forms of anxiety that define contemporary human life and that have invaded the most intimate domains of our individual and collective lives (Bauman, 2000, 2003, 2004, 2005, 2006a, b).

Bauman's dystopian world seems a far cry from Marshall McLuhan's cosier 'global village' (1964). According to McLuhan, among the first seriously to articulate relations between global time–space and modern, electronic communications systems: 'Today, after more than a century of electric technology, we have extended our central nervous system in a global embrace, abolishing both space and time as far as our planet is concerned' (1964, 3). Since McLuhan, a powerful and often negative discourse on communications technologies and their effects have heightened a sense of danger in terms of both identity and security. A rapidly changing 'plug and play' world order, comprised of radical shifts in the capacities of communications systems, including the exponential growth of computer processing power, digitalization, fibre-optic cabling, global satellite coverage, high-definition television, has meant a dizzying proliferation as well as an uncontrolled and perhaps uncontrollable domain of 'media'. The power of these technologies was already becoming visible in the so-called first Gulf War. In conjunction with new mobility of peoples and migrant populations of modernity, these technologies seem to seriously threaten national borders and local ways of being in the world. Consider how social media transform our sense of our connectedness and challenge the very idea of being locally rooted in any essential way.

Movement of people and peoples strongly contributed to the mingling of cultures giving rise to the condition of hybridity associated with the postmodern (Lyotard, 1985), complicating relations between global, national and local, changing these dimensions of 'being-in-the-world'. Location, including our own being-in-the-world, can no longer be simply a matter of topography. Where we 'are' has become a complex matter. Our 'place' involves multiple aspects of being. Globalization involves meta-regional convergences including integrated world markets; global system of communications, knowledge and culture; accelerated mobility of people; and the export and import of policy norms. Global flows transform practices and institutions as well as identities: and in many visible cases work towards a normative convergence. According to Arjun Appadurai, it now makes more sense to divide the world into spheres of operation than geographic continents. The world can thus be defined in terms of (1) the ethnoscape, (2) the mediascape, (3) the technoscape, (4) the financescapes, and (5) the ideoscapes. The suffix 'scape' refers to 'fluid, irregular shapes' (2008, 52). To this we should also perhaps add the 'eduscape' in order to remind ourselves of the importance of education as a world market, a world phenomenon of considerable puissance and scope.

Changes wrought by globalization in terms of consciousness have transformed both our sense of the world and in our experience of it (Harvey, 1991). Time–space compression is an important dimension of this. It refers to both physical travel and communications connectivity. A major effect is the disruption of the local by presence of the 'Other'. Cosmopolitanism is dispersed, no longer the special condition of particular locations. We experience the cosmopolitan in supermarkets, through radio channels, via our self-organized media flows. It is generally palpable in the material substance of our lives, wherever we are. We might say that a certain global consciousness promotes an increased awareness of the 'world'. World politics, world culture and world ecology discourses proliferate. Such 'globe-talk' heightens uncertainty. 'Alien' forces are no longer far away. They impinge on our world while remaining beyond our control. Where exactly, are they? Our fate it seems has become subject to distant political, economic and cultural forces, processes and institutions. The illusion of being in control of our world is perhaps now less sustainable. We collectively run the risk of a dire political autoimmune condition in an effort to safeguard a probably mythical collective identity.

The sense of shadowy political forces at work in the new morphology of globalized economic powers is palpable for some; at the same time, new resistant political forces, it's claimed, arise in the agonistics of conflict between the dark forces of 'empire' and the manifold, self-organizing, positive and resistant identities of 'multitude' (Hardt and Negri, 2000). Communities may have died, but the new force of networks – by no means all on the side of the rich and the powerful – have given rise to a new articulation of politics. We have to review our very idea of how politics works it works, where and even what it is (Hardt and Negri, 2005, 2009). David Harvey's influential, now well-worn, account of *The Condition of Postmodernity* likewise proposed a global shift in the very nature of economics and culture and seeks to identify a new political world order (Harvey, 1991). Jean Francois Lyotard in *The Postmodern Condition* offers a radical critique of metaphysics, rethinking the very nature of identity, meaning and history in the light of changes in the global world order. Lyotard indicates that totalizing descriptions must be handled with care. After Nietzsche, all 'global' descriptions must acknowledge their own provisional and positioned nature. As a self-professedly anti-totalizing position, postmodernism makes claims about the 'new' condition of the world while recognizing that no such descriptions can claim transcendental authority (Lyotard, 1986). This is a tricky but necessary balance to maintain in 'our' world.

Educational dimensions of globalization

Globalization has given rise to the idea of education as a generalized human right, drawing on the 1948 Universal Declaration of Human Rights, the United Nations' 1959 Convention on the Rights of the Child and the UN International

Covenant on Economic, Social, and Cultural Rights (1976). All of these declare education a fundamental human right. In recognition that universal access to education remains unrealized, further discussion has continued at the Education for All conferences held in Thailand in 1990 and Senegal in 2000 as well as in the International Commission on Education for the twenty-first century's report 1996). There is, however, no universal agreement on what amounts to an education to meet the minimum requirements to fulfil that right. Questions arise about who should provide what form of education to whom and about how the right to education might be claimed or enforced. There is a complex but important story to be told concerning globalized education or education in the new world order. Caution might be advised here, but there is no question that education has been caught up in globalization and the two cannot disentangled.

Is globalized education a function of neo-liberalism, imposing governmental education policies and practices, while eroding 'proper' enlightenment ideals? Education, some might claim, has been distorted into a tool for managing the social division of labour and for promoting market ideology, an arena for neo-liberal ideological forces on a global scale. The impact of supranational institutions like the Organization for Economic Co-operation and Development (OECD) on national education systems, promoting convergence, can be seen as hostile to local identity and community (Burbules and Torres, 2000). 'World education' represents the opposite of equal access, on this view. In a new, competition-driven hierarchy, powerful institutions dominate. A deficit discourse identifies poorer national contexts as educationally deprived. At the same time, all national contexts enforce a national system as education is represented as an economically necessary form of governance. As a key institution of population management, the school has been globalized. The university, similarly, partakes of the global knowledge economy. The form of that economy is pitilessly on the side of capital and accumulation (Hatcher, 2001).

Globalization and the school

Globalization can be seen right at the origins of schooling in modernity in the process whereby the school becomes the paradigm institution of socialization in the more powerful and wealthy, industrialized areas of the world: Europe, North America, Australasia and Japan. The UK example is highly instructive, given the colonial and postcolonial dimensions of globalization. In her account of education in nineteenth-century India under the British Raj, Gauri Viswanathan describes an interesting relation between colonial and home practices. Examining the rise of English as a school curriculum subject, Viswanathan demonstrates how the English curriculum first took shape in India as a vehicle for the enculturation of subaltern population in the process of education for administration of British rule. Ironically, English was imported 'back' into the 'home' country after the First World War as a way of re-enculturating the working-class population. Fears of the contagion of Bolshevism, a concern for the cultural integrity of the nation, a fear of the 'corrupting' influence of popular culture and a moral panic about the corruption of the English language impelled this reformation. National coherence, it was felt, was at stake in this project to construct a national culture through the now well-established education system (Newbolt, 1921; Viswanathan, 1989). In this counternarrative, Viswanathan turns the conventional wisdom concerning English teaching in England on its head and makes us rethink any simplistic assumptions we have unthinkingly entertained about what is fundamental in the curriculum subject. In some ways, Viswanathan's work provides an object lesson about the process of rethinking. The object, in this case the history of English teaching, or English teaching in its origins, is rethought and redefined by bringing new knowledge to bear upon its formation.

This vignette illustrates how education has long been a feature of globalized geopolitical relations. As the modern form of the school took shape in the nineteenth century as an essential feature of the modern nation-state, it began to permeate national borders (Green, 1997). As modernity emerged and established the distinction between developed and developing sectors, levels and modes of schooling became a significant measure of 'development' for nations, an index of prosperity, economic potential and relative well-being. In national contexts of relative poverty, access to schooling became and remains a specific index of political status and puissance. The meaning of access to and acquisition of education, at national levels, as well as it the level of the individual, however, is not simply a matter of redressing a deficit. Excluded or disadvantaged ethnic, class or gender groups struggle not only to 'receive' education, but also to shape its content and form. In Foucault's terms, education is the most powerful example of 'bio-power' – a far-reaching social technology. One significant effect of this technology is the distribution of status: a process that works in general in schooled societies to distinguish between different levels of access and status; but this process also, we must remember, works at national and global levels to distinguish between zones of educational plenty as it were and zones of educational need or poverty. From this perspective, the idea that education is or can be a remedy for poverty – again at both individual and international levels – is rendered problematic through a rethinking of its ontological status.

The form of the school is an index of globalization. As this paradigm institution has been adopted, and adapted, as the key instrument for development in virtually all global contexts, significant points arise from this metastasis. As schooling becomes ubiquitous, so the model of education it carries with it also disseminates. While the specific form of the school may vary, consistent elements of the institution and its purposes have become pandemic. The meaning of this process is not straightforward at all. Many benefits of schooling for children would be hard to contest, such as systematic pastoral care, concern for personal development, a degree of freedom from labour and access to non-local knowledge as well as some significant protections. But we have to acknowledge that schooling as we know carries with it loss or negation of local identity, linguistic domination, subjection to regimes of knowledge and collusion with the social division of labour that may systematically discriminate against significant segments of the population in the name of just but culturally biased processes of assessment and selection (Bernstein, 1971). Education is never simply a gift: in its modern instantiation, education always enacts governance. In contemporary terms, however, education has become a dominating concept in terms of development, prosperity and well-being at local, national and global levels. Formal, systemized education is seen as an absolutely essential dimension for any and every nation state. This state of affairs, that naturalizes education as an essential good, in spite of much of the evidence to the contrary, is indicative of a powerful metaphysics.

An example from the oil-wealthy Middle East illustrates one aspect of the impact of educational development on national life. In Qatar, recently, the Supreme Education Council, established by decree of the Emir, made educational reform a government priority, referring to the need to 'modernize'. The iconography of the public literature disseminated to promote this process juxtaposes references to traditional local identities with hypermodern images of hi-tech learning environments: 'Best practices from around the world combined with Qatar's unique culture are ensuring a bright future for every child.' 'Best practices' in this case include the sustained intervention of the RAND Corporation, a California-based NGO. In terms of the structure of school governance, the form of the curriculum, assessment systems, the dominant model of professional development and ideas about learning, the new, reformed 'Qatari' education system follows a thoroughly Western model. It is hard in this case to see how RAND-led modernization has enabled 'local' identity into the 'new era' initiative. The curriculum includes Arabic, but is dominated by English, mathematics and science. The public message promoted by the Supreme Education Council emphasizes global competition, giving prominence to 'performance levels' and 'scale scores' to drive 'school improvement' with publicly published results and cohort comparisons. In other words, Qatar has imported wholesale a Californian ('Western') educational ethic and system.

The salience of English in Qatari education signifies a characteristic aspect of global education. South Africa after apartheid furnishes a problematic and illustrative case of complexities in this field. One of the first decrees of the post-apartheid government was to recognize eleven official national languages. Nevertheless, English soon became recognized, although disputed, as the dominant language of government and education. Arguments about the rights of minority languages versus the de facto hegemony of English were symptomatic of the global, local, national torsions at work in the arguments the policy engendered. Neville Alexander, one time member of the Interim Governing Board of the African Academy of Languages, has focused recent work on the tension between multilingualism and the hegemony of English in the public sphere. Alexander, an educationist with impeccable ANC credentials, and fellow prisoner on Robben Island with Nelson Mandela, has become a champion of alternative education arguing for resistance to any simple acceptance of the hegemony of English. Alexander's independent organization, Project for the Study of Alternative Education in South Africa (PRAESA), argues that while accepting 'the immediate and obvious economic and social benefits of English' it is vital to sustain 'home languages' for cultural and political reasons as well as for economic and social reasons. In this case, the hegemonic form of education has met with some powerful resistance, for urgent socio-cultural and political reasons. The outcome of this resistance remains to be seen, but it is worth noting that the form of educational reform in South Africa after apartheid, in terms of institutions and curricula, has followed a globally hegemonic model often despite explicit policy intentions.

Indigenous education may struggle to retain its indigeneity, impelled to follow the hegemonic model of powerful nation states (Green, 1997). Manuel Castells offers an example of a struggle over education arising with the Indian insurgency in Mexico. Hitherto 'an absent actor' in the current Latin American modernization process, constitutional reform granted rights of access to education to Indians. Castells claims that health and education services improved for Indian communities, and that 'limited self-government was in the process of implementation' (Castells, 2004, 86). What this apparently cheerful story indicates is that hitherto excluded communities may gain 'access' to education through political intervention and changes in rights legislation within national contexts. But what is also indicated is that entry into the sphere of education is not necessarily empowering. Local populations are included within the norm-related practices of national institutions of socialization. An excluded population in being brought within the ambit of education becomes subjected to – and subjugated by – the institutionalized ordering of identity. Such processes – including the excluded, in order to better manage them and their potentially disruptive presence – occur in wealthy and powerful nations to the less wealthy and powerful population segments (Peim, 2006).

Globalized higher education

In contemporary philosophy, there is a strand of thinking suggesting that the very idea of the university is under threat from forces driven by globalization. According to this narrative, the liberal enlightenment ideal is what is in danger. This ideal of the university, as essentially a place of freedom, demands independence from national governments and global economic powers. This independent university, guaranteeing academic freedom, stands for 'communicative rationality': its task is to promote the values of scientific thinking as a model for the public sphere and as a mechanism for the production of objective and politically neutral knowledge. This story claims that it is essential that key knowledge producing institutions in modern societies affirm and enact the values of freedom, objectivity and integrity (Derrida, 2004; Habermas, 1987). While universities in all national contexts face pressures to be or become more economically efficient and 'relevant', the counter-discourse seeks to reclaim the special educational role of the university against the dominance of 'technological enframing' (Heidegger, 1993c). Such discourses have seriously questioned the proliferating tendency to orient research and teaching towards a programmable and profitable end.

One problem is that there are many ideas of what the university and higher education (HE) should be. The university, as we know it, is largely a product of modernity. As modernity mutates, so our understanding of this powerful institution will have to take into account the global dimension. Universities are increasingly globalized institutions: with networks, flows of students, a global hierarchy, as well as global convergence of practices, aspirations and orientations to knowledge. For Jacques Derrida, the question is how can the university develop the legacy of its enlightenment ideal in the face of globalized lines of force and operate as a properly cosmopolitan, 'hospitable' institution, open to 'Others' in the form of both cultural identities and knowledge. How might the classic functions of the institution – teaching, research, training, transmission of culture – sustain both rigour and hospitality in the face of rationalizing tendencies and competition that have taken on a globalized character?

The history of the university as we know it is aligned with the history of the rise of the modern nation state. Universities have been seen as key institutions in the construction of the nation state, in the development of secularization, industrialization, in the promotion of public culture, influencing civil society, and creating significant forms of citizenship along with the emergence and development of the 'knowledge society'. Neo-liberal market forces have been seen to influence this history and to have given rise to a new era of globalized HE dominated by market forces and an instrumental, managerialism, displacing the classic form of the institution with its monstrous new progeny, the 'multiversity' (Sun-keung Pang, 2006). According to some, on the other hand 'higher education remains a primary source of cultural and social innovation in modern societies' (Rhoads and Torres, 2006, xviii).

The enlightenment version of the university promoted by Kant and von Humboldt, the liberal vision articulated by Newman, Eliot, Jaspers and the more recent 'radical' visions of Dewey, Habermas and Gouldner, have all had to come to terms with the functionalist perspective that dominates much of the impact of global market forces on HE. The university remains central to what remains of the project of modernity, including both its rationalizing and its liberalizing tendencies, but also to the postmodern, globalized, university of 'liquid modernity'. While it may be that the university retains a degree of 'relative autonomy' from the state and from the pressures of the neo-liberal hegemony (Ball, 2004), new regimes of university governance – including emphasis on financial accountability, formal audits, and rankings for research, internal review, appraisal schemes and self-assessment – all impact as constraints on the productivity of academics. Current measures of professional competence, including peer review, citation indexing and the new emphasis on impact draw their power to define the work of universities from global forces (Delanty, 2005; Rhoads and Torres, 2000). Such performative pressures are symptomatic of the global self-consciousness of the university and its standing in the global education market (Brown and Lauder, 2004).

The three main exporters in the global knowledge economy – the United States, the Unite Kingdom and Australia – promote their educational exports as part of their foreign trade interests. Government departments in these countries encourage, represent and even coordinate activities that enhance the global reach of their HE institutions. Quality, status and cultural questions arise in relation to the double flow of exported courses and programmes and imported students. Larger cultural effects of such global educational flows might be understood in terms of some of the work done in media theory. The simple thesis of cultural domination is challenged by detailed ethnographic work indicating that aspects of the local 'life-world' are not necessarily negated as cultural products, such forms of knowledge, pedagogical relations and the production of identities, get exported from one – frequently more dominant – cultural context to another (Tomlinson, 1991).

Globalization as ontology

Most accounts of globalization emphasize the 'new global disorder' as a process to be resisted, demanding a critical stance towards 'neo-liberal' reorganization of global capital and power. Hence the rise of the anti-globalization movement, an alliance of disparate forces and itself, paradoxically, a globalized force. For many theorists, globalization carries with it a duality of power and possible resistances. Derrida has identified the ten 'plagues' of globalization, but has also proposed the idea of a 'new international', as an informal association with common interests and purposes coming together in the name of social, cultural, political and economic justice. For Michael Hardt and Antonio Negri, the new hegemonic global force of 'Empire' is balanced by the rising force of 'multitude' informed by a series of democratically oriented concepts they refer to as 'commonwealth' (Hardt and Negri, 2000, 2005, 2009). In both these cases, education is identified as caught up with the flow of powers and the struggles between forces, as an instrument on the side of the forces of 'Empire' *and* as a means for resisting 'negative globalization'.

The term 'globalization' must always be problematic and in need of deconstruction. To describe 'the world' all at once is the impossible dream of metaphysics. The world as a totality can be apprehended, or surmised, from a specific position, as both Wittgenstein and Heidegger articulated at length in the first half of the twentieth century. At the current point of the twenty-first century, the borders between the 'global', the national and the local, and between the overarching structures and the possibilities of play, remain areas for exploration. Heidegger, Wittgenstein, Derrida, Spivak, and Foucault, among many others, have all problematized the idea of 'the world' as a Eurocentric construction. In the context of education, the fact of the convergence of curricula, institutions, hierarchies and values must be seen against the specificities of local practices and cultures that invariably operate against any simple, one-way flow of 'cultural imperialism'.

It is now generally agreed that the bold enunciation of 'the end of history' and the triumph of liberal democracy and market capitalism made by Francis Fukuyama was not just premature but also misguided (1992). The question of the condition of the 'world' is not settled but remains in play. Similarly, the question concerning education is very much alive. Education appears in an increasingly 'ontotheological' mode, a globalized force defining both 'lifelong' personal development and fuelling the global economy. Education is seen as the driving force to redress corrosive inequalities and solve the practical problems facing the human species. In this elevation of education to a powerful principle of being, enlightenment versions of education struggle against the general culture of performativity. On aspect of future debate may be to address the present hegemony of the idea of education as the solution to all the world's problems. While globalization has sold education as the dominant ontological principle and has made the reach of education ubiquitous, questions may still be asked about the rights of this hegemony.

The meaning of globalization

Globalization remains, of course, contested as a way of giving an account of the current condition of the world. Space–time compression, postcolonialism and the rapid rise of powerful communications technologies are no doubt powerful forces that have changed relations between national, local and global dimensions of existence and impacted on cultural identities. Education has been globalized as systems have experienced convergence, institutions have been imported and exported and what counts as effective knowledge has been defined beyond local contexts. Globalized education seems to carry with it a double movement of (1) the extension and amplification of hegemonic power and of (2) the countermovement of globalized forces of resistance. Local contexts have expressed some resilience in the face of global incursions. The reign of performativity has yet to entirely displace the enlightenment ideals of objectivity and freedom for education. The still-growing geographic and cultural reach of education as a governmental force, however, may encourage educationalists to rethink the current emphasis given to education as global ontological principle.

Chapter 6

Data Narratives

The narrative dimension

This chapter addresses narrative but really is about the mode of representation proper to educational (or social science) research. It addresses genre, claiming rhetoric as a significant dimension of research. This is not rhetoric as opposed to reality. Rhetoric concerns how we make claims for research to be valid, be truthful and accord with how the world is. Such claims must represent their own cause. The presentation of a case is always required, no matter how secure, convincing, detailed and consistent the argument and evidence. Every research project depends on textual affirmation.

There is a tactical element to genre. To present a plausible case demands alertness to the ruses of representation, to the modes of appropriate rhetoric. An educational research project will have to present itself in a certain format with the implicit rules of genre being attended to. There is some flexibility in this genre according to one's orientation. But the business of presenting a coherent case consistent with the academic genre is essential to its reception by the academic world. There is also a powerful force of constraint in this. To deviate from the established norm may be dangerous, running the risk of rejection. 'This is not a research thesis' may fall as an excluding judgement – legitimate or not – made against a work that violates the law of genre.

The production of research is a balance between following the conventions of the genre and the equally important requirement to produce something new. Most research, in Thomas Kuhn's terms, does not break with the dominant genre. Workaday research may never even address the paradigm question, resting content within its own assumed world. Countless instances of educational research remain within the well-established mode, reproducing and reinforcing its own premises. This is a powerful consequence of the kind of the thinking in the thesis handbooks. Such repetitive research practice reaffirms its own validity. We can see this in educational research dedicated to school improvement, for instance, or much research that's dedicated to 'critical pedagogy'. The pattern of the research follows a well-worn path. Modifications in practice are determined to generate more efficient learning, or more effective interventions into character, or more just means of delivering a reformed education agenda (Arthur et al., 2016; Gorard, 2013). In some cases, improvement is displaced by an ethic of redemption: the vision of education freed from its neo-liberal fallen self is offered as pure self-realization at both personal and social levels (Apple, 2014). That these repetitive, rote ways of understanding education can be questioned from another perspective is never be entertained by these genres. To do so, in fact, may threaten their very continuation. So, key ontological questions remain foreclosed.

Thomas Kuhn, writing about science, proposed the idea of paradigm shifts in a historical sense. In the world of educational research, different paradigms exist side by side. Such differences are so strongly entrenched that research produced within one paradigm may not recognize the validity of research produced in another. So, the question of genre is fundamental to the researcher. Understanding where one stands in the world of research production is highly significant. It determines the reception one may expect and demands knowledge of the world one is addressing. In this sense, the use of the word 'narrative' in the title of this chapter may be controversial and may signify a particular orientation towards research that some might find inimical.

But this chapter does not seek to promote mode of research that is at heart and fundamentally narrative, as one option among a range of predetermined options, as many research manuals suggest. It aims rather to address the *question* of genre through the idea of narrative as an essential dimension of knowledge that has been privileged by some serious and far-reaching theory in recent times. This idea of narrative as mode of knowledge is not to be confused with storytelling in the usual sense. Narrative has acquired a special sense through the work of Jean-Francois Lyotard, author of the most influential version of the postmodern condition (Lyotard, 1986). For Lyotard, narrative is associated with the overriding ideas or principles that govern – often unconsciously – modes of knowledge. Lyotard uses the phrase 'grand narrative' to signal a dominant world view or ethic. Lyotard argues that such forms of knowledge have their roots in specific anthropological perspectives, specific 'forms of life' that can be analysed in terms of collections of specific 'petits-recits' or small-scale language games. Lyotard's case challenges all positions that claim a privileged relation to reality – as though there could be forms of knowledge (science would be the paradigm case for our world) that could be uncontaminated by the socio-anthropological dimension. Lyotard points out that while science may claim to be free of such contamination, in fact, it must be organized as a system by narrative knowledge as much as by cool ratiocination or by neutrally construed 'method'. Nevertheless, science as neutral persists as a key idea in research including social science research.

Narrative in the Lyotard sense relates to myth. A tradition of modern and postmodern thinking has seriously revived the role of myth as an essential component of all thinking. This revival negates the idea of myth as pre-rational naivety. According to this position, myth informs all knowledge, despite efforts of formal knowledge to claim otherwise. Myth is an essential dimension of thinking implicit in the stories that cohere forms of knowledge. The rationalities that inform our quest as agents of knowledge or science are powerful myths of our time. Lyotard demonstrates the logic of myth at work in modern and contemporary science. This element of myth, according to the logic of Lyotard's thinking and of the tradition I refer to above, must also inhabit all those apparently essential categories of knowledge pursuit such as research design, the repertoire of research techniques or technologies that enfold the dominant practices of research. Within the field of education – a field heavily populated by myth – the modes advanced of acquiring, verifying and justifying knowledge belong essentially to the domain of myth. While this claim may seem scandalous, it does not seek to suggest that researchers who subscribe to the given formulae are more deluded than others. It merely changes the status of the belief systems that underpin research practices. All research practices must, at some point, as we saw in Chapter 3, rely on an element of faith, which is after all an essential feature of myth (Barthes, 1973; Peim, 2013).

In the Attic world, where thinking was dominated as much by myth as by Socratic rationality, when Thucydides wanted to claim that he had reinvented history as a form of knowledge, he sought to free historical data from the taint of myth. In modernity, reverse moves occur. Anthropology reinterprets myth as symbolic of social and cultural meaning, rather than as the primitive residue of primordial modes of thinking such as animism. Myth in this view signifies a symbolic system expressive of a way of life. Mythology in this sense is not to be equated with the opposite of truth just as it is not to be directly equated with *the* truth. All modes of cultural meaning come to be realigned with the mythological dimension, as in the work of Roland Barthes. The anthropological perspective discloses myth in the element of faith necessary to the pursuit of knowledge.

Understanding the narrative dimension in all modes of knowledge is an essential move in developing a keen sense of what is involved in engaging with that world. In education particularly, this is strongly the case. Educational institutions, practices, discourses and ideas are beset with various forms of narrative, dominated by powerful mythologies. Identifying such narratives is crucial to getting to grips with the motor forces of idea that sustain the educational world. Consider the array of quite powerful narratives that lend their force to educational thinking, often with scant explicit articulation or recognition. So powerful are these implicit narrative elements that they often take on the guise of natural truth, appearing to be self-evident and therefore unquestionable:

- Education as a positive force in the world
- Education as a form of enlightenment
- Education as capable of delivering social redemption
- Education as essential to self-realization
- Education as necessary to democracy
- Education as a vehicle for social justice
- Education as essential component of economic development

While there isn't space here to explore each of these categories of myth in turn in detail, there are powerful arguments and positions available that suggest that they should be granted the status of myth rather than taken as self-evident truths (Wolf, 2002).

The question concerning data

The role of narrative in education research raises the question of data. An educational research project might tell a story – perhaps concerning the persistent inequalities that schools enact in relation to social class. To verify this story, to shift its status from 'mere' story to authentic narrative of truth, the research project will generally reach for the validating resource of data.

In data we seek clarity, perhaps also truth and finality. Data settles arguments and overcomes ambiguity. Data signifies the response of the Real, in loosely Lacanian terms (Belsey, 2005; Lacan, 2006). Social sciences research programmes that tend to separate the quest for data from considerations of issues, definitions of problems and surveys of existing commentary or knowledge. This is the consequence of the domination of the field of social science, including the field of educational research, by a dominant although mostly untheorized, model of knowledge. The dominant genre offers a model for the researcher, from the summative 'literature search and review' through the determination of method in the already-established data gathering procedures, perhaps via the interesting detour of theory, to the neatly arrived-at conclusions. The model suggests a natural order to the progress of the research project. And yet, key modes of thinking are suppressed for this order to reign.

It is useful to rethink our relations to data as well as to interrogate what data is and what its proper role is in the structuring of research, though this is not common procedure. This is not simply recognizing that data may take different forms and thus require different approaches for its generation, nor simply to assert that the difference between data and what is not data – narrative, interpretation, say – is not at all as clear as we may either want it to be or as others consider it. It is the 'ontological status' of data that can be usefully to put into question. The term wants to separate something ontologically distinct from other elements in research production and representation. In data, we often invoke something deemed essential to research validity. We might think that data, in its difference from other research terms, signifies a necessary and essential separation between dimensions of research. Perhaps problems about the essence of data only arise when we complicate our practice and approach with such questions that always tend to blur the lines between entities.

I will suggest here that we can take contrasting approaches – and find that both will be legitimate in the eyes of the research collective so long as we can find an authorized context to present them. We can simply abide by the dominant paradigm for educational and social science research. This is the paradigm that divides the research process carefully into a staged journey with its discrete elements, as proffered in the handbooks. Or we can take a more open exploratory approach to the question of data, putting data itself into question, while at the same time we may seek to use its authorizing status as a move in our argument in the presentation of a case. In this latter case, our approach to data is ambiguous, but not dismissive. We may grant data a different ontological status from its usual, unthinking determination as what guarantees access to 'the Real'.

Data signifies desire, we might say, perhaps oddly, drawing from a Lacanian perspective. The desire that is expressed in the production of data is the desire to access the Real. In LacaSnian ontology, the Real is that dimension of being beyond the reach of the Symbolic, the crude materiality of what is, the undifferentiated pulsing of matter in the world or some similar but necessarily nebulous formulation. The problem with the Lacanian Real is that it is both formless and elusive to our apprehension. We are mostly cut off from any direct contact it. The Real is accessible only through the veil of the Symbolic. While we may seek to ground knowledge in the hard core of material reality, the means for that must belong to the already-ordered realm of the Symbolic. What's more, our relations to the Symbolic are permeated with the other ontological dimension that Lacan refers to as the Imaginary. Rather like overlapping sectors in a Venn diagram except that we cannot separate out any one of the three dimensions from the other. We are doomed, as it were, to inhabit all three simultaneously. The mildly good news here though is that the Symbolic, while strongly configured and beyond the full comprehension, reach or manipulation of individual will, is nevertheless structured by a degree of mobility – otherwise there could be no instances of the production of new knowledge, no paradigm shifts and no recognition or realization that different worlds (horizons of knowing and being) are possible. Another piece of possible good news is that the Symbolic itself constitutes a domain of data: how we symbolize the world and the things that are important to us within it is highly significant – and it is perfectly consistent with a Lacanian ontology to suggest that the Symbolic is exactly the domain that we experience in our necessarily mediated encounters with the Real. If we follow Lacanian ontology – or use it for our own purposes – the intricacies of the relations between Real, Imaginary and Symbolic may provide us with some useful material for articulating something significant, if not essential, about the nature of the knowledge we are in the process of producing and something about our own relation to it. In doing so we will be addressing what are conventionally known as method and methodology: both these dimensions of research are concerned, conventionally at least, with data (Benvenuto and Kennedy, 1986; Bracher and Ragland-Sullivan, 1991; Lacan, 1986, 2006; Weedon, 1987).

So, we may begin with a question concerning the provenance of data. While we tend to think, as citizens of modernity, that data is another word for 'the facts', what we refer to as data cannot be entirely immune to the interrogative mood. This seems to be especially the case with research data and even more especially the case with research that claims an empirical identity. In all officially sanctioned research training (e.g. in ESCR-sponsored research centres), there is an assumption that real research, research that wants to engage with the realities of the social world as it is, will include a component of data that is generated by the researcher or by the specific research project in hand. The collection and interpretation and presentation of data are the clinching elements (Gorard, 2013). Everything else, it is implied, is either preliminary to data or supplementary to it. This way of thinking, strongly embodied in practice, has become an implicit orthodoxy – hence the great emphasis that research training courses give to modalities of method, and to the element of 'research design' that invariably includes reference to 'data sets'. In Lacanian terms, this emphasis on data is a symptom of anxiety. The anxiety in question is the fear of a failure of the Symbolic Order to fully mesh with and express the essence of the Real. Data belongs to something more solid, it seems, than a mere sense of things or an interpretation or an already-received idea or a reorganization of ideas. Ideally, data is what checks our ideas about reality. Data may disturb our sense of how things are by demanding that we rethink the order or the nature of things. And it is hard to think otherwise, so strongly engaged is this model.

The Symbolic Order is best considered in relation to language. Ferdinand de Saussure (1857–1913) had introduced the idea that language is – essentially – a 'system of differences', meaning that we have to abandon the idea of language as correspondence. While we may amble along through life happy that we know what we mean and that what we mean roughly accords with what there is, there may be occasions and times when the ambiguity essential to language makes us stumble for the right expression. There may be times when we come to be aware of the failure of language to express an essential experience, emotion or an intuited knowledge of things. At such points, we are forced to confront the disjuncture between language and the world, the radical separation between the Symbolic and the Real. The problem is compounded by the way that knowledge works in the field of the social sciences, including of course the production of knowledge in research.

Knowledge of the social is peculiarly difficult to locate precisely in the Real, to continue with the Lacanian vocabulary. No one has ever seen a 'habitus' as such, nor have they ever been able to bring an aspect of social injustice into the laboratory for inspection. In the same way, no one has ever seen intelligence, nor have they ever seen an institution or an institutional practice. We have all seen what we take to be signs of habitus, pointers that enable us to make coherent sense of what it is as a 'thing'. We all probably have a sense of how education relates to questions concerning social justice, especially when we see the data that indicates severe social class bias in the distribution of social goods. And we have all seen buildings that house institutions and have all experienced the effects and have all probably been caught up in institutional practices. The upshot is that we must resign ourselves to the fact that we can get access to the Real of social practice only through the symbolic repertoire that is available to us: the semantics and syntax we inherit, learn and become adept at deploying are elements of this Symbolic Order, that acts as a network of embodied ideas. Through it we 'see' (in the Kantian sense) and we experience and we make sense of the social world. Our explanations, theories and descriptions, and even our most mundane words for simple components, belong to this rather spectral element of signification.

That is not to say that there is no 'reality' to the social or that the social isn't real. The social partakes of the Real in all its operations. But this Real is not identical with the language we use to describe it. Language produces meanings that express intentions, desires, reasons, truths, but there is no way to guarantee that the representation we offer and that shapes our thinking is a precise and faithful rendering of what is there. Lacan tells the parable concerning two Greek painters who compete to paint the most realistic picture. Zeuxis paints grapes so lifelike that birds come to peck at them. When his rival Parrhasios reveals his picture, Zeuxis asks him to show what was depicted behind the veil he saw before him. Parrhasios had depicted the veil and so won the competition (Lacan, 1986, 103). This could serve as a parable of representation as it arises from de Saussure's distinction between the signifier – the material component of the sign (or language) – and the signified – what it signifies or points towards. The implications of this difference are enormous. For the painting, photograph, mathematical equation or logical notation, narrative or thesis or even a simple word acts as a kind of veil for the very 'thing' it seeks to signify. It stands both for it and in the place of it. The symbols involved in all cases constitute a kind of evidence for what is being represented, a substitute element that stands in its place. This is the very condition of data. For while the way that we seek to use the word 'data' may want to imply something hard, clear and unambiguous, all data must also partake of the *spectral* dimension of the symbolic where it finds its form and expression (Derrida, 1994). Material reality itself partakes of this spectral ontology (Derrida, 2001).

In this account, the idea of data as the essence of knowledge seems to have evaporated. And yet, there is more to it than that. We cannot simply dismiss data, even though we might be inclined to problematize its identity and status. Many kinds of data remain commonly agreed as significant and even vital. The problem is that we cannot finally distinguish between data that is the product of discursive formations and events and data pure and simple. And this indistinction is really, in the end, the result of the inescapable fact of representation. We cannot find any way of presenting data that does not necessarily entail some system of mediation: whether linguistic or numerical or in some other form such as photographic. In all these instances, there is an inevitable gap between what is being represented and the medium of its representation. It is not simply difficult to stand before the object-in-itself (noumenon) without the interplay of our own consciousness, ready-to-hand ideas or symbolic order. Data cannot give us such direct, unmediated access. The dimension of representation is a complication we cannot get around. Our experience of the world is phenomenal – not noumenal. In other words, the most robust data sets and the most rigorous methods of gathering them cannot stand outside of a system of classification and a deeply held syntax. In the end, our knowledge belongs to the order of language, the order of discourse.

One far-reaching consequence of that fact is that knowledge, data, research findings and their interpretation are all necessarily shot through with desire. As we've seen, and this is particularly the case with much educational research, our engagement with things is predicated on 'care'. We are always already oriented towards the very thing we seek to research – to know anew in some way. We cannot erase what Hans Georg Gadamer would refer to as our 'foreknowledge': it is part – a very significant part – of what makes us what we are and of what makes us capable of knowing anything at all (Gadamer, 1989). And we cannot step outside of what Heidegger might refer to as the 'clearing', the clearing of the specific mode of being that we find ourselves 'thrown' into by the historical, topographic and cultural accidents of our origins (Heidegger, 1962). At the same time, we cannot neutralize our desire, the very motive force of any quest for knowledge.

Empirical theology

It's important to get some sense of the extent that social science research has become tied to a model that includes and even privileges the empirical. This is a product of modernity and of the model of science that has tended to dominate thinking about how knowledge gets generated and secured. It is also a function of the domination of research by the demand for 'impact', a demand that seeks to guarantee that the research undertaken by universities is not merely knowledge, but that it is useful knowledge and that it is somehow tied to the real world (Denicolo, 2013; Reed, 2016). Such an ethic results in a shallow conception of research and seeks to delimit the category of the useful to what can be calculated and managed in the distribution of material resources. In this ethic, the empirical, ironically, acts symbolically, to ground the ideas or hypotheses that all progress or shift in knowledge requires. Certain kinds of data are felt to be particularly robust insofar as they can be tested and the results from such testing, ideally, will be repeated, thus clinching the sense that reality – even where that reality belongs to the wholly relational social world – is consistent, is answering back and is speaking the language we have devised to communicate with it. Questions about the solidity, validity and objectivity of data really belong to the modern desire to get in touch with what is really 'there', with the materiality of the material as we encounter it. There is in this a deep-seated fear that to think otherwise is to surrender to relativism and to give up on the very idea of truth. This desire and its misplaced fear are expressed also in the will to rationally calculate the use value of research and to allocate funding accordingly in research institutions. The modern state invests significant resources to shore up the attempt to determine what is 'really useful knowledge', the elusive category that nevertheless dominates contemporary research thinking (Johnson, 1981). The problem for such thinking is that the material reality that lies outside ourselves has to be grasped and represented through the same symbolic apparatus we use to do a host of other things with, some of them far from rigorous and far from concerned that they have a decisive link to material reality. The dimension of myth cannot be banished from such apparently rational calculations.

A major problem concerns this recognition of the symbolic and the source of its specific shape or form and the range of possibilities it may encompass. Here we must return to Heidegger or at least to the somewhat anthropological position that is implicit in Heidegger's account of fundamental ontology. If human knowledge cannot stand outside itself – and how, really, could it? – and if the apparatus it gets mediated through is tied up with the prevailing symbolic order – as it must be – then it must belong to a specific world order. Any data used to ground that knowledge – to provide it with a ballast that belongs to some other, non-symbolic space – must be generated and rendered intelligible in the terms that belong to that world. Even while we acknowledge that that terminology changes and can be viewed as dynamic, its possibilities for change are constrained by its specific semantic range and its syntactic ordering, its grammar. In Heidegger's terms, our world offers us a particular clearing onto Being (Heidegger, 1962). Being itself withdraws and we 'see' or know 'the world'; but we always know it from within the clearing. In this sense, the absolute distinction between the intelligible and the sensible – or ideas and data – is not really sustainable.

In the end, this way of thinking that problematizes the concept/data distinction is likely to eschew all forms of absolutism: and this is in line with modern theories of science. Karl Popper's theory, for instance, is predicated on the very idea of falsifiability, that is on the assumption that one day, sure enough, our knowledge will be modified, displaced and transcended and that what we take to be a true and proper account of reality no longer stands; just as Kuhn's model of scientific knowledge incorporates a historical sense that knows that models of knowledge of reality shift; and Feyerabend's model suggests that there is no essential core to method nor any 'proper' procedure or mode of verification in science. The field of science for Feyerabend is essentially fractured but at the same time powerfully institutionalized. The social dimension prevails over any determinate method (Feyerabend, 1975a, b; Kuhn, 1959, 1970).

One of the consequences of following the basic phenomenology of research relations (outlined in Chapter 1) is that there is no strict divide possible between what constitutes data and other elements that must be considered to establish the 'being-in-the-world' of the object in question and the question raised about its nature by the researcher. Playing the data game is about making decisions about what element of the object in question will furnish what will come to be represented as data, while a great deal of other contextual information and insight, that might also be considered to constitute data, will be defined in other terms. In an important sense, what determines how the elements of a research project get separated and dealt with very much depends on how the researcher manages the genre of the research statement. The role of genre is a vital component in defining data within any research project. In the context of contemporary education, we are very used to the idea that statistical information constitutes a 'data set': and that this kind of object is taken to have special properties of revelation for knowledge about education. Vast sums of money, in fact, are dedicated to funding projects that seek to return to familiar educational objects – forms of inequality, for instance – to define their conditions and modes of being differently. Such data is deployed to present a case usually about refining understanding of forms of inequality, often in relation to the shifting sands of policy (Ball, 2005; Brown et al., 2015). Such projects may offer new interpretations of sources of inequality. In most cases, they will seek to do so by providing data to clinch their case, and most usually what they will claim is 'new' data. So funded research projects will in many ways repeat and reinterpret existing knowledge but will frequently want to verify their case by presenting what is claimed as data that will confirm the interpretation they offer, thus again confirming the idea of a distinction between data and other elements of a research project.

The upshot is a kind of endless repetition of what has been known for a long time: that education systems generate inequalities. Such accounts rarely, if ever, address the ontological conditions that guarantee this continued story of inequity. They are honour bound, in fact, not to do so, as they must retain an attachment to the idea of reform, although the reforms that have been enacted through the history of education have brought little or nothing in the direction of social justice or equality (Bowles and Gintis, 1976). But researchers continue to produce data that confirms the thesis of education beset by inequalities. Such studies are invariably predicated on the – sometimes implicit sometimes explicit – assumption that present inequalities can be redeemed and that at some time in the past education took a wrong turn, became dominated by neo-liberalism and that ultimately education is salvageable as a liberal and egalitarian project. This entirely relies on an ethic of salvation and a (misplaced) faith in education and its modern apparatuses as vehicles for self-realization and social transformation (Ball, 2013; Power, 2003). All the data in the world, and all the subtle recalculations of data, and all the newly defined sources for data and the data they may generate cannot disturb the essential logic of reform and redemption that such studies perpetuate. It would take an ontological breakthrough, as it were, to effect such a rethinking. Those who perpetuate this logic – drawing large publicly funded grants in many cases – cannot countenance such a transformation. To do so would be to undermine their own existence. This sober lesson for the value and ontological status of data has far-reaching consequences and constitutes an important part of the argument of this book.

To declare that practices of revisiting familiar fields of research are essentially rhetorical might run the danger of being accused of scepticism. In other words, acknowledging or foregrounding the fact that such 'formulaic' practices are more about presenting a plausible case and following an already-legitimated procedure to produce an already-legitimated position. But this is not necessarily a negative charge. All social science research, and all educational research, could be seen as an intervention into an open field of debate where the characteristic gesture of the contributor to the field of knowledge is: What if as appears to be the case and if we revisit this through these perspectives or change our lenses in this way, the thing (that we are interested in) appears differently and we have revealed another or a different aspect or dimension of its being? This is quite different from the mode of presentation that says, in effect: this data demonstrates that this is the case. This speculative gesture is analogous to the kind of practice in textual studies that declares that, read rightly, a text will reveal certain insights and truths. 'How we must read *Great Expectations*' is the title of a chapter in a book published in 1970 by the Leavises, notorious for their insistence on certain incontestable modes of reading and interpretations (F.R. and Q.D. Leavis, 1970). A great deal of subsequent theory indicated that such an approach is essentially theological and belongs to a closed order of thinking. It might seem scandalous to suggest that the contemporary privileging of data in educational research within an ethic of improvement, reform or redemption belongs to a similarly theological mindset. But it does. The dominant paradigm of knowledge corresponds to what Heidegger identified as 'technological enframing', within an arena dominated by what Weber identified as 'instrumental rationality'. This dominance means that more speculative and inquisitive knowledge production in the interrogative form that asks 'What if ... ?' struggles to survive or at least to receive much credit.

The prominence accorded to data in the standard handbooks and in the dominant research model opens important questions about educational research and its most habitual ways of working. It opens an ethical question in the larger sense of that word, relating to matters of commitment and 'care'. A great deal of educational research that follows 'the standard model' actually misses out on some serious and important questions that are likely to be raised if the alternative, basic phenomenology model is followed.

Knowledge and narrative in Lyotard

Jean-Francois Lyotard's *The Postmodern Condition* (1986) is entitled a 'report on knowledge' but really is much more than that. In it Lyotard explores the effects of certain technological changes since the Second World War. Lyotard claims that these changes (that have intensified and accelerated dramatically since 1986) have produced a new relation to knowledge in transformed global information conditions and relations. The defining element in these technological changes is computerization, but in a context where the distribution of powerful knowledge is already geopolitical. Digital knowledge, as it were, puts us as a species in a different relation to knowledge but also means that the distribution and control of knowledge change form. One upshot of this transformation is that there arises, along with other tendencies we have noted throughout this book, the problem of legitimation of knowledge that does not emerge from a universally agreed authoritative source. How do forms of knowledge – especially when knowledge proliferates and accumulates within a relatively new and rapidly changing technological framework – claim legitimacy for themselves? In this movement, knowledge becomes intricated very visibly with power – scientific and technological power, for sure, but also with the power of institutions and the power of the archive – the power to determine what powerful knowledge is, what really counts and where such knowledge may reside and may be generated. For Lyotard, there can be no form of knowledge that isn't caught up with a kind of ideological power but more insistently perhaps with an institutional power that isn't identical with but that is strongly related to state and corporate power.

Anyone working in or attending a contemporary Western university will know the kinds of power issues at stake in the determination of knowledge. Elite Western universities operate as global centres for the accreditation of knowledge that they have deemed worthy of recognition on the global scene. Universities in the United States and in the United Kingdom have assumed this globalizing force. Shifts in the ordering of knowledge occur at global knowledge management centres. Such centres decide what knowledge is legitimate and who has access to such high-status systems and through what processes legitimation of knowledge may occur.

The knowledge economy runs in parallel with financial economy. It is indubitably the case that global satellite communications, with all their potential to reconfigure modes of communication, are managed by influential commercial interests that may have a significant say in the forms and even the kinds of data that are communicable. Access to the kind of data provided by satellite systems can be crucial as was made very visibly evident as early as the so-called first Iraq war in 1991 when images of satellite-guided missiles stunned Western TV audiences.

At the centre of Lyotard's account of the shift in knowledge is the idea drawn from Ludwig Wittgenstein concerning modes of communication. Lyotard proposes that the postmodern period is characterized significantly by a concern with language – and this correlates with Derrida's idea that writing becomes a metaphor for Being itself (Derrida, 1976). Leading sciences and technologies became concerned with language: theories of language itself, semiotics, communications theory, deconstruction are all centrally concerned with the centrality that language has for technological transformations in the dimension of knowledge.

Lyotard chooses the idea of *language games* to characterize developments in postmodernity. Wittgenstein's notion of the language-game expresses a cogent linguistic ontology, one that is hard in fact to argue against. Language games operate according to rules that are internal to themselves. The rules of any language game do not appeal to something external to that game for their justification or legitimation. They rely rather on the tacit agreements – agreements that always precede any individual use or user – for their binding power. One important aspect of this is the detachment of data from knowledge and the change in the ontological topology of knowledge: so that the time-honoured principle that knowledge inheres in individual minds and is associated thereby with judgement and wisdom can no longer apply.

Because of their relative autonomy, it turns out, according to Lyotard, language games are incommensurable: they operate quite differently from one another, according to different protocols, in line with different rules. Moves in one language game cannot be transposed simply into another language game. While language games are held together by social convention and the momentum of practice, they reveal at the same time an *agonistic* dimension. The games being played may be fraught with internal and external differences that involve quite different ways of being positioned for players. The element of contest means that even within language games interlocutors deploy strategies and tactics to affirm their own take on things. This account of social life as working through language games highlights the implicitly political nature of language and the inescapable bond between knowledge and power. For Lyotard, power and knowledge are held together in decisions about what legitimate knowledge is. The ontological implications for knowledge here are powerful. Despite our tendency to idealize certain forms of and orientations to knowledge, what counts as knowledge cannot be disentangled from the determinations of power.

Scientific knowledge lays claim to authority by its essential difference from narrative. In fact, in its privileging of method, scientific knowledge claims to make a purchase on reality that corresponds to the nature of the referent, the thing it refers to. Hence, science will make claims about the nature of nature that does not depend on some other authorizing source for its truth value, but that depends on the validity of method that can reveal a truth that is verifiable about the thing-in-itself. Latterly, science is seen to depend rather on falsification for its claim to validity, shifting its ontological status claims (Bacon, 1620; Popper, 1992). Scientific verification and scientific falsification both require a relation between a 'sender' and an 'addressee'. In other words, a scientific process requires a social context for its verification or falsifiability. Scientific procedures rely on the consensus of those who belong to the specific, synthetic scientific 'community' in question. Consensus is essential to this process, although science also must concede that consensus does not guarantee truth. A community must be generated and sustained – and this must be essentially a community of equals that is independent of other, non-scientific, community interests. Already things are getting complicated. Such disinterested communities are hard to find no doubt; insofar as such communities constitute 'worlds', they are necessarily beset by the same issues that attend any sphere of social existence. Such worlds require internal bonds and a framework of ideas to enable them to be coherent and consistent. It turns out that while such scientific communities seek to banish extraneous narrative elements from their practices, at some point they must resort to narrative to secure their bonds and express allegiance to some overriding purpose or meaning.

Modernity itself may be expressed as the retreat of narrative modes of knowledge for the more cognitive, abstract, denotative and logically rigorous kinds of procedure general associated with 'method' that science claims as its distinction from other, less rigorous modes of knowledge (Bacon, 1620). In Lyotard's vocabulary, science requires denotative language to be the order of the day and to effectively banish connotative language. Scientific language cannot afford to be contaminated by the connotative, that is open, indeterminate, poetic. These – denotative and connotative – are different poles of language that obey different rules for their arrangement into statements. The two forms of language are essentially incommensurable. For the scientific consciousness, narrative is connotative and belongs to a more primordial form of knowledge properly to be associated with myth, custom, ideology – not science.

But Lyotard insists that science itself cannot exist without recourse to narrative knowledge. Despite all efforts to banish narrative, science ends up being dependent on it. This is a characteristic way of thinking for deconstruction.

Lyotard's argument deconstructs the strict division between science and narrative. The point at which science and narrative most dramatically meet is perhaps in relation to matters of legitimation. Science relies on a certain myth or set of myths for its continuation. A range of narratives can be detected in the grand ideas that inform scientific practice and that lurk within the institutions that must justify their continued championing of science. There is an epic element to this myth. Science heroically and unselfishly works towards the liberation of humanity. Science is key to progress, to prosperity, to general well-being and, ultimately, to the survival of the species.

One further implication of Lyotard's position concerns an essential feature of the postmodern condition: that is, the end of grand narratives. Lyotard claims that in our time, grand or master narratives are no longer plausible. Grand narratives have lost credibility. The grand ends of modern thinking concerning the emancipation of humanity from its various ills and its realization of ideal condition have not only faltered but have been ultimately found out as empty promises. In the meantime, techniques and technologies of production and management have proliferated, shifting the emphasis from the pursuit of now implausible ends to the efficient management of processes. So it is, declares Lyotard, that 'performativity' becomes the order of the day. Technology serves the efficient rather than the 'true' and serves efficacy rather than emancipation. The input/output equation is the means to measure the goal of performance. This has become very much evident in educational institutions. All forms of knowledge on degree courses, for example, now have to demonstrate their value in terms of 'transferable skills'. The knowledge that such courses may purvey is not and cannot be an end in itself. Ultimately, it must be seen as the occasion for qualities that can be taken out into the world of production and activity for the function of sustaining prosperity. Performative then becomes the measure of the 'truth' of a practice, the 'proof' of efficacy. According to Lyotard, there is a very dark side to this tendency. Scientific ideas or insights that threaten to destabilize the order of things may experience suppression. Lyotard goes so far as to suggest that such actions can be 'terroristic' in that they may banish legitimate players from the game if their contribution threatens to interrupt the efficient flow of knowledge as perceived by the 'community' whose world order has been threatened.

Lyotard deployed the term 'modern' to refer to 'any science that legitimates itself with reference to a metadiscourse', making an appeal to 'some grand narrative' often in the name of 'a great progressive odyssey' (Lyotard, 1986, xxiii). The grand narrative mode Lyotard refers to frequently entails a teleological vision of mastery, expressing faith in progress, celebrating the conquest of nature. Lyotard argues that, on careful scrutiny, modern forms of knowledge cohere only vaguely and in practice subscribe to no specific narrative of meaning. Fragmentation is the order of the day, as Paul Feyerabend claimed; residual grand narratives are exhausted and have been displaced by the 'petits recits' that inform the micro-practices that constitute a decentred world social, intellectual and cultural order.

One of the powerful fictions that sustains educational research is the ethic of improvement frequently tied to a narrative that education is essential to the well-being of the individual and the collective at the same time (despite evidence that education hierarchizes the social). The fiction of educational research to be progressive, to work towards social justice, to be central to any positive vision of the future is written into the very fabric of educational research practice. But Lyotard's way of thinking disturbs this educational research order. Problematizations arise instantly when the various modes of research are considered with their borders and discrete orientations and practices that have the potential to contradict one another. History, philosophy and the politics of knowledge in educational studies all have the potential to undermine the pretentions of the grander narratives of reform and redemption that dominate. For researchers, finding themselves within the differentiated field of educational research but also confronting the myths of reform and redemption decisions must be made concerning this condition. If grand narratives remain, education is perhaps the best example of a residual 'master' narrative. That does not, of course, mean that the grand narrative of educational discourses is legitimate. I would suggest that there are powerful reasons for thinking otherwise. But it remains dominant.

At stake in this question of education and grand narrative is the ontological status of education in modernity/contemporaneity. On another, anti-grand narrative view, education appears not as the neglected or misshapen modern product that has turned against its proper Greek or enlightenment ideal form but as that extensive, productive apparatus that has in modern biopower become the most pervasive instance of 'the secret matrix and nomos of our time', to recontextualize Agamben (Agamben, 1997, 106). Contemporary education provides the occasion for a revisiting of the ontological legacy of modernity. This revisiting cannot avoid questions concerning what is proper to both philosophy and history. Further, neither of these domains of knowledge can avoid confronting the question concerning the politics of knowledge. The institutions of knowledge and discourses of education appear in our time as quintessential expressions of the contemporary state of the global world order.

Education as a discourse of knowledge rarely acknowledges its complicity in a global politics of knowledge, a complicity that compromises its own positive self-image (Peim and Martin, 2001). In approaching the politics of educational knowledge, the Derridean distinction between 'avenir' and 'futur' has seriously deconstructive, even catastrophic, consequences for currently dominant mode of thinking in key fields of educational knowledge – where the residual grand narratives still hold sway as expressions of an anachronistic allegiance to a project that is evidently no longer plausible.

Ways of thinking beyond the 'technological enframing' of 'educare'/ biopower are perfectly possible, however, and may reach beyond the ontotheological commitments of current educational discourses. That space beyond might be characterized as 'the empty space of truth', to paraphrase Derrida. It necessitates thinking in terms of an unprogrammed 'avenir' as opposed to a determinate 'futur' predicated on ways of thinking and an apparatus that are caught up with the 'instrumental rationality' of predicted management (Dick and Kofman, 2002).

Knowledge, archive, spectrality

If data is not to be thought of as equivalent to knowledge, we might ask, What is knowledge? Since it is what we seek in research. We might also, being historically mindful of ourselves, ask, What is the structure of knowledge in our time? Asking fundamental questions like this can be useful and illuminating, although it can also be frustrating as the object of our quest, as Plato's dialogues frequent reveal, seems to recede the more we interrogate its very essence.

We are often invited to think of a stock or store of knowledge, representing the accumulated data garnered by generations of agents and long-standing institutions of knowledge. In many cases, such storehouses are venerated and carry great symbolic authority and status often related to national identity and prestige. We may think of the British Museum (established in 1753) or the Smithsonian Institution (established in 1846 'for the increase and diffusion of knowledge') as embodiments of this phenomenon of the archive. These venerated institutions hold items that carry with the cache of culture and knowledge.

In Derrida's *Specters of Marx*, 'the spectral' signifies the appearance of something calling for an unfulfilled or disturbed past to be fulfilled in some redeemed future (Derrida, 1994). The spectre – 'revenant' – apparently coming from the past at the same time, paradoxically, represents a call from the future towards fulfilment of unfinished business, disrupting linear time. Knowledge, as representation where one 'present' element stands in for another, absent, element, shares this spectral structure. Insofar as knowledge is communicable and belongs to the order of representation, knowledge has a spectral, incomplete, future-oriented ontology.

Derrida coins a term for this, 'hauntology', to get across the dual ideas of ontology and the spectral, an idea that clearly echoes the deconstruction of the metaphysics of being-as-presence in earlier writings: 'the spectral, says Derrida, is what exceeds all ontological oppositions between absence and presence, visible and invisible, living and dead' (Rottenberg, 2002, 5). In an interview, Derrida remarks on the deconstructive dimension of 'hauntology' invoking an earlier lexicon:

> the concept of the spectral has a deconstuctive dimension because it has much in common with the concepts of trace, of writing and differance, and a number of other undecidable motifs. (Derrida, 2001, 44)

Recollecting that

> The play of differences supposes, in effect, syntheses and referrals which forbid at any moment, or in any sense, that a simple element be present in and of itself, referring only to itself ... Nothing, neither among the elements nor within the system, is anywhere ever simply present or absent. There are only, everywhere, differences and traces of traces. (Derrida, 1987, 26)

Knowledge cannot, according to this logic, answer to a desire for the revealing of 'beings themselves', in Heidegger's terms, in full presence. Data does not constitute such a revelation and is literally meaningless without the supplement of narrative. The dimension of time, the interplay of what is present with what it signifies (that is absent, although signified) indicate the spectral: a presence signifying an absence, both haunted and haunting. There is something incomplete in the very 'nature' of the spectre (Abraham, 1994, 171). The spectre, classically, conventionally understood, is the past returning: an incomplete life, an unresolved issue, some uncanny thing, something to be tested, verified and confirmed or 'falsified'. Spectrality problematizes truth as present in the very object – or data – that supplies it: 'the thinking of the spectre, contrary to what good sense would lead us to believe, signals toward the future' (Derrida, 1994, 245). The future comes to demand attention, and often action, to reveal the untold or unconscionable truth. Hence, the spectre is restless, unquiet and demanding, but demanding of a truth to come, not a truth arrived at. Surely this resonates with the ontology of data, where data cannot be seen, on its own, as constitutive of what we call knowledge. Knowledge, as we know it, requires the embrace of narrative, as Lyotard insists – and as we may amplify here. Narrative is what shapes data in its spectral form into coherence, logic and meaning that partakes of temporal logic. The narrative dimension in research is inescapable.

The archive as store of data and repository of established knowledge stands as a bulwark of authority. 'Commencement' and 'commandment' are invoked as co-ordinate principles of order and containment in the early pages of Derrida's account of the logic of knowledge in *Archive Fever* (Derrida, 1996). The archive is expressive of the power to both institute and to maintain authoritatively. Derrida's exploration of the archive renders problematic any logic of knowledge that expresses itself in terms of a revealing of an absent presence, of the disclosure of the being-as-presence of the past. Rather the logic of the archive that Derrida rewrites suggests that the archive is structured by inherited power, is constantly in need not only of protection but also of carefully monitored and scrutinized renewal. This indicates something of the logic of research that must both produce something new – 'an original contribution to knowledge' – and that must, at the same time, conform to the law of genre, to obey the established canon of knowledge.

Two key insights of *Archive Fever* – (1) that technologies of communication determine the archive (Derrida, 1996, 16) and (2) that 'archivization produces as much as it records' (Derrida, 1996, 16) – suggest productive possibilities for rethinking a philosophy of knowledge as well as, I would suggest, for rethinking a historical ontology of education in our time. 'Archivization' indicates a process, an ongoing work of reproduction. If we recall Foucault's statement concerning the relations between truth, fiction, history and politics that appears in Chapter 4, we can see a similar sense of a mobility of relations between these key dimensions – in Foucault's terms, at least – of knowledge. What comes first is not clear, nor is the order of production between these dimensions ordained in advance. In Foucault's statement, we can perhaps 'hear' a message to the future of Derrida's spectrality – or hauntology – providing a series of resources for rethinking the temporal relations of history, truth and identity in relation to what knowledge is (Derrida, 1994).

The recent history of educational research has included a discourse of preservation, a desire to return to a more purposeful and ordered past where the functions of the discourses of philosophy and history of education were more clear and where their clear separation was regarded as both proper and productive (Hammersley, 2007; Herbst, 1999; Pring, 2000). The age of Hirst and Peters, often referred as the founding 'fathers' of the philosophy of education, now looks, surely, like the time of a naively positivist fantasy where philosophy could serve and explain, illuminate even, and refine the practical business of education, defining the true categories of knowledge and the most appropriate pedagogies (Hirst and Peters, 1970). The self-appointed archons enjoyed an untroubled faith in the virtue of their project as well as in the order of knowledge that they guarded. Many have since lamented the intrusion of modes of thinking and ways of knowing that appear to dissolve the very function of history and philosophy in their proper relation to the grand project of education. Hospitality to potentially disturbing and disruptive discourses (in the Anglo-Saxon context often referred to negatively as 'continental') has not been unequivocal. Canny advocates have often reclaimed such disturbances to the established project of educational research – predicated essentially on progress and improvement – as new theoretical tools to be deployed towards the same-old purposes.

Derrida's rethinking of the ever-decaying and renewing archive provides a way of thinking, to address the preservation of knowledge. What is to be preserved? What knowledge is 'proper' to the field of education? Practical researchers privilege the practical business of empirical research, subordinating theory to that greater purpose (Ball, 2013). But that assumption of a given order of purpose avoids confrontation with the ontological question, 'the question of questions' that as Heidegger suggested transforms philosophy and problematizes all questions of the meaning of Being. Security of genre, security of priorities, a clear sense of purpose: these safeguard the proper, what belongs, by right, within the place that is protected from improper intrusion by the procedures, processes and ceremonies of entry. Officially sanctioned writing must have passed through a complex series of *rites de passage*, structured to guarantee that the writing in question warrants acceptance. But this ambit, this apparently bordered space, is always, necessarily, uncertainly bounded, except by the conventions and protocols supervised by the 'archons' kept intact by their actions and decisions. The archons are empowered to decide what's in, what's out. Beyond the proper lie possibilities that signify the danger of transformation.

History provides an interesting example of the relations between narrative and the idea of a proper identity for a specific form of knowledge. Traditionally, it is Thucydides's *History of the Peloponnesian War* that marks the moment of the origin of a history that can – and does self-consciously – claim itself to be free from the vagaries of myth. The insistence on the empirical is accompanied by scrupulous attention to a temporal ordering, as though narrative itself could replicate the truth of sequence. But even the godless Thucydides constructs his narratives and his analyses in terms of a dominant idea that the driving force of history is a force powerful enough to displace the Homeric gods. The problem with Thucydides is perhaps the faith the text expresses in its own method. But the genre is clearly dominated by its own categories that, after Barthes and Ricoeur, for example, would themselves be reinterpreted as mythical – and as fraught with faith as Homer (Barthes, 1973; Ricoeur, 1990; Ricoeur and Kearny, 1978).

In modernity, myth, apparently banished by Thucydides, returns to the field of knowledge to distress any Liebnizian vision of order as the triumph of 'the principle of reason' (Heidegger, 1991). Of course, it should not be necessary to remind ourselves that Liebnizian reason is not reason itself and that the project of engaging with reason may have long been associated with instrumental rationality but that that is not its only nor, indeed, its best and most productive modality. Let's not forget, too, that one major form of reason or, perhaps we should rather say, of reasoning, is deconstruction in the sense of an interminable engagement both with specific concepts and with the conceptual apparatus that sustains such concepts at the same time, without resting at either premises or conclusions that ever enjoy the status of first cause or final terminus (Derrida, 1978). As with Foucault's engagement with history, truth, fiction and politics outlined briefly above, there is neither original origin nor ultimate teleology.

For education, with its frequent assumption of a necessary grounding in practice, one major problem is that much research is and has been conducted as directed towards the practicable as the authenticating substance or meaning of the work (Carr, 2007; Thomas, 2007). Any hint of fiction, or 'fictioning', must be met with disapproval for the evidence-based-practice movement and its marriage to the ethic of research as improvement or redemption (Fullan, 2001; Hopkins, 2001).

But for Foucault, it seems, 'fiction' can never be a charge levelled against the truth of any writing. Fiction is not a measure of inadequacy. But Foucault's strangely rich and provocative statement – ostensibly about his own writing – has powerful implications about the relations between (not the nature of) writing, politics, reality, fiction and truth. For Foucault, there can be no eradication of fiction as an improper element, or genre, within this knotty series. Fiction is a route to truth. If we find this uncomfortable, and perhaps we should, we might recall the commonplace association between narrative and fiction. Fiction, in Foucault's sense, means fashioning, or making something – or making something up.

We can identify examples of this necessity of fiction immediately. In the field of educational research, a powerful fiction reigns: a fiction strongly embedded in the practices and ethics of the institution; a fiction that defines the truth for the production of writing that seeks to guarantee its relation to truth. This fiction has a generative power: it defines and determines the proper form, style, type of contents, mode of address and relations between elements. The proper form of writing in the official discourses of the academy, its organs, institutions and inhabitants is organized in relation to this dominant fiction. And there can be no doubt that this production and reproduction of a procedure for truth – as Foucault has now indicated – is political in character. In Foucault's ontology of truth, the political is an inescapable feature. In the context of contemporary mainstream educational research discourses, the dominant political character is tied to the ethic of improvement and to the continued faith in instrumental rationality.

The current emphasis on impact is a symptom of this politically powerful, strongly enforced ethic. At the same time, we can also see that in oppositional discourses there reigns another powerful fiction: the fiction of the redemption of education and the restoration of its 'true', enlightenment function. While fiction, it seems, from Foucault's logic, is necessary, it is not necessarily this fiction. This particular fiction can only hold sovereign sway by keeping its fictional status secret. But this secret is what is known as an open secret, and it soon becomes a matter of commitment, of faith in the proper deployment of the power of reason, that sustains it as truth. The fiction in question is intricated with the ontotheological faith that dominates contemporary discourses and practices in the field of education. That faith sustains the myth of education as the essential vehicle of sustainability and improvement.

Writing and research: Anxieties and the necessity of myth (narrative)

Narrative is not really an optional addition for the researcher, a mere supplement to data. Narrative means writing: producing a coherently articulated, inscripted case. For Derrida, ontological questions have a necessary relation to writing. Grammatology, Derrida's proposed 'science' of writing, begins from the insight that writing increasingly has become a metonymy for Being, including the expressions of code and grammar in life sciences. Grammar in this grammatological sense, in spite of liberal disavowals, is significantly a matter of good manners, of etiquette, requiring a certain obeisance to the unwritten as well as the explicitly codified rules of the game. Identity, in terms of becoming an initiate member of a group or, more grandiosely, a community, involves induction into this social grammar (Derrida, 1976, 1978).

In Heideggerian terms, identity is the outcome of aligning one's being with the 'mitwelt' of shared ideas, values and ways of doing and being in the world that precedes any individual existence. Any privileging of the individuality of individual existence is a kind of error of thinking it forgets or negates this dimension of being-with. But this is not to fall in with a naïve version of community as warm, nurturing soil of identity. 'Dasein' – the term designed to avoid positing a purely subjective subject – inhabits a world of worlds. The 'world' of dasein is specific. It makes a claim on identity, demands commitment. In the world of the academy, dasein always stands in a defining relation to genres of subject identity (Heidegger, 1962).

In Heidegger's fundamental ontology, any vantage point, any specific way of being in the world is organized by a structure of anxiety, a structure that is predicated on the relations between the world of one's being and the nothing that necessarily borders that world. Anxiety is the relentless driving force that invests the concrete fictions of our worlds with truth. It is against this contingent nothing, against the threat of nihilation that a world is constructed, developed and subjected to an attitude of care. The bits and pieces of any world constitute a set that requires generic knowledge to manage, to inhabit and to dwell within (Heidegger, 1962). In this sense, genre expresses a relation to, perhaps always a commitment to, such a gathering and such a grammar of existence. Narrative is a mode of realizing this grammar.

The question of genre in educational writings can be read as a symptom of an anxiety – never far away – that is particularly acute in the humanities, where subject identity is always problematically bordered. It is particularly pressing in educational studies, where the very right to exist and to qualify depends on the adherence to certain generic reassurances. Most commonly in educational studies is the reining in of flights of theory to ensure its subordination to the demands of practice and impact.

If the purpose of educational studies cannot be solidly grounded in the empirical world of practice, so the story goes, then the game (in the Wittgenstein sense) is in danger of being up. Hence the necessity to restore the focus to the proper. This anxiety, which frequently finds fully explicit expression within the strange domain of the philosophy of education, is also evident in all the ready-to-hand assumptions about the proper nature of educational research. In educational studies, research statements frequently labour under an assumed requirement to be more than 'merely' constative. The performative has become a kind of proper mode of educational research. What else might guarantee the value and integrity of the work? Educational research often feels itself under an obligation to positively 'make a difference', to effect improvement within the grand project of the relatively grand narrative of progress.

While established knowledge has to guard against the dangerous incursion of the other, at the same time, knowledge has to guard against the monumental tendencies of the institution. It must replenish and renew itself. Knowledge is always a body to be both respected and violated, held in place and disturbed, revered and assaulted. The archive, perhaps, is the name for this process, rather than a place of stabilities. The archive is a place where stability and tradition labour against destruction and renewal. The archive is a fictional bulwark against and a victim of the constant and remorseless transformation of the present into the past. The institution monitors this process and safeguards its propriety. Knowledge dwells within the institution. What lies outside of the institution cannot claim the identity of institutionalized knowledge. The metaphor of the 'oikos' or hearth inspires the identity of the archons, those who preserve and sustain the archive. In the early pages of *Archive Fever*, as indicated above, 'commencement' and 'commandment' are invoked as co-ordinate principles of order and enclosure, expressive of the power to institute and to maintain in order. In this account, the metaphor of place is aligned with the idea of knowledge as event, and with the idea of things in their place: an archive is, ideally, a place where things can be held, organized and defined in their proper relations: an ontological order, in other words (Derrida, 1996).

Order is always problematized by the movement of time. In *Archive Fever*, the problematization of the metaphysics of presence that is habitual in Derrida's thinking concerns the preservation and reproduction of knowledge. The movement of time corresponds with the movement of meaning that generates the danger of dissemination, the dangerous proliferation of meanings that threatens to escape the order of the archive.

The archive raises a question of domiciliation: What threshold is to be maintained for this residence, and maintained by whom through what process? The etymology of 'archive' indicates a resonance with residence – 'arkheion' as the residence also of the archons, the guardians who operate under the 'law' and who themselves are enclosed, as are the archives, under a 'house arrest' and subject to a labour of interpretation. The practice of consignation (Derrida, 1996, 4) implies putting into order, keeping 'in place' and 'institutionalization' as well as a history of this gathering, ordering and guarding: but there is, in relation to the archive 'a deconstructable history', leading to the statement that where the archive is concerned: 'Order is no longer assured' (Derrida, 1996, 5). There is a crisis of order in the field of knowledge (see Chapter 5). This crisis is productive.

Education as myth

The insistence in educational research on a determinate genre is expressive of a technology of knowledge seeking to determine what belongs where within a normative mode. It provides a framework and logic for the writing of research that is already programmed. It operates as a closed system that discourages invention and creativity.

Unconditional openness, what Derrida has referred to as 'unconditional hospitality', allowing for otherness and difference no matter what, is an impossible condition. Even thinking this thought momentarily, Derrida insists, negates its possibility. Unconditional openness of the borders is not possible. There are always conditions. There will always be decisions as to what and who may pass, implying, in turn, that there must always be some exertion of force and authority, at the borders, checking the papers, scrutinizing the credentials. In hospitality, there is the force that moves to embrace the other and the force to restrain, to remain untouched and retract from the other, trying to keep the threshold carefully guarded.

The controls that render unconditional hospitality an impossibility in the institutions of knowledge are the effect of a more or less arbitrary power and force. This might seem shocking but reflects the logic of knowledge as it is in our world, dominated by powerful university interests under the injunction to demonstrate 'impact'. Such controls must always stand both in need and in receipt of criticism: they must be 'deconstructed'. But deconstruction is not ever sufficient to achieve completion: it is not a state, present-to-itself and fulfilled. It is necessarily interminable. Deconstruction can never deliver justice. The guardians and the terms of guardianship of what belongs and what, in the form of the new, can be welcomed, must be subjected to the interminable deconstruction that is the necessary condition of a movement towards a hospitality that can never arrive. At this point in the argument, questions concerning the ethics of research arise, for the researcher must ask themselves, at some point, surely, Where do I stand in this ordered order of things?

Many commentators now claim, since Lyotard, at least, that the world of knowledge is in a state of crisis. The cultural critic Walter Benjamin's relatively early twentieth-century theses posit a condition of crisis that is always already with us (Benjamin, 1999). What if we were to take this condition of crisis seriously, as the ontological condition of modernity/contemporaneity? And what if, following hints from Benjamin's acolyte, Agamben, we were to see this condition of crisis as being, in an essential way, related to if not a product of, the dominance of the social by education (Agamben, 1997)? Would this thought not impel us to rethink our relations with both the world-dominating fact of education and the discourses that serve it. The world of education is fuelled by research that renews its right to claim a privileged purchase on knowledge.

If modernity and contemporaneity are characterized by the extension and magnification of education and by the elevation of education to an ontotheological principle, then surely the purveyors of the research ethic should ponder the meaning of this condition and render some account of it and its role in the world. As researchers are we not honour bound, as it were, to engage with such questions? We are not likely to be confronted by them when we are asked by the formal procedures of the university to fill out an ethics form designed to minimize harm and embarrassment. Where do we stand in relation to the 'archive', to the established order of knowledge, to the narratives that dominate our present horizons? These questions are neither hard nor too obscure for any researcher to answer, and to answer without reaching for the everyday clichés of educational research (e.g. to 'make the world a better place').

Education has become the primary ground for the political: a panacea for social ills, the context for schemes for improvement, the driving force of the economy. Education, we are constantly told, will effect social justice and in the new politics of happiness will redistribute well-being as well as securing national cohesion and puissance. Education has become a dominant myth in the deep sense, that is, as the ontotheological principle of reason, virtually foreclosed to interrogation. At the same time – and this is the darker corollary of its mythic status – education functions as a now globalized biopower, a transnational mechanism of governance, determining identities, forming selves, defining collectivities, enclosing knowledge, distributing cultural capital – a vast, unbordered technology of information and population management. No longer seeking to mask inequalities, education discourses now constantly highlight them within a mythological structure that sustains the very inequalities it claims to challenge with the empty promise of redemption through improvement.

Despite the essential governmental function of post-1800 education, despite the persistent history of education-sponsored inequality, the myth of education as salvation persists. The figure of the teacher–hero offering both social and spiritual redemption remains a powerful mytheme driving the desire that informs its more technological supplements. Similarly, the mythic 'science' of pedagogy justifies the vast extension of population management through bureaucracy that is schooling. Here, where the 'iron cage' of bureaucracy is conjoined with the spirit of individual and collective salvation, Michelle Pfeiffer, who stars as the redeeming teacher in the Hollywood film *Dangerous Minds*, and Max Weber, dark thinker of the 'iron cage' of life in modernity, join hands.

No amount of data can redeem this analysis I have offered above; at the same time, this is not what 'counts' as significant within the prevailing regime of research in education.

The dimension of language

The dimension of language is complex, subtle and interesting. For the researcher, it is inevitable: there is no escaping language. It is the medium of existence, the 'house of being' (Heidegger, 1993b). It is certainly the medium of research. Each research enterprise makes an intervention into language. A research thesis is a new account of something, an intervention into discourse. Language is there from the outset, demanding that we explain ourselves, insisting that we lay claim to the significance of our project, inviting us to 'give an account' of our object, its conditions of existence, its claim to attention, our point of intervention, demanding we explain our interest, even ourselves (Butler, 2005). Language determines the nature of the object we seek to explain.

Language is metaphysical, and is bound up with our thinking, much more than we conventionally realize (Derrida, 1978, 1976). Language gives identity to things, sets them in order, taxonomizes the world (Foucault, 1977b, 1981). Language is the grammar of our thinking, organizing the connections we can make between things. Language constitutes the symbolic order that shapes our world, determines categories of things and differences within categories. Language is a complex series of differences that articulates the world – breaking it up into separate entities, constituting how we see, experience and even feel about the nature of things (Lacan, 2006). Language mediates the world outside: its grammar and its protocols define our relations with the Other. Language constitutes a horizon for us. At the same time, in a very powerful, ontological, way, language is inside us. It shapes the substance of our being. It is the medium we experience our identity in: our heritage, our status, our individuality and our connections with those to whom we are most connected. How we speak, what we say expose who we are.

Knowledge itself is very much a matter of language: to know a field of knowledge or practice – from carpentry to nuclear physics – is to know your way around a form of language, a specific vocabulary and discourse (Foucault, 1981; Wittgenstein, 1968).

But language is also mobile. It changes. Language has and is history. Language is obviously also social and cultural. While it signifies belonging and identity, it also signifies difference. It is socially stratified. Subcultural groups generate their own forms of language and require members to be inward with specific modes of use. Language is also the field and occasion of dispute. In common parlance, we often hear the phrase 'You say that …', meaning that while you contend such a thing or such a state of affairs to be the case, we might speak or write differently of it, contesting the account you offer, suggesting that your language is open to contest, even perhaps that you or your way of speaking or writing have misrepresented the nature of the thing of which you speak (Lyotard, 1988). It is a function of the social that in the world of activity and practice differences of language are acted out (Bourdieu, 1991). The identity of any thing is not given. Identities are forged in language.

There are powerful reasons why the researcher, particularly in the social sciences, and perhaps more particularly in the field of education, should be attuned to matters of language – and to the relations between language, identity and discourse. From the very beginning, research seeks to rethink the object it addresses. It must do so in and through language.

The mobility of language, its uncertain point of reference, its changing interpretation, its structural openness and its social dimension are all aspects of an indeterminacy – a spectrality – that, as recent history of modern linguistics and modern philosophy demonstrate, is ontological. We know that different languages engage with the world differently but it is also the case that different aspects or arenas of language, different language games or different discourses, represent the world according to their own specific and very varied determinations and logics (Sapir, 1929; Whorf, 1956). Consider everyday practices such as football or carpentry. These have their own discursive formation their own vocabulary often designating the special objects they speak of or refer to. A good deal of modern thinking about language suggests that these discursive practices are actually 'world' forming: they do not so much reflect entities that are already out there in the world; they represent a certain way of being in the world, a certain configuration that expresses a specific range of interests and concerns. Hence the necessary bond between language and the identity of things, or metaphysics.

The mobility in language operates at many levels. The things of the world are not simply given over to language: language determines the nature of things – hence we can speak of a politics of language, a political element in discourse insofar as language has a hand in defining 'the Real', or reality. And we all know that these things are open always to difference and dispute (Lyotard, 1988). What's more, the thinking of language that characterizes much intellectual effort of the twentieth century reminds us that the systemic nature of language, its grammar, does not have any necessary correspondence with the world that it is purported to describe, define or analyse.

When we speak of language, though, we are using an abstraction. No one can reveal or lay out in from of themselves 'their' language. Language in that sense is not a given property of an individual – or group or culture – but is always emergent, a totality we can only glimpse in temporally disjointed specific instances. Here we encounter something elusive in language, a totality that is imagined. The famous distinction in language between 'langue' and 'parole' (general and particular, system and utterance) is predicated on what is in effect an imaginary object: the whole of language (de Saussure, 1922). A specific instance of language always thus refers to and is dependent on something other than itself – and something that cannot be demonstrated, only suggested by a further instance of the specific. In this sense, language must be always incomplete and each utterance, no matter how extensive and elaborated, will remain in a state of incompletion. Even *War and Peace* cannot say everything there is to say about war and peace.

When we speak of language, we often imply an entity out there that corresponds to the world, some 'thing' that has consistent properties, a delimited existence, and stands in a determinate relation to the nature of things (Russell, 1918; Wittgenstein, 1961). In fact, language as a whole is an abstraction. But language is also a convenient fiction or perhaps a necessary fiction, something that is not 'there', although something that is constantly in use and active. We know that it's not 'there' in any conventional, demonstrative sense and yet we need to refer to in order to be able to make sense of an absolutely important dimension of our world and our thinking.

There are languages of course, and we can apprehend these entities in terms of their grammar, their semantic content in relation to their characteristic syntax, the rules that govern the combination of different semantic elements they deploy. We've known for some time that different languages have different ways of representing even quite fundamental dimensions of the world, like time, place and spatial relations. It has been suggested that different language represent different ways of *being* in the world and that in some cases these differences can be quite marked (Wittgenstein, 1968). In this we encounter the unsettling realization that the common idea that languages represent things out there in the world is not sustainable. Something quite other is going on. Consider the fact that translation is always conceived of as a business of approximation; one translation of a text may differ radically from another. The indeterminacy that there is in translation tells us something fundamental about language and its ontological status.

Jean Francois Lyotard, author of *The Postmodern Condition*, explored the ontological dimension of language in T*he Differend* that carried the subtitle 'phrases in dispute' (Lyotard, 1988). Lyotard proposed thinking about language in specific contexts as 'phrase regimes', in other words as an ordering what could be said and a determination what cannot be said. Such a view of language implies strongly that what language designates may be quite different in different phrase regimes. In one example, Lyotard explores a dispute about land in Australia. A mining conglomerate defines the land as a quite different something from an aboriginal group. What's more, there is no mediation possible between these two positions. Each side, in some fundamental sense, occupies the world differently, or, we might say, equally, occupies a different world. In Lyotard's terms, borrowed from Wittgenstein, we might say that the two disputing parties are playing different language games. Yet another way of putting this radical difference is to say that the conflicting sides in this dispute are expressing themselves in relation to different discourses. A discourse in this sense shapes what it is that you understand to be the nature of the thing it refers to; but discourse in this sense also indicates something of a way of thinking and feeling about an element of 'your' world. What's more, discourse indicates something about who you are involved with and what your primary attachments in the social world are. In all of this, world and discourse are strongly correlated (Bernstein, 1971, 1973; Bourdieu, 1991).

If, for Heidegger, language is a horizon of being we can make sense of that idea in terms of understanding both that and how language shapes our being in the world, in the most inward and far-reaching ways, as the 'differend' case above, and many others that Lyotard elaborates. Noam Chomsky, writing from a very different perspective, offers another angle on the ontological provenance of language. For Chomsky, language is hard-wired into the human organism. Not that we are all born with language. That is clearly not the case. Rather, Chomsky asserts that we are all born with something he referred to as a 'language acquisition device' and this is something that belongs to our species-being, a product of evolution that is universal. This language acquisition device is what enables children – when very, very young – to acquire language extremely quickly and in such a way that they become creatively proficient users in an otherwise inexplicable time span (Chomsky, 2000). Chomsky has powerful reasons for claiming that there is this inbuilt propensity to language. Where he faced great difficulties, in spite of the inventive brilliance of his efforts, was in demonstrating what he thought must be there – an underlying, universal grammar that lay 'behind', as it were, all existing, specific instantiations of language.

Why is this engagement with the very nature of language important for the social science researcher, for the researcher who might be interested in exploring some crucial aspect or element of educational practice, for instance, in order better to understand how it works and perhaps with a view to suggesting improvements? The point here is to emphasize the extent that language constitutes a horizon for our being but also, of course, a horizon for our knowledge (Gadamer, 1989). The process of acquiring language happens to us when we are very young, too young to be in control of what is happening. We find ourselves caught up in the mesh of language, given a position, an identity and within a world that is ordered for us in and through language and that includes, crucially, a social world. Language carries with it a sense of our place in the scheme of things – a scheme that has its own specific syntax and semantics. When we were young, we were hardly aware that we were being lured – or interpellated, as Althusser would have it – into way of thinking, feeling and knowing that would provide the grounding for future attempts to understand the nature of things (Althusser, 1984b). Coming to consciousness of this fundamental feature of our being-in-the-world is one significant component of becoming a researcher who might be aware of the constitutive role that language plays in defining the object and context for a research endeavour.

Discourse in education: Reform, redemption

What do we mean by discourse? Provisionally, we can perhaps agree that discourse refers to language used in specific contexts of practice and meaning. The element of discourse is inescapable. But in research practice, it can be approached with varying degrees of self-consciousness: from being ignored to being the entire focus of the work in hand. It's worth recalling, though, in what ways discourse can be mapped onto a research project, what elements of the mapping of the project can be addressed from a perspective that is sensitive to the dimension of discourse. Discourse is such however that there can be no neat mapping of discourses onto the topography of the research project, no matter how carefully that might have been drawn. For reasons outlined above, though, it is worth identifying the various discursive areas that any social science research might address, returning again to the basic phenomenology of research relations that identifies possible aspects of any research project. In the field of education, discourses proliferate. Policy, literacy, behaviour management, information technology, pedagogy, ontology – and thousands of others are possible discourses within the field of education.

In the first place is the overarching discourse that pertains to the field of enquiry. There is a global discourse of education, in two senses, at least. First, there is the discourse that dominates the 'world' of education, the discourse that projects a series of ideas and ways of knowing, understanding and feeling about education (Brock and Alexiadou, 2013; Yin, 2005). This is the hegemonic discourse of education as a whole. This is the discourse invoked when anyone makes an assertion about the general significance of education in the world. This is the discourse at work when anyone claims that education is an end or a good-in-itself. In general, the world of education affirms that education is a supreme value and that – whatever the real world of educational practice with its specific institutions might be up to – overall and in general education is a force for good (Ranson, 1994; Roth, 2013). In this we encounter the ontotheological dimension of the discourse of education: the world embracing faith that education is a force for good. In this implicit order, education is frequently represented, automatically and without any recourse to argument or critical analysis, as offering salvation for the individual and for the social (Fullan and Hargreaves, 1998; Gorard, 2002; Tooley, 2009). Because of its established power, it is difficult to argue against this position, although it might be very important to do so, especially where, as is often demonstrably the case, educational institutions and educational practices do not have salvationary effects and may well be complicit with more negative aspects of the social formation.

The idea of education appears in discourses of our time configured according to a number of factors. One is the history of the rise of education. Education becomes a concern for governments in the nineteenth century and gradually enters powerfully into the domain of the political – initially in very different form from how we experience it now as a privileged element of a discourse of economic competitiveness, social cohesion and social progress (Donald, 1992; Hunter, 1988, 1994). The development of the general discourse of education follows an interesting history. The pioneers of nineteenth-century installation of schooling for all in the United Kingdom were concerned with providing basic literacy, social cohesion and a form of self-governing self-management useful for the demands of a globally powerful industrialized culture. The foundation of *elementary* education, as it was known, had nothing to do with ideas of equity or access or social mobility or self-fulfilment or self-realization. It was brazenly, if mostly unconsciously, socially divisive. It wasn't until well after the Second World War that discourses of social equity entered into the field of public education, although they had been rumbling away in the background among certain counter-hegemonic groups for a long time (Jones, 1977, 2003; Lowe, 1997). In the 1960s, implicit discourses of equality of opportunity became significant and influential in public discourses on the provision of education. Almost at the same time, education as a public discourse was beset with questions concerning relevance, efficiency and national puissance. In the 1980s, for many the comprehensive ideal, dedicated to equality of opportunity, was displaced by discourses seeking to restore a competitive, selective and ultimately elitist view of education at the level of both policy and practice within a neo-eugenicist idea about intrinsic ability and aptness for the academic pathway. The Education Reform Act of 1988 turned against the comprehensive ideal, installed a national curriculum and led to an inspection system that led to an ongoing insistence on performance against norms of attainment as the essential meaning of education 5–16 (DES, 1998).

Against this historical perspective, we can also chart the assumption of an enlightenment-inherited idea that education provides the key to human progress in general. In those systematically economically depressed or marginal parts of the world, education gets configured as the saving power. In specific national contexts education is often represented as the essential arena for development and for the healing of social ills. Education and the promotion of knowledge is seen as offering progress, even salvation and ultimately redemption (Tooley,

2009). This tends to work in two powerful, if often implicit, ways: (1) that education can be redeemed from its present failings; and (2) that education can redeem the social from its arbitrary inequalities and injustices. While neither of these positions can be justified by any evidence and certainly does not accord with the history of education as we know it, and while the sociology of education confirms time and time again the complicity of education with persistent forms of inequality, these ideas remain powerful throughout the sphere of education, even within its institutions and in general public and political understandings. Recently, President Barack Obama affirmed that education would be the grounds for equalizing and offering all the 'god-given right' to 'realize their potential' (Obama, 2009). While this is an old and sociologically discredited idea, it gets reaffirmed in public discourse and in many ways organizes ideas among educators and educational researchers.

This dominant discourse of redemption, progress and enlightenment proclaims that education is a necessary force for good and is rarely subjected to wholesale critical analysis. Critical education perspectives have tended to suggest that education – in some pure or ideal sense – is essentially the grounds for fulfilment. It is the failings and the political biases of policy makers and intrusive non-educational features that ruin the grand social goals of equality and enlightenment (Apple, 2014; Giroux, 2011, 2015). This position does have the advantage – especially for educators – of sustaining the idea that education can be and should be redeemed in order to fulfil its 'God-given' function (Obama, 2009). In fact, the ontotheological affirmation that education is redeemable, and is itself a form of redemption, may close off alternative modes of knowing and understanding. The problem is that the very idea that education might be an instrument for inequality, that education represents in itself a kind of social and cultural bias and that its hegemonic position is entirely mythological – this radically critical perspective has been entirely foreclosed so that it cannot even enter into contemporary arguments about the purposes and proper directions for education in practice (Peim, 2011, 2013a, 2013b). The myth of redemption sustains the world of education and educational research as it is.

The point of this discussion is to indicate an overarching discourse shaping our understanding of what education fundamentally is. Both education and the redemptive view is very much a global and globalized phenomenon. According to certain, rare, but nonetheless serious, versions of this view, education can be seen as a new kind of imperialism carrying the ethic of inequality through the world in the name of enlightenment. This is a discourse rarely heard in education, of course, in spite of its evident validity (Peim, 2011; Peim and Martin, 2011).

Discourse in education: An illustration

Any aspect, dimension or specific object that we might research in education falls within the discursive arena that frames education at large. But there is also a discursive framing for the specific object of study, the particular focus. My own doctoral research concerned English in secondary schools, in the 14–19 context that I taught in at the time. There were, I discovered, many dimensions to the interpretation and identity of this phenomenon. I had hardly considered that 'my' subject had a history, for example. That English was formed in response to various pressures, and institutional machinations during the late nineteenth and early twentieth centuries had not been part of my consciousness of things, of my understanding of the 'object' in question. According to some perspectives, English as a subject was originally formed as a dimension of colonial rule in India, being deployed to enculturate a subaltern population (Viswanathan, 1989). Essentially, the message was that English had emerged as a subject in parallel with the rise of a schooled society (Wardle, 1974). It emerged in different educational contexts and took shape differently in those contexts. It was shaped significantly by a discourse of national identity and cohesion from an early stage. The affirmation of a relatively recent – twentieth century – formulated idea of national culture and of cultural heritage gave a strong moral sense to English (Anderson, 1992; Doyle, 1989). It was to maintain the 'proper' distinction between real culture and popular culture and to work against the corruptions of language that non-standard forms threatened (Batsleer et al., 1985).

To understand English historically there was also a more recent history to take into account characterized, partly, by a conflict between traditional models that sought to maintain the privilege accorded to cultural heritage and a more liberal version seeking to promote creativity and seeking to recognize a wider sense of what literature might be to include, for example, the 'multi-cultural'. Curriculum history reflected these differences and tensions (Mathieson, 1975). At different levels, subject English was configured differently, representing different modes of existence for the subject that could not then be seen as a tight or consistent unity based on central and fundamental principles. Its existence, oddly, was both contingently juridical but surprisingly ideologically consistent.

During the 1980s, various critical positions emerged that impinged on subject identity questioning its historical formation, seeking to reinvent its substance and to review its ideological privileging of favoured elements. Similarly, sociological perspectives suggested that the constitution of English favoured certain social groups above others and claimed that despite rhetorics of inclusion informing the subject, it was deeply socially divisive and excluded significant cultural perspectives and denigrated certain linguistic orientations. Adjacent subjects challenged the hegemony of English. Cultural studies and media studies emerged to represent culture and cultural preferences differently offering alternative modes of textual engagement. Philosophy and linguistics also proposed different modes of textual analysis and understanding from those favoured by dominant models of English. Feminism affirmed the scandalous gender biases ingrained in the subject's very practices (Peim, 2003).

Turning to English to review its constitution in the light of these insights, things were not so easy to analyse or make sense of. For one thing, English varied from institution to institution. Even while we could see perhaps that there were consistencies, the subject held enough flexibility for one kind of practice in one kind of institution to differ greatly from another kind of institution in another sector of education. English in universities was more attuned to new ideas and challenges in the 1980s than English in schools, for instance. English was not consistent in either universities or schools, although it was more regularized in schools. In universities, changes occurred addressing some of the political questions of subject identity that never really appeared in English in schools. How could we make sense of this structural difference? Perhaps we would need to explore something of the features of the institution. After all, the context that the subject found itself in would significantly influence the nature of its being, surely? Would we then have to take a historical look at the university and the school? We would also not have to engage in some kind of institutional analysis of both? Despite much educational research, not much had considered providing any account of these institutional contexts. To understand English in schools, surely it would be important to understand schools; but the school did not feature as an object of research. There was little ready-to-hand thinking about what a school is, as most research assumed that a school was a certain type of thing with a certain type of mission (Peim, 2001).

On the question of the school, what perspective might address this? A basic phenomenology? Such a thing didn't exist for the school. Some philosophical promptings then might enable the construction of such a phenomenology so that we might be able to engage with a historical, social, cultural analysis or description at least, pausing perhaps to ask why this kind of question about basic apparatus had not previously been asked or explored.

Significant sociological discourses about the processes of schooling did exist (Bernstein, 1971, 1995; Bourdieu, 1991; Macherey, 1978). These put key assumptions of the subject, English, and of its practitioners into question. Practices were acted out in historically situated institutions that sustained value systems within a generally constrained, strongly patterned environment. So the question about what a school is, what its characteristic modes of operation are, how it configures learning, how it organizes identities, its overarching 'ethic' – again, appeared to become vital to any understanding of the context of operation for a school-based practice.

I came to feel that I needed to engage different discourses in any attempt to offer an account of the subject's being. For the school, I needed to construct a discursive topography of the institution to understand its symbolic spaces, its ideological structure and its division of identities as well as the variations in these that might pertain. Drawing on various sources, almost all outside the domain of English as a subject, I could begin to make sense of the spatial organization of the school, as an abstract entity and for schools that really existed in historical, social space.

Each of these elements of English could be explored through discourse, acknowledging the role of language in determining and sustaining the order of things as well as providing the means for a critique alternative positioning. In addition, my research asked me to revisit the question of where I stood among all these strands. What had been particular about my understanding of English teaching, accumulated through my subject orientation, developed through my formative engagement with the subject, my induction into the teaching profession, my professional experience with recontextualized versions of subject identity? Again, these significant elements have a linguistic, discursive dimension.

Language in the twentieth century: Implications for educational research

It is difficult to overestimate the importance of language in twentieth-century thinking. Latterly, discourse came for many to be essential to understand the meaning of any practice, its ideational structure, its limits, its distribution of identities and its contribution to knowledge. Any practice, from cosmology to knitting, it seemed, could be approached, interpreted and known through the specific form of the language it deployed. The world itself could be subdivided into its various discourses. The concept of discourse could cover more or less everything where meaning was in play: from football, to domestic life to the most rarefied practices of abstract thinking. Discourse seemed always to be at work. The discrete areas of social life as well as the most intimate conduct of personal life became illumined by the idea of discourse (Jorgensen, 2002; Macdonell, 1991).

The notion of discourse relates to the realization that the language we speak varies not only in terms of its overall grammar and syntax – as with English or Chinese or Hopi, say. Language also varies socially, according to different positions within the 'social division of labour' (Bernstein, 1971). Language use also varies according to what we are doing and what social and cultural space it occupies.

The dimension of language, or discourse, engages various ways of thinking that themselves can expand our articulation of the object we seek to explore and know in research practice. The thinking of discourse and the vast significance attributed to language is a major element of twentieth-century thinking. That thinking is far from exhausted. Language remains central to key issues and questions – and the dimension of discourse constitutes a field of 'data' rich in possibilities for exploration.

In modernity, language becomes an ontological principle. As the notion, Man, displaces God in the order of things in enlightenment thought, so in the twentieth century Language displaces the sovereignty of Man (Derrida, 1978). In this latter shift, as Lacan insists, 'Man' is not 'master' in 'his' own house. The twentieth-century focus on language signifies a decentring. Language, both inside and outside of the body it inhabits, comes to represent a controlling symbolic force, but one that no one can control. Again, as Lacan might put it: language uses me more than I use language (Lacan, 2006). Language is a kind of enclosure or symbolic net through which I come to know the world. I can't step outside of it. Language is uncanny, impossible to locate finally and to delimit.

The often strange case of Ludwig Wittgenstein is illustrative. Wittgenstein produced two philosophies in his life: the first an attempt to clarify what could and what couldn't be said logically and therefore meaningfully (Wittgenstein, 1961); the second addressed 'the rough ground' of actual language that Wittgenstein came to describe as comprised of different 'language games' (Wittgenstein, 1968). In both of philosophies, Wittgenstein sensed strongly that language represented a horizon for understanding. In the early *Tractatus Logico-Philosophicus* is the standout statement: 'The limits of my language are the limits of my world'. In the later, posthumously published, philosophy, Wittgenstein affirmed the ontological primacy of language: 'to know a language is know a way of life'; 'if a lion could speak we wouldn't be able to understand what it said' (Wittgenstein, 1968).

Wittgenstein's thinking extends beyond philosophy. We can see how this ontological thinking of language applies to the nature of research, including educational research. The dimension of discourse can be seen to embrace everything significant about educational research. In the first place, research itself makes a linguistic intervention into the field of knowledge. No research product does not make a claim on a new and special purchase on the world, on reality or on the truth of some significant matter. Every research product is an instance of and intervention into language. All the possibilities for the meaning of such productions – relating to world, reality, truth and significance – belong to the order of language. This rather obvious truth is perhaps so self-evident that much of its implication is passed over when we think about the nature of the research process and about the ends research might be directed towards. And yet everyone who engages with the world of research must labour with the production of text. Every research endeavour needs to find its own form of expression, must be aware of the discursive field it is entering and must also be aware of its own contribution to a shift or adjustment in that discursive field. These matters are, of course, linguistic: they are language based not just in the sense that the appropriate language must be found to express such truths as may be told. They offer to change the very language of knowledge: to extend, modify, refine or redefine the discourse they contribute to.

The ethic of knowledge that attends research depends on the idea of transformation. Research contributes to the transformation of the semantics and syntax of the domain of knowledge in question. This textual/linguistic element is obvious in that doctoral qualification depends on the production of a book, an extended statement that complies with the law of genre.

There is an analogy here with the idea of a generative grammar: the potential of a language constituted of finite components to generate endless variation (Chomsky, 1965). The would-be contributor must first become inward with the language of practice and field, must get to know the key defining statements, the differences, the conflicts, the subtleties of position and the precise forms of expression that belong to that practice and its field from the inside. At the same time, the initiate may feel at odds with a dominant language, may seek to contest its favoured modes, its determinations. There arises a textual component here, of course: research is textual in the many ways. Research requires significant reading: fields have their canonical texts, texts at many different levels, of different types. In addition, there are all the less canonical, perhaps mundane, perhaps oppositional texts to be considered. Then there are texts from overlapping and adjacent fields and practices, texts that may exert influence on the object in question. Making sense of such texts is essential to very possibility of entering the research process; fields of practice and the knowledge that inhabits them are fundamentally linguistic in different modes including the spoken and the textual. Subjects are positioned; objects are determined in their fundamental nature through and in various language practices. What's more, linguistic interventions change understandings of the very nature of things. It is in the nature of discourse itself to allow for this very mobility – or play – even while we must acknowledge the power of language to shape things including the very intimate power in determining the identities and possibilities of subjects who will always be differentiated according to language.

Chapter 7

New Bearings in Research Thinking

But what is thinking?

In some contexts, philosophy is represented as a practice working towards the refinement of ideas in general: its purpose to serve the interests of practical, useful knowledge. This tendency is evident in social science research. A powerful imperative decrees that research, being funded by public money, be useful, dedicated to the improvement of practices and the betterment of the world. While this may seem to be an obviously good thing, the domination of thinking by an ethic of improvement distorts the pursuit of knowledge or 'wisdom'. Education is the field of study perhaps most afflicted with the call to improvement. Educationists themselves often see the world as in need of more education or a refined, reformed version of education. It is hardly ever the case that the domination of the world by education is challenged on philosophical grounds. The assumption that education is the means towards an improved world prevails.

It's wise, though, to review critically all our assumptions, especially the ones we hold most nearly. This is possibly an originary principle of philosophy. If we want to engage with thinking, we must undergo some radical questioning of ourselves, our beliefs, our world. This is the point of Heidegger's attempt to resuscitate 'the question of the meaning of Being', a project that might seem absurdly metaphysical in its ambition. Actually, it affirms the place of the question in thinking. One practical implications of the question of the meaning of Being is that it introduces the interminable into the business of thought. For deconstruction, the process of questioning, interrogation of the conceptual is endless. There is no resting place for thinking. But this isn't merely accidental nor a matter of choosing what sustains the activity of philosophy for its own sake. It rather, I think, claims to correspond to something in the 'nature' of both being and thinking. Before Socrates, Parmenides had declared they were the same (see Chapter 6).

It has been my contention that thinking has not been a dominant mode of engagement in philosophy, particularly in research philosophy and, more particularly, in the philosophy of education and the research practices promoted in that arena. Heidegger prompts the interrogation of thinking in a 1951–1952 lecture course 'Was heist Denken?' The question concerning thinking has at least two significant dimensions. The translation suggests, 'What is called thinking?' but that sounds a rather awkward construction in English. The question has another resonance that suggests something like 'What calls for thinking?' (Heidegger, 1993e).

The first part asks us to think what we mean by thinking. Thinking can mean several things including calculation, rational reckoning, planning, problem setting and solving – elements we might associate with the world of activity. But that isn't the kind of thinking in question. What do we know about thinking? We acknowledge that there might be specialist thinking, associated with specific academic discourses, say: historical thinking or thinking historically. Some thinking may be more technical, and some entirely abstract as with mathematical logic. We must acknowledge that thinking has different modalities and different techniques for its pursuit, but also that thinking isn't exclusively rational. The realm of the rational is compromised by all the other modes of thinking – unconscious, undirected, unanticipated and often unknown – that intrude into consciousness.

Heidegger's thinking wants to go beyond the rational organizing kind of thinking that dominates worlds of practice, beyond the processes of conscious, deliberative control. We might think here of being troubled, of brooding on something, of being possessed by a thought that we can't shake off. But there is another kind, a thinking that might be free from the practical concerns of everyday living or even from the grander designs and projects that motivate elements of our existence. This kind of thinking is not exactly beyond our control yet may sometimes haunt or trouble us with its force. This thinking we do in contemplating the meaning of things in the larger sense, as when everyday things we encounter on occasions may appear in estranged or troubling form. This is perhaps the kind of thinking our logical and technologically oriented training does not prepare us for and that cannot be easily organized into a programme. Yet, it may be a kind of thinking we yearn for and also shrink back from.

The question that threatens to disturb the current hegemony of practices, attitudes and ethics within philosophy of education is the fundamental question: What is philosophy of education? This is the very question, oddly perhaps, that education – supposed to be concerned intimately with questions of knowledge, disciplines and the organization of thinking – seems reluctant to ask seriously enough to trouble its most cherished, hard-core assumptions. In general, educational philosophy is what serves to clarify issues to enable a refining of our sense of the purposes and practices of education (Hirst and Peters, 1970). It is a form of not thinking. Philosophy of education has been largely dedicated to an improvement ethic, taking it for granted that education has a rightful place in the world order and operates essentially, if potentially, as a force for good. Where education fails to live up to its redemptive mission, it is for philosophy of education to indicate the adjustments necessary to set it back on the path to righteousness. This is essentially the ethic of educational philosophy in its institutionalized, hegemonic form.

This ethic has already excluded much thinking, having already foreclosed ontological questions that put education itself into question. The Heidegger title mentioned earlier, 'What calls for thinking?' includes another possibility concerning what calls us to thinking. This perhaps less-obvious dimension concerns the impetus to thinking. What makes us want to think? What impels us to think in the reflective, ruminative mode that can invite us to call into question the meaning of things even as we experience them as endowed with meaning, semiotically laden with significance? Heidegger's account of thinking includes an invocation of something that calls us. Thinking calls partly because it is not present among us in any immediately accessible form. In fact, Heidegger contends that in modernity, and perhaps for long before, thinking has withdrawn from the reach of human beings. But it is also Heidegger's case that in withdrawing, strangely but plausibly at the same time, thinking calls to us or rather draws us towards its withdrawn self. We miss it.

If this sounds mystical, it is perhaps because the account I have given echoes some of Heidegger's flirting with the mystical. But I think the point resonates with a fundamental issue that faces 'we contemporaries' and that has particular relevance to the present condition of education. This concerns the role of education as a secular religion, a new faith or ontotheology. The language of redemption still haunts the present period, whether we call it late modernity, postmodernity or liquid modernity. We still collectively, as a species, as it were, express the tendency to believe that the present may be redeemed by some technological fix of the future, that instrumental rationality remains the most rational and most fruitful way to organize our collective lives. Education now takes a central role in this ongoing 'technological enframing' where even populations across the world are seen as resources for economic development.

The call to thinking is something specific to 'dasein' or human being-in-the-world. It is like a question or questioning from far off – far away from our present immediate concerns, a call that reminds us what we may have forgotten: our finitude, our fragility, our need for meaning and our desire to make sense of being here, now. The possibility of thinking, rethinking or thinking differently is expressed in the secret desire of the researcher towards discovery: the prospect of the transformation of our understanding of ourselves in our world. Here I use the word 'prospect' advisedly – as a caution against the idea, now so common in research practice in the social sciences and particularly in education, that seeks to find the solution to a question, the answer to a problem, that seeks to make known and explicit the direction for practice and that leaves the essential business in hand alone as if it were a self-evident thing. This attitude opens enquiry with a view to shutting it down in the name of improvement.

Symptomatic of currently hegemonic research thinking are the handbooks setting out various positions for the researcher in advance of enquiry proper. These manuals offer, as a menu might, a range of possible positions corresponding to an already-established orientation for the researcher. This approach negates the specificities of concern and care arising from worlds of practice and fails to accommodate thinking as a process that may engender new and surprising way of looking at things: in other words, thinking that may enable research – the realization of new understandings, new knowledge, new orientations to existing knowledge – to be research in that more interesting, exciting sense.

In order to explore the possibilities for thinking that are on the horizon, if receding, as Heidegger suggests, but drawing us forward, we might want to revisit those handbooks and see what they are telling us about the state of research thinking and its relations to contemporary philosophy. This will be a short excursion. Such manuals represent thinking as already ordered, known and packaged for the consumption of the would-be researcher. This is why this book urges its reader to throw the handbooks away and to engage in thinking.

Against this framing of research thinking, we can turn to consider the state of modern philosophy. In fact, no consistent authoritative view of thinking will be found there. The world of philosophy is divided against itself, fragmented into domains and specialisms. These differences often take a critical form: they mean that different branches and 'brands' of philosophy can't communicate with one another. Different orientations see the task of philosophy itself differently. The history of these schisms can't be explored here, but if Paul Feyerabend describes the world of science as essentially anarchic, the same, at least, is true of philosophy (Feyerabend, 1975a). Philosophy is far from being a world of ordered progression. The world of philosophy is fraught with radical differences, hostilities even, and cannot be summed up as to its overall condition from some neutral standpoint within philosophy that would give a sober and coolly reflective account of these differences and their meanings. At the same time, there are a series of far-reaching tendencies in modern and contemporary philosophy that hold out the prospect of renewal for thinking.

Philosophy today, now?

The present condition of philosophy is not simply that philosophy has expanded and divided its domains but rather that schisms have occurred that divide the world of philosophy into ways of thinking that appear to incompatible with one another, operating different language games with quite different orientations to meaning.

In this sense, it is perhaps no wonder that the domain of philosophy seems to have been kept out of the explicit account so research practice in education. But it isn't just philosophy as institutionalized that has been excluded. The dimension of metaphysics, thinking concerning the nature of things, has been significantly excluded. Several reasons can be posited for this. One relates to the way that education has become an ontotheological principle of our time, a domain considered to be beyond the petty arguments of professional philosophers about what matters, about whether Wittgenstein or Derrida is the one true 'master'. Educational research, the consensus agrees, is more serious, more immediate and more practical: it is dedicated to the improvement of the world. Its urgency has intensified now that education carries the burden of being the vehicle for social justice: at a time when differences in access to social goods is increasing, when the divide between rich and poor is increasing, the social causes of the world seem urgent and demand an approach to research that seeks to determine what steps can be taken, what measures to be implemented in the great cause of improvement – of education and of the world that education necessarily serves.

This argument, this position is self-defeating, of course. Practically oriented, improvement-directed research can no more guarantee that its findings are firmly grounded in the soil of truth than can any other, say, self-avowedly speculative mode of research. What's more, research that gets undertaken in all confidence in the name of improvement, or in the name of social justice, can no more claim to be effective than any other just because it wants to be. In addition, famously, there is no necessary link between the world of educational research and the world of educational practice. Policymakers, practitioners of education are not waiting with excited anticipation for the latest findings of researchers. And even if they are, they will have to sift through the voluminous, often contradictory material to discover no definitive consensus for the path to redemption.

More than all that, for the purposes of this book, that wants to rethink the relations between philosophy, metaphysics, thinking and social science and educational research, philosophy of education has limited its scope significantly. It is my contention that the history of the philosophy of education, as embedded and embodied, say, in the history of its key organization in the UK context, PESGB, has been as concerned as any other domain of education to keep itself uncontaminated by forms of thinking that it perceives would be hostile to its project. That project is represented by the work of its founding 'fathers' [*sic*] whose patriarchal heritage has been recently celebrated as indicating the proper role of philosophy in relation to education (Hirst and Peters, 1970).

Deconstruction

It is as though the philosophy of education has resisted the possibility that in the past century and a half philosophy has undergone a kind of 'queering' from, say, 1872, the date of the publication of Nietzsche's *The Birth of Tragedy*. This 'moment' is provisional. No doubt many other moments and events will have contributed to the change in orientation marked by Nietzsche's first book. In any case, the precise date of its publication did not create an instant swerve in the meaning of philosophy. But, for the sake of argument, I affirm that *The Birth of Tragedy* initiates deconstruction.

Nietzsche's effort in and from *The Birth of Tragedy* is to rethink the Western heritage, to revisit the Attic sensibility to critique the Platonic/Aristotelean inheritance and its rationalist ethic, to rethink in effect, the meaning of philosophy. Nietzsche's project caused a stir leading to the ontological disturbance in Heidegger. From 1927 (see above regarding dates and moments), Heidegger's project was dedicated to rethinking philosophy, metaphysics and thinking. The urgent question emerges as: Is thinking possible? In this movement, Western philosophy turns back on itself, problematizes its own history, its entanglement in metaphysics, its tendency towards ontotheology and its forgetting of the question of being. Maybe thinking is possible after philosophy. But this is by no means a certainty.

Derrida, in *Writing and Difference*, wondered if philosophy had died. Could thought have a future? Both were unknowable, he declared. But these were the only questions capable of founding a community of 'those who are still called philosophers' (Derrida, 1978). What follows in Derrida's various rethinkings of philosophy becomes 'deconstruction', an elusive but decisive approach, echoing with meanings in relation to questions concerning meaning. It is futile to seek a single authoritative source for deconstruction's strict interpretation. Trawling through the work and statements of its putative author doesn't finally stabilize deconstruction into crystalline clarity. It does help, though, to give sense to the orientation referred to by the word. Definitions cannot substitute for Derrida's extensive, rigorous rereading of Western metaphysics – and the many lines of enquiry it opens up. What deconstruction is can be productively described in terms of enabling processes of rethinking, redefinition, unhinging, or 'queering'. It is a rereading of Western philosophy, of a significant line in our heritage of thinking. What may have seemed settled is reopened. The interrogative cast of mind it enacts revitalizes what may have seemed sedimented in the archive of moribund knowledge, immobile thinking. Deconstruction offers a range of strategies and examples for interrogating the conceptual apparatuses within the ontological horizon for our thinking (Derrida, 1976, 1978). Deconstruction, amazingly perhaps, also realizes the resuscitation of the dead: it returns to what had seemed 'dead thinking' and breathes new life into it. Deconstruction is rethinking, queering and revitalizing the philosophical tradition.

Deconstruction is exemplified – not uniquely – by Derrida as a kind of rereading (Derrida, 1987; Malabou, 2015). The notion of reading here is useful. Most of Derrida's work in philosophy consists of returning to key texts in the history of philosophy – as well as in the history of thought more generally – to re-examine specific articulations and conceptual structures that enfold their thinking. Deconstruction is a kind of re-reading that gives close attention to the precise formulations that come down to us in the established works – the archive – of what is often reckoned to be 'our' intellectual heritage. Derrida has written about this process of archive and reception, reminding us of some of the fundamental processes involved in actively making sense of a legacy (Derrida, 1996). To paraphrase all too briefly, we find ourselves 'thrown' arbitrarily into the world, confronted with an assemblage of texts, a symbolic inheritance that is also at the same time a kind of debris, the leftover bits and pieces of various 'pasts' that bear various relation to our own specific present. Such texts may be protected by 'the archons', authorized to safeguard, to preserve and to protect from improper influences that might endanger authorized versions. Deconstruction mines (or re-mines) the archive and produces something kind of new out of the relatively solidified materials it confronts (Derrida, 1996; Foucault, 1977b; Malabou, 2015).

Attending to the language of ideas, deconstruction reminds us that language and ideas are not separable: the most mundane, everyday language is freighted with metaphysics (Derrida, 1978). In turn, it reveals that the language of metaphysics – the very language of reason – is not free from the contaminations of everyday language, the inexplicit assumptions, ambiguities, slippages, contradictions, unintended associations and non-sequiturs that beset all linguistic practice. Adept at finding the strange torsions in the logic of language and in the language of reason, deconstruction undermines any assumption of a pure, clear language of reason. Deconstruction, though, does not decry reason: it's actually made from it, but makes us rethink the conditions of such reason that we might aspire to. To the essential categories of philosophy (ontology, epistemology, hermeneutics, phenomenology, ethics) for example, deconstruction adds 'the aporetic' (Derrida, 1993).

Deconstruction epitomizes 'negative capability': everything that's knotty, intractable and irresolvable potentially gets foregrounded, including the necessary dimension of 'madness' in reason. Derrida's account of the decision – however weighed, however meticulously considered – reveals the kernel of undecidability in all the operations of reason. At the same time deconstruction is – interminably, remorselessly, intricately and voluminously – dedicated to the pursuit of reason. It simply will not let things lie. Its remorseless pursuit of reason uncovers reason's very own aporia (Derrida, 1993).

Deconstruction's semi-droll sister invention, hauntology, rethinks ontology (Derrida, 1994). Emphasizing the complicity between presence and absence, Derrida's hauntology insists on the spectral, invoking mourning as an element of the ontic and ontological. Mourning belongs to that essential experience of change and the inexorable, destabilizing movement of time. Derived from Derrida's earlier, extensive series of concepts arising from the deconstruction of being-as-presence – supplement, trace, differance, dissemination – hauntology foregrounds the spectrality that constantly disturbs any stable, determinate relation between present and absent, present and past, intelligible and sensible. The spectre is never itself but is the return of something previous; but 'the spectre is [also] the future, it is always to come, it presents itself only as that which could come, or come back' (Derrida, 1994, 11). Past, future and 'present' move in an intricate dance destabilizing secure temporal order. Spectral deconstruction carries us back to Nietzsche's account of the Attic sensibility – before Euripides in unholy alliance with Socrates reduce tragedy to the rationality of the classroom (Nietzsche, 1956).

The heritage of the philosophy of education is at odds with this 'queering'. Its foundations in 'conceptual analysis', its dedication to a rationalist ethic, its fidelity to its founding fathers (see the recent spate of festschrifts, for example), its commitment to an ethic of improvement, or to an ethic of redemption betray its patriarchal will to a truth far from its own assumption of self-evidence.

I want to explore now some tendencies in contemporary thought and philosophy that promise to carry the force of deconstruction forward to thinking and that have important resonances for all forms of research but, for me, at least, speak strongly to educational research in its present, hegemonic form.

Catherine Malabou's 'plasticity' and the rethinking of biopower

Malabou's thinking has most been associated with the idea of plasticity, derived from Hegel's preface to the *Phenomenology of Spirit*, elevated to an ontological principle. Her idea of plasticity is derived from Hegel but is not simply Hegelian – and this is an important point about her example (2005). It is inflected with sustained ontological readings of both Heidegger and Derrida, but goes beyond all three. For Malabou, these names signify necessary points for articulating ontology beyond the key positions she inherits, uses and exceeds. An important dimension of Malabou's thinking is that plasticity remains a dominant idea but is itself always a changed, changeable and changing idea – as she reflects on certain dimensions of personal experience, on a serious engagement with psychology and neuroscience and on experiences of abjection that she uses to enhance an account of what she comes to call the 'ontology of the accident' (2009). It is perhaps an obvious point that Malabou's plasticity is itself subject to its own ontological movement, that it is essentially deconstructive. To put it another way, Malabou's work, that makes frequent use of the term 'deconstruction', in its will to rethink and review ensconced modes of thinking, suggests that plasticity is another name for her expanded articulation of deconstruction. Deconstruction is interminable, as thinking is (in principle, at least)

Malabou defines plasticity as a principle of being to displace the hegemony of writing that associated with Derrida's rethinking of Heidegger (Derrida, 1976). Writing is here conceived of as the primary condition for thinking and being, but is always deconstructable. Malabou is not attempting to claim that she has superseded Derrida by displacing writing with plasticity. She acknowledges the historical justification in Derrida's privileging of writing. Derrida features throughout her work as co-presence, 'a transformational mask', as a thinker whose contribution to philosophy is far from exhausted (Malabou, 2009). The relation between plasticity and writing is not a question of Malabou's negation of Derrida, but rather rethinking a heritage, remodelling a highly suggestive, productive model.

Writing appeared as a powerful ontological principle as a means to deconstruct the metaphysics of presence. Derrida's strange but compelling articulation of writing compels us both to rethink our essential relations to language and to rethink ontology. Writing is used in a special sense here and actually operates as shorthand for 'arche-writing' – the condition of possibility for language. Derrida argued for the 'semantic enlargement of the concept of writing' revealed in the form of programme, information and code and in the reading of genetic information, cybernetics and all linguistic-graphic inscription (Derrida, 1976, 59). Hence the possibility of writing to rethink ontology; hence also, the emphasis given to both 'play' and spectrality in Derrida's work (1978, 1994). Derrida's rethinking of language clarifies and heightens the relations between metaphysics and language – confirming the increasing sense, from Heidegger particularly, of the inheritance of Western metaphysics as a form of enclosure we both live and think within.

It would be ridiculous to attempt to summarize what writing is for Derrida, but the title of an early major work, *Of Grammatology*, indicates a desire to engage seriously with the possibility of a 'science' of writing. For Derrida, though, 'writing' can never be the mere supplement to speech that so much Western logocentrism has willed it to be. Rather writing must be seen as the very condition of language itself, as arche-writing, the conditions of possibility that enables language and that shape and determine our apprehension of things, including ourselves. Derrida early on acknowledges, though, the paradoxical impossibility of a science of writing, given that any science would have itself to already be within writing to be a science at all (Derrida, 1976). This is one of the starting points for Malabou's address of Derrida's privileging of writing and her suggestion of the 'dusk' or twilight of writing and the 'dawn of plasticity'. But she also finds inspiration in biology to suggest that writing as a metaphysically privileged idea, even if it is an idea that has deconstructive and anti-ontotheological force, is not adequate to describe certain essential phenomena that arise in contemporary neuroscience, psychoanalysis and in theories of identity.

The 'plasticity' (*plasticité*) that Malabou posits as an alternative to Derrida's writing is elaborated variously and in relation to objects as different as the history of philosophy and our emerging idea of the brain. Plasticity draws from and transforms the idea expressed in Hegel's preface to the *Phenomenology of Spirit* (1977). For Hegel, plasticity belongs to the realm of ideas signifying both the presence of a concept and the historical and contingent form that enables its appearance and that also destabilizes its form. The original move that Malabou makes is to align plasticity with deconstruction, but, at the same time, to suggest that writing as ontological principle must be displaced.

Malabou's plasticity forces us to rethink what we might mean by 'self' or any ascription of identity. Holding onto while also redefining the deconstruction of presence that reached its climax in Derrida, Malabou's 'plasticity' teases out the implications of the renewed thinking of form articulated Heidegger's fundamental ontology where the condition of 'dasein' is to be always caught or caught up in a plastic movement between modes of being: between, say, anxiety, concern and care wherein those modalities overlap and co-exist and where there is no outside, no transcendental external vantage point (Malabou, 2012).

The anthropologically significant 'transformational mask' (coined by Levi-Strauss) is borrowed by Malabou to provide an account of her travelling through the questions she addresses concerning writing and plasticity. It provides a useful way of thinking also about her relations to the philosophical tradition and its key figures for her. She explains that Levi Strauss's account of the structure and meaning of the 'transformational mask' demonstrates a union of the graphic and the plastic (Malabou, 2015, 2–8). So it is that the graphic is not displaced as the mask operates by bringing together the graphic and plastic in a new form of meaning (2009, 3). Malabou then invites us into what she calls a 'twilight' that involves 'the symbolic rupture between the plastic and the graphic component of thought', suggesting that this opacity offers an affordance to address philosophical issues and questions anew. In effect, it seems that Malabou suggests here the possibility of what Heidegger thought possible at the end of philosophy: the emergence of thinking freed from the ontotheological inheritance of Western philosophy.

Clearly, the evocation of the transformational mask speaks to Malabou's sense of her philosophical self and what she borrows from others. It is a feature of Malabou's work as a whole that she variously returns to rethink subjectivity in this double sense: rethinking the sources she draws on and redeploying plasticity as recognition of a form that is constantly changing itself but is also subject to change and to explosive destruction. Hence her interest in the 'ontology of the accident' with its unusual focus on trauma and dispossession as illustrative cases of fundamental ontology. For Malabou, fundamental ontology merges with general ontology.

Plasticity arises from Heidegger's destruction of metaphysics and Derrida's deconstruction. Malabou's plasticity does not so much displace as galvanize and rearticulate these philosophies. Malabou considers the temporal dimension of her relation to the history of philosophy as a radical temporalizing where, as with Derrida's hauntology, the strict separations between past, present and future cannot apply and their assumed order is destabilized, rethinking our grasp of time. The point is to indicate the realization that, for us, at least, past, future and present are in a mobile relation with one another; what we take as given in terms of being present is always hovering in a relation to some form of otherness. So Malabou argues that a continued approach to Hegelian dialectics, Heideggerian destruction and Derridean deconstruction will 'forever' bring these perspectives into our efforts to put any singular one into play: so there is another Hegel, another Heidegger, another Derrida – 'a childhood to come in the text' (2009, 54) that lives on through the processes of reading.

Plasticity is a deconstructive notion, rethinking thinking and drawing 'dialectical reason' into a 'dusk' where knowledge cannot assume poise, stillness or completion. Plasticity retains a strong relation to a central feature of deconstruction: that there is strictly speaking no outside to the enclosure of Western metaphysics, to the metaphysics enfolded in language. But neither plasticity nor deconstruction therefore mean that we are entirely caught in a trap. What deconstruction aims to do is to lubricate the internal mobility in metaphysics available through the play of signs in language. Following Heidegger's thinking of form: 'Being is none other than changing forms; being is nothing but its own mutability' (Malabou, 2009, 43); Heidegger points to the lack of an outside for both 'dasein' and Being as a whole: suggesting, for Malabou, a certain necessity for plasticity: 'Nothing happens except self-transformation' (2009, 44). But this is significant.

Recently, Malabou has taken on questions concerning biopower, Foucault's idea about the transformed mode of government that holds sway through 'capillary power' in modernity and beyond, and that is concerned, above all, with the 'life' of the people. Biopower is the force that seeks to manage in minute detail (mostly through education, interestingly) the grain of identity, forms of selfhood and the orientations to knowledge of populations (Malabou, 2009). Rethinking the formulations offered by Derrida, Foucault and Giorgio Agamben concerning the nature of the distinction between biological life and cultural life, Malabou points towards a deconstruction of that very opposition. Deconstructing biopower may enable us, she claims, to think differently about what we are in relation to the dominant form of collective life that shapes our world and our form of being. This rethinking affirms the continuity of life (with culture) and promises to deconstruct the always powerful distinction between biology and culture – with the promise of a 'deconstruction of sovereignty' as we know it (Malabou, 2013). Recently, Malabou has expanded this line of thinking, returning to Kant to address questions concerning the noumenon/phenomenon distinction addressed in Chapter 1 particularly in relation to Quentin Meillassoux's affirmation of 'ancestrality' that suggests the existence of things that precede consciousness, things that clearly have existed without benefit of human knowledge (Malabou, 2016a).

Clearly, Malabou's continuing oeuvre represents a renewal of philosophy that revisits classic philosophical themes but that also draws on other modes of thinking (biology, for instance) to regenerate philosophy. Her work addresses key themes concerning the contemporary politics of life that, although not addressed in philosophy of education, has far-reaching implications for education as deeply implicated in the heritage of modernity.

Giorgio Agamben's political ontology

An extreme, though plausible, perspective on the contemporary role of education can be taken from Agamben's account of the paradigm nature of the camp in modernity (1997). Agamben claims that what he refers to as 'the concentrationary universe' signifies something essential about the juridical structure we live in now. The camp constitutes an exceptional space outside of or beyond the law that is at the same time instituted by a constitutional action. According to Agamben's shocking affirmation, the camp is a paradigm case: a camp may refer to a variety of exceptional, but legally sanctioned, places, spaces such as Guantanamo bay, 'ordinary' prisons, detention centres for asylum seekers and possibly more apparently homely but nevertheless exceptionally governed spaces. Hence, we can see the school as a form of 'camp': an exceptional, although ubiquitous, governmental space. The possibility of occasions and spaces of exception is for Agamben an indication that even the most liberal democracies of our time carry with them a totalitarian thread. In following the outline of this argument, I am not, of course, trying to draw some absurd or offensive analogy between schools and concentration camps, but seeking to follow the logic of Agamben's account of the political ontology of our time.

Agamben's account of this dimension of the political order suggests that we reconsider the function of the education in our time, although this is rarely, if ever, done. A political order characterized by 'biopower', with its extensive governmental concern with the life and quality of its population, necessitates the modern (post-1870) form of the school.

The school, I argue, constitutes the paradigm institution of our time. Key aspects of the school offer significant points of analogy with Agamben's metonymic interest in the camp as a feature of biopower. The school is a highly exceptional space – juridically speaking. While utterly mundane, normal and dispersed, much of its internal practice is immune to law, despite the power it is endowed with to make decisive decisions about the very nature – and the social trajectories – of its subjects. Conclusive decisions the institution makes in terms of identity are beyond the reach of law. There is no recourse to extra-institutional authority to challenge life-defining determinations and distribution of social identities made through schools and other educational institutions.

At the same time, schooling operates under the compulsion of the law. Schooling in Europe is obligatory. In many countries, 'home-schooling' is illegal. This legally enforced dimension of the school hardly warrants comment in current discourses on education. It is clear that schooling – although much more frequently represented as a 'right', or a 'gift' or a space for national and self-realization – is the essential space of modern and contemporary government. The constituency of the school is not free to determine its own relation to time and space: being in school is far from free in a number of ways. Schooling operates in contexts of confinement, enacting the restriction of association and the strict organization of time and space. Perhaps one of the most interesting features of the school's 'dislocating localization' is its deterritorialized ubiquity: its non-special enclosure of space as a 'zone of indistinction' or a 'hybrid space of exception' (Agamben, 1997, 113).

In the nation state of modernity, schooling has also been configured explicitly as an agent for national belonging and cohesion, from Empire Day to more recent and more subtle attempts to organize collective culture – through the rise of 'citizenship' programmes – and through the ongoing governance of language. This cultural governance parallels the 'government of the soul', the dimension of schooling concerned with inculcating deep-seated modes of conduct and orientations towards the self as self-managed project. And, of course, in their strict hierarchy of authority, schools model a specific organization of power in the name of ingrained, 'proper' authority. The deterritorialized governmental force of the school operates also as a dimension of security: in Hannah Arendt's rather odd phrase, 'to protect the child from society and to protect society from the child'. The school can further be related analogically to the camp insofar as its denizens have a special, non-citizen (not-yet citizen) legal status.

The camp, like the modern school, is a European invention, has colonial origins, and has been concerned with displaced national security. According to Agamben, the camp constitutes the 'fundamental biopolitical paradigm of the west' (Agamben, 1997, 181). The same claim can be made for the school. The school as fundamental institution of governance has been exported increasingly, often in more explicitly violent form (Harber, 2004). Agamben claims, as I claim for the school, the camp constitutes 'an event which decisively signals the political space of modernity itself' (1997, 113). The camp according to Agamben is 'the hidden matrix and nomos of the political space in which we are still living' (1997, 106). The school is not hidden, although its governmental essence is obscured in educational discourses by its mythical identity and status. For example, while it is often claimed that education is an essential component of democracy, it is obvious that the paradigm institution (and virtually all the other known examples) of modern education, the school, is far from democratic in structure, practices and effects. Insofar as the school constitutes the key instrument of government – the production of citizenry, the management of population, the technology of identity, the myth of meritocracy – its characteristic modality expresses the political order of our time. We can see this essential, ubiquitous governmental presence as an example of what Agamben elsewhere refers to as an ontology of the rule of rules: when it becomes impossible to distinguish a way of life from the following of rules and the performance of rituals (Agamben, 2013).

Agamben's view suggests we rethink education in our time. In its cradle-to-grave attempt to give meaning to life, education represents itself as the supreme principle of reason. Education has become an ontotheological principle by force of 'reason', the major defining power in the lives of individuals, social groups and in the destiny of nations, perhaps in the destiny of the world. That philosophy of education has tended, always and necessarily, to avoid any consideration of this ontological condition can be partly attributed to the triumph of the idea of education as ontotheological principle, contributing to its supremacy. The automatic assumption of the rationality of education indicates a limited understanding of rationality and its contribution to modernity (Hirst and Peters, 1970). While any direct association of national education performance with either economic or global political puissance is highly doubtful, individuals, institutions and nations increasingly understand themselves in terms of their educational orientation within a global distribution of socio-cultural and economic authority (Harber, 2004; Wolf, 2002).

Something of this global force can be understood through another concept Agamben proposes to challenge hegemonic thinking, Agamben's articulation of 'impotentiality' offers a disruptive resource for thinking education differently. Impotentiality resists the implication of necessity that attends contemporary general ontology. Impotentiality arises for Agamben as a key idea partly in relation to a desire to resist what he sees as the nihilistic possible implications of Nietzsche's 'doctrine' of the 'eternal return', the idea that the world is condemned to repeat itself endlessly, to continue in the form that we see before us as though this way of being is necessary and inevitable.

Education habitually emphasizes the realization of potential. At the same time, education organizes its programmes towards the eradication of the contingent and the determination of the necessary, in spite of the glaringly obvious contradiction here between a relatively open idea of potential and a relatively closed system of knowledge. Education takes its own contingent arrangement of things, however, as necessary: its knowledge, its modes of being, its deportments, its determinations of identity and its institutional structures.

The dominant discourse of 'the learning society' renders the meaning of life in terms of labour towards self-development. This strongly embedded though mostly unconscious ethic depends on a metaphysics that distinguishes between what it defines as essential differences: human and animal, for instance, adult and child. These distinctions also operate as principles of inclusion and exclusion. In contemporary discourses, those who are outside the magic circle of 'the learning society' exist in a state of partial inclusion. Learning is represented as essential to being human in the fullest sense. The learning society offers education as essentially a kind of 'social orthopaedics' that is concerned above all with 'improvement'. This model of improvement concerns itself with maximizing competencies and efficiencies. Hence the emphasis at all levels in education on the cultivation of 'transferable skills' where knowledge itself is reduced to being a vehicle for more 'useful' purposes. Here, the value of activity is in its *potential*, its capacity to be rendered useful in the future. In this we can see how lifelong learning is strongly implicated in the transformation of the state itself into an invasive force that operates ostensibly at the level of the individual. Self-organization and self-development are key to realizing the potential of the self and of the social collective.

Impotentiality is other to this process. Thinking impotentiality involves a challenge to the logic of the established cliché of realizing potential through education, the idea that is so powerfully implicit in official and in critical discourses that privilege education. Agamben soberly reminds us that potentiality can only be thought properly in relation to impotentiality, that impotentiality is the dark shadow that haunts naively positive affirmation of potential. In the first place, Agamben simply states that potentiality negates itself in its very realization. 'The potentiality that exists', Agamben writes in Homo Sacer, 'is precisely the potentiality that cannot pass over into actuality' (Agamben, 1997, 45). Potentiality must exist in a relation to impotentiality – understood as the capacity to not do or not be. Currently embedded thinking that dominates educational systems, and that determines that education is the key to self-realization, cannot know about impotentiality except as lack. What is expressed as impotentiality gets exiled to the zone of failure. The maintenance of this zone of failure is essential to the system of education for the realization of its positives. Hence its remorseless determinations of identity along a continuum of success and failure. Hence, also, its relentless imposition of a drive to self-realization (of one's 'potential') – always according to its own limited understanding of what potential is and can be.

Agamben is interested in what he takes to be the paradigm figure of Herman Melville's story, 'Bartleby, the Scrivener', a figure who fascinates through a constant refusal to do and to achieve. Bartleby is the 'strongest objection against the principle of sovereignty' (Agamben, 1997, 48). Bartleby's case can be seen in terms of a refusal of the normative dimension of instrumental action and production. The normative dimension of contemporary education – the drive that relies on a determinate notion of potential – produces exclusions based on norms of achievement. The self is configured through schooling's processes as essentially entrepreneurial in relation to norms of achievement but also and more fundamentally perhaps to a required way of being.

In relation to this exclusionary ethic – refusal means failure – impotentiality can be seen as a component of freedom. While education as the realization of potential gets strongly represented in positive, redemptive, teleological terms, the recognition of the spectral nature of potentiality may indicate resistance to the dominant instrumental rationality of performativity. In contemporary education and political discourses, potentiality passes over into actuality in a measured and determinate process that actually excludes the other dimension of potentiality: impotentiality. The topography of thought here sees the realization of potentiality in the zone of activity as the necessary movement towards self-realization at the individual and the social level. This determination necessarily excludes possibilities.

Every teacher has probably at some point had to embrace the well-worn aspiration: 'I want to help my students to realize their potential' – an embedded common-sense notion. The reflex affirmation of the idea of potential is echoed in grand public statements about the significance of education – in spite of the fact that long years of attempted educational reforms continue to produce grimly predictable inequalities of attainment. Under the 'No child left behind' mantra of recent US educational policy, for example, the national leader declares: 'Let them fulfil their God-given potential', as though this potential existed in some determinate space in some determinate form and could be released, or realized, in spite of generations of repeated and apparently systematic inequality. The idea of potential as 'God-given' surely doesn't bear thinking. But the repetition of this gesture to the non-concept of potential is commonplace. The impossible call to bring the marginal into the mainstream via education is offered as economic duty as well as divine justice. In this context, in the face of all that we know about this call, the fulfilment of potential sounds like the mere repetition of a hollow, wish-laden mantra. This is especially troubling when we consider that it is in terms of determinate attributes that such bearers of 'potential' as are invoked by the national leader are most likely to be sacrificed – in social terms – by the processes of an education system that will, in the not very long run, define them negatively. After all, education seeks to translate potentiality into actuality – and, in that process, to foreclose the impotentiality it cannot recognize in its well-organized scheme of things. As a resource bank for thinking in relation to the contemporary condition of education – and the world, therefore – Agamben offers several key lines of research-rich enquiry.

Slavoj Zizek's Lacan and the parallax view

Some of twists and turns of deconstructive thinking are evident in the work of the Slavoj Zizek that addresses the contemporary condition of things in relation to a desire for political transformation. Rethinking the philosophical heritage or inheritance through a Lacanian lens, Zizek's thinking offers a mercurially perceptive contribution to political ontology, especially from rethinking the Marxist inheritance through the articulation of ideology that comes through Althusser (see Chapter 3). Zizek's rethinking is powerful and illuminating. It is highly suggestive for educational research.

Zizek follows a critique of Marxist false consciousness through an awareness of the unconscious in shaping thought, knowledge and perception. Important for Zizek is Lacan's 'foreclosure': ways of knowing are occluded from conscious or unconscious apprehension but may nevertheless appear through the Real. Essentially for Zizek, ideology is unconscious and quite fundamental. It is as much about what we don't know that we know as anything else. It is never for Zizek possible to think in terms of unmasking ideology to reveal the unvarnished truth of things. Rather ideology is what has always already shaped our thinking. Ideology is what precedes us to shape our thinking, to delimit its possibilities.

Following Lacan, language is implicated here – as the symbolic order that carries with it stabilizing pressures that represent themselves as carrying the truth of things. When we encounter such pressures, as with, for example, certain determinations in law, or certain unquestionable political precepts, we know we are in the realm of ideology. At any point when we encounter the experience that we cannot think otherwise, we are in the grip of ideology – and whenever we reach for some common-sense point of reference, we are similarly calling on the authority of an ideological system. Not of course that we can escape to an ideology free zone: that is the whole point. Our being-in-language is what ensures that we experience, know and perceive the world and its things in ways that are ordered well before our coming to them

Ideology for Zizek is entrammelled in our everyday thinking and embedded in our everyday rites and rituals, the 'normal' behaviours that we take for granted and assume as natural to the social world. It is there in discourse, powerfully, in the ideas that dominate our thinking: freedom, the individual, democracy, education – all terms of our time laden with meaning that we use automatically as though they are self-evident. On this view, ideology is a virtual system that sustains our understanding of the world. We can think about just about every aspect of education as belonging to this virtual order even while it takes material form in the world: in institutions, practices, texts, procedures and habits. Ideology in this sense is necessarily related to power; but the position expressed by Zizek, via Althusser following Lacan, is that ideology is not controlled by some committee of the powerful. On this view, ideology is pervasive, less accessible and more invasive. It is also significantly inescapable: we cannot pass through ideology to reach the Real on the other side.

For Zizek, being thoroughly Lacanian, the Real is not the same as what might understand by 'reality' – what we experience as a meaningful and ordered totality that simply is out there and accessible to our conscious examination. That is not to say that the Real isn't there. There are two important dimensions to the Real that inform Zizek's take on Lacan. The Real appears to us at point when the Symbolic Order breaks down or fails or comes apart from its moorings. Such an occasion might be death: where the material entity (my father, say) ceases to exist as such and vanishes from the Real but remains powerfully present in the Symbolic (I still think and speak of my father). Or when we glimpse what was once a magnificent symbol of plenty and order (the Titanic, say) and see that it has become reabsorbed into the amorphous substance of the world. We bump up against the Real but mostly we experience the Real as overlaid by the Symbolic. The Symbolic though itself is significantly material and also partakes of the Real. Already we begin to see how for Zizek, as for Lacan, the Real is not simply one dimension, consistently occupying one discrete topological space. The Zizekian Real eludes singular definition. Its implications are powerful for subjectivity, especially for rethinking the subject as through the Symbolic Order rather than as prior to it.

Zizek's ontological matrix invites us to reconsider ourselves in fundamental ways as non-transcendental beings. Within this uneven and fractured view of the world and of the subject's relation to it, Zizek develops the idea of a 'parallax' view: our seeking after truth can only be formulated through a switching of perspectives to get some purchase on the mobilities of perception and meaning.

For Zizek, power operates mostly through institutions designed to regulate both behaviour and thinking. And this power belongs mostly to the Symbolic Order. It is the power of law and interpellation. One of the implications of Zizek's general view is that the political extends beyond the official realm. In fact, the Real of the political is more to be found in the institutionalized meanings and perceptions that we engage with than the operations of liberal democracies, for example. At the same time, what is *most* political – our very understanding of the nature of things – has become depoliticized and tends to be couched in a language of inevitability, necessity or natural or social law (Zizek, 1989, 2009). Again, this has enormous implications for how we read, know and make sense of education and our knowledge of it.

Bernard Stiegler's prosthetic ontology

Much of the rethinking offered so far in this chapter affirm the centrality of belief – albeit unconscious belief – in our ordering and understanding of the world. Bernard Stiegler provides a description of modernity that puts faith and fidelity at the centre. For Stiegler, both are understood essentially from a social, rather than individual, perspective. The arguments in this book have sometimes tended to put into question our collective faith in education, not in order to promote a universal faithlessness but to re-examine the ontotheological commitment to an apparatus that seems, in so many ways, to do the opposite of what it promises or at least to contradict its mythical mission. If the privileged status of education is derived from discredited or untenable modes of thinking or vision, we may not want to rethink education and educational research – not in order to redeem it from its fallen self, and certainly not to reform it into a better, improved more efficient version of its present formation, but to more thoroughly put into question its privileged status as an idea and as a global social project.

For Stiegler, who closely follows, extends and develops Heidegger's fundamental ontology, society can be understood as 'an apparatus for the production of fidelity'. Stiegler notes, following Weber, that in the modern era capitalism transformed fidelity (Stiegler, 2013, 59). In modern societies, 'trust understood as fiduciary calculability' became the order of the day; and more recently, Stiegler claims, the crisis of 2007–2008 turned what credit was left in this 'fiduciary' faith into discredit, giving rise to a new form of 'disbelief' – a condition of social nihilism.

Our era experiences the 'disenchantment brought about by rationalization' in more intense form. For Stiegler, for whom human life is always strongly characterized by a 'prosthetic ontology', the apparatuses of meaning-making have a strong bearing on questions of fidelity, belief and faith. We experience the world to a significant degree through such means insofar as we experience life as 'worth living'. According to Stiegler, contemporary loss of faith correlates with a long process stemming from the renaissance 'reading revolution'. For Stiegler, the real meaning of the renaissance is in a transformation of prosthetic memory via the printing press and access to 'grammatization' that leads into modernity. This process is recently enhanced, transfigured by the digital revolution that extends the textual world, producing 'an internet of things', the 'hypermaterial structure' of the contemporary life-world (Stiegler, 2013, 60).

Following Heidegger, Stiegler notes that the rise of rationality occurs not only in the register of reason but also, significantly, in the register of calculation that comes to stand as a prosthetic extension of what reason is. Through reason and rational calculation, 'Divine logos' becomes subject to secular reading (law is mystical; text is everyday), and this in turn concurs with the process whereby, according to Heidegger's reading of Nietzsche, 'the suprasensible' is put into question. Stiegler points out that Nietzsche knew that his declaration of the death of God was premature and that its meaning was 'to come'. For Nietzsche, it would be a long time before 'those who murdered God would be capable of comprehending their gesture': 'I have come too early ... This tremendous event is still on its way, still wandering; it has not yet reached the ears of men' (Stiegler, 2013, 61).

Oddly, perhaps, Stiegler's 'strong nihilism' arises from the analysis of the thing as a central figure in his account of *things*, his 'prosthetic ontology'. Taking a Lacanian-Althusserian position, Stiegler reminds us that relations with things are fundamental to our being, are always freighted with meaning, loaded with desire. Things populate our world(s) neither as neutral debris lying around nor as pure functional tools that serve other, thing-less purposes, but rather as expressions of a symbolically rendered imaginary relation to the world that also binds us to one another. The primordial 'thing' or object of attachment and desire is cathected onto things: the world is shaped and ordered by things in this sense. Things have world-forming functions and express an aura of the absolute other. At the same time, at the heart of 'the thing' there is an essential nothing without this aura of attachment that is not a property of the 'thing itself'. The thing of desire is the impossible (although essential) object: a kind of nothing that is at the same time 'the a priori of desire'. This idea of the thing and things in general as both fundamental ('what makes life worth living') to 'relations of fidelity' (Stiegler, 2013, 62) and as existentially empty is partly drawn from Jean Baudrillard's 'system of objects' and partly from Derrida's logic of the 'pharmakon' (Derrida, 1981). The very constitution of a specific world and 'mitsein' is characterized by a collective relation to things that operate as transitional objects in the Winnicott sense: things exist in the form of a tie or seal within a system of things that holds the world together (Winnicott, 1953). Such things accrue value within the realm of symbolic exchange and mutuality. They are otherwise devoid of content or empty, characterized by a necessary 'nothing'.

For Stiegler, one serious problem is that under capitalism the aura of things shifts as things become increasingly disposable, even structurally obsolescent. Their symbolic value becomes more transitory and uncertain to a radically different degree. Hannah Arendt had foreseen that this 'systematic infidelity' destroys 'the sustainability of the world'. This description of the present order of things – where 'everything solid melts into air' – strikes a chord with Lyotard's 'law of adaptation' that holds under the postmodern condition as well as with Zygmunt Bauman's condition of 'liquid modernity' (Arendt, 1958; Bauman, 2000; Lyotard, 1986; Marx and Engels, 2015). Liquid selves live in a world of liquid fear where the basic unit of the social bond is hollowed out and the ultimate, nightmare scenario is made of 'consumers without object'. Stiegler's account of things is predicated on a historical sense of radical shifts between orders of 'techne' – or technology – towards the present, digital order populated by 'internauts' who occupy, engage with, exchange and find meaning in an 'internet of things' (Stiegler, 2013, 63).

Stiegler's argument is couched in terms of crisis: as though the present condition or the condition of the present represents a historically new condition of loss. It is lapsarian: it projects back, by implication, at least, to a time of more finely attuned relation between human and 'techne' encapsulated in the rather romantic image of the 'sealhunter who carves his harpoon' (Stiegler, 2013, 84). Accordingly, Stiegler's account of contemporary global conditions is organized around the idea of salvation based on the metaphor of healing, referring to a 'pharmacology of the spirit' and 'a pharmacology of symbolic relations' meaning, effectively, a return to a prior relation to the world through the things of human production (Stiegler, 2013).

Stiegler is one among many – Weber, Heidegger, Marcuse, Adorno, Derrida, Bauman and others – who have updated Freud's discontented civilization through an account of the present condition (Adorno, 1990; Bauman, 2000; Derrida, 2004; Heidegger, 1977; Marcuse, 1964; Weber, 1991). After the death of God, after the discovery of the unconscious and the formless 'thing' it harbours, after the various crises of modernity – including Derrida's 'twelve plagues' but also the general loss of meaning that comes with the end of grand narratives, the awareness of radical finitude, the acknowledgement of solar death to come and the perhaps humbling recognition of a necessary turn to animality: after all of these apparent falls, we are perhaps left with the big existential question that is not simply about how to improve things; the big existential question, surely, is an invitation to reconsider, above all an invitation to 'thinking'.

Adriana Cavarero

Adriana Cavarero offers an interesting instance of deconstruction in her feminized rereading of Hannah Arendt whose work both guides Cavarero's thought and provides the occasion for a quite radical and far-reaching rethinking. Cavarero's career is an extended example of such rereading in order to reconceptualise ontology, especially political ontology, through a feminist lens, expressly inspired by Luce Irigarary's discourse on identity (Irigaray, 1993). Inheriting a rich vein of feminist thinking, Cavarero is able to meticulously work through some of the key concepts of her chosen philosophical loadstone, Hannah Arendt. In a parallel with Malabou and Derrida, Cavarero takes some key lines of thinking from Arendt and utterly transforms them, providing a provocative rethinking of the tradition of philosophy. Her feminist perspective offers not only a fulcrum of critique but, more importantly, a position and mechanism to shift the grounds of essential thinking. In that sense, Cavarero is an ontologist who returns to key philosophical and mythological texts in order to review and renew their meanings, often providing an utterly transformed reading that recovers the unrevealed significance of figures and themes that have been occluded or masked by patriarchal readings.

Cavarero's practice illustrates the hermeneutic principle of horizons well. In her first book, Cavarero takes on the venerable status of Ancient Greek thinking in the figures of Plato and Parmenides particularly but does so through the inspiration of Irigaray's feminist-inspired deconstructive philosophy. Cavarero's approach is figurative and imaginative, and highlights the carceral character of patriarchal discourse in order to propose a symbolic female order. One highly inventive move she makes in this process is to take Arendt's pronouncement that it is *natality* that characterizes human uniqueness as a way of affirming the primacy of the feminine without presenting a strict programme or totalized system of thinking.

With an immediate and practical political significance, Cavarero's work explores the politics of the body, looking at both political metaphors deploying the body and asking questions about the exclusion of the body from the foundational categories of politics, again indicating her desire to re-examine and extend the inherited ideas of Arendt in rearticulating political ontology. Her work insists on the political (for Heidegger, simply 'mitsein', the very fact of being together) as fundamental and draws this sense from its expansion of ideas of self and other, construing the self as 'narratable' but also in need of the corroborative narrative engagement of others. Reciprocal relations suggest that being is networked, intricately drawn out through exchanges that are always at work, provisional and mobile. Her thinking on identity came to influence Judith Butler – as it holds an unusual tension between the immersion in language that is the collective medium *par excellence* and the physical embodiment of language through her redefinition of 'voice', a redefinition that much research that is oriented towards 'voice' as a privileged carrier of identity has not touched on.

Cavarero has also given us a highly charged account of the contemporary: basing her thinking here on the prominence she gives to the phenomenon of 'horror'. Cavarero's arguments here are intricate and complex, but she reveals an inherent – ontological – vulnerability that is a feature of bodily existence and that on the one hand reveals a need for the care of the other (or even Other). At the same time, vulnerability is, intriguingly, I think, for Cavarero, the condition of possibility for an essential dignity both in the unique body and in the reciprocity that this vulnerability carries with it. This is a powerful position that may have (as yet unexplored) connections with Catherine Malabou's 'ontology of the accident'.

The effect and implications of Caverero's thinking are far-reaching. As indicated, she draws a great deal on Hannah Arendt's ontological stance as expressed in *The Human Condition*, but she modifies it, rethinks its implications and gives it a specific turn that turns it against the depredations of historical patriarchy and that also enables fresh thinking concerning contemporary political ontology.

So, what calls for thinking?

I've argued throughout this book that educational research has been beset by a limited technology. As the handbooks proliferate, the dimension of thinking, as here defined, retreats and is displaced by a predictable format that eschews what is most proper to philosophy, as defined, or at least suggested, by some key figures that I have privileged throughout.

This final section is mostly dedicated to the suggestion that there are rich resources for thinking in modern and contemporary philosophy that are not much informing the practices of educational research, and that don't – and can't – get recognition in the dominant models of research that prevail. I have only here been able to touch on some of the implications of some key ways of thinking that offer to deconstruct the inheritance of philosophy, that therefore revive the significance of that inheritance and offer a possibility that what Heidegger refers to, without defining, as 'thinking', may be possible and may be a productive, alternative resource for the metaphysics of research – and that may therefore enable researchers to engage with their interests in a more ontological mode, seriously grappling with what is most near to their interests in a fundamental way.

Note: Another chapter, another book, indeed, might have been dedicated to some of the most powerful strands of contemporary thinking that address the 'anthropocene' and its implications to any thinking of human and non-human futures. Global warming appears in philosophy as a symptom of 'technological enframing' (Heidegger) as the expression of the runaway effects of the burgeoning human presence on earth. Increasingly, thinking posits the finitude of that presence. In the immediate sense, there is the danger inherent in the ecological crisis that has already transformed the very substance of the world, that calls for a rethinking of human 'stewardship' (if that is what it is that is called for) as a matter of drastic urgency. This theme occurs especially – and very cogently – in the work of Bruno Latour, Donna Harraway, Timothy Moreton and Bernard Stiegler (Haraway, 2016; Latour, 2013; Moreton, 2013; Stiegler, 2013). Educationists will argue that education can provide the knowledge and learning required to transform present conditions. Others, myself included, will indicate that education has not achieved such a conversion so far, and that education itself, with its own technical rationalities, its intrication in biopower, is part of the problem. I hope to address this question in further works.

Final Theses

This book has presented what it takes to be an original case for the reconsideration of research in education, although its thinking applies more generally to the social sciences. It has done this by focusing on essential elements of thinking that are available through some strands in modern and contemporary philosophy. It has also offered a critique-explicit and implicit-of the handbooks that offer a set genre for the writing of theses in education. It has been predicated on the idea that thinking has a significant role in the production of knowledge. Thinking, it claims, is a form of knowledge. Thinking in the sense used here is not merely ruminating but is an active drawing on and use of the resources of the legacy of thought in order to think anew. If metaphysics is always all around us, then thinking may arise in unexpected places and may offer insight and knowledge in such guises as much as in the more formal arenas of philosophy.

This final section summarizes some of its claims that are here offered as provocations to displace the formulaic approach to educational research that has become so common and restricts the scope and the significance of the field.

- The dimension of thinking is always present in research whether acknowledged or not.
- Philosophy can provide a useful series of terms to address fundamental, essential dimensions of research. I have suggested phenomenology, ontology, epistemology, hermeneutics, ethics, aporetics. I have suggested that these categories, once understood, offer more productive points of entry for real researchers in the context of their interest.
- To put the above terms to active use (and to render research productive in terms of the researcher's immediate interests and predilections) does not require voluminous philosophical knowledge.
- At the same time, contemporary thinking, in the form of philosophy, is rich with powerful resources. Engaging with such thinking offers the possibility itself

of generating new knowledge concerning familiar objects. It may on occasions be essential for going beyond or getting outside strongly entrenched received wisdom – or ideology.

- There can be no such thing as a literature review as commonly conceived of by the research manuals and the genre of research they have come to sanctify. The literature – and therefore the thinking – that bears upon a subject cannot be so bounded. To suggest that the appropriate literature that bears upon a subject already exists in determinate form is likely to lead to restriction of thinking and repetition of research clichés. The literature review in effect plays its part in relegating thinking to a second order activity, at least.
- Common oppositions of research perspectives, for example:

  Constructivist/positivist

  Quantitative/qualitative

  Empirical/theoretical

  are much less useful and productive than the organic categories of thinking offered in Chapter 1 in this volume.
- Theory is another name for thinking, often dismissed by advocates of practical, impact-driven research. This is a serious mistake. Theory is essential as what offers an alternative horizon to the embedded way of thinking and seeing that inhabit a practice and determines its objects. This relates to the hermeneutic dimension that enables the displacement of the subject and the redetermination of the aspect of the object in question. To eschew theory is to be a victim of non-thinking.
- A useful starting point, which any researcher can engage with, is to produce a basic phenomenology of research relations.
- From this, the ontological dimension is brought into play by the force of the simple question: What is ...?; this opens onto the historical, social, institutional dimension of the object in question.
- The dimension of subjectivity – while avoidable – is always present but is rarely well understood in research, either by those who seek to banish its presence or those who seek to embrace it. No research, of course, can be undertaken without an orientation towards its object or without a powerful element of desire. Both require a subject and engage subjectivity.
- The subject is not the static agent of research, but is transformed by the phenomenological encounter with the object and in the meeting – or collision – of horizons. Neither is the subject ever neutral in relation to the object and

the world both inhabit. Giving an account of subjectivity is a significant form of thinking.

- Subjectivity is never as subjective as we are trained to imagine. Giving an account of ourselves – our subjectivity – requires that we objectify ourselves, our experience, our knowledge, our desire. We can do this by focusing on history, sociology and other aspects of context. In addressing these dimensions, we transform ourselves by transforming our self-understanding. This process includes the strange effect of objectifying our own subjectivity.
- A consideration of ontology opens questions concerning the identity of things and of any specific 'thing'. 'What is …?' acts as a kind of loosening agent that is productive and is fundamental to any research seeking.
- Any consideration of ontology (of what is) is likely to encounter or call forth the ontotheological: the determination of what is – and any settlement of identity (of the identity of things or of any *thing*) must acknowledge this.
- Ethics relates to the subject of research. Ethics in research must include questions about purpose and about orientations to questions of truth and the 'institutions of truth' – or thinking: 'There is nothing either good or bad, but thinking makes it so' (*Hamlet*, II, ii). Educational research manuals and university practices have tended to restrict ethics to a prophylactic, usually bureaucratically governed process of legitimation with no positive content.
- Research that engages thinking demands decision-making. Decisions are more interesting and complex than we may commonly believe, as deconstruction demonstrates. Taking responsibility for the decisions we make as researchers engages with the dimension of the ethical: and this is ever-present. Research involves – at every major stage – major decisions. The logic of the decision escapes the enclosure of pure rationality. This introduces the inescapable element of faith.
- Ethics also goes beyond the subjectivity of the researcher. It necessary engages with the 'ethnos', with the dimension of belonging to a world and standing in a position of responsibility for one's productivity in a contextual sense.
- Knowledge and research (as we know these things), as indicated, cannot escape entirely from the dimension of faith. Our being-in-the-world and our essential relations with others are significantly predicated on various forms of collective faith, as recently demonstrated by Bernard Stiegler (2013).
- Hermeneutics provides an essential dimension for research (especially in terms of originality). The awareness of horizons of knowing and horizons of understanding offers rich possibilities for the production of knowledge.

- The issue of originality is not at all trivial. It is essential for research to constantly revisit knowledge – and the grounds of knowledge – to remain vital.
- The relations between an object (or a topic of research) and its context open the possibility for infinite expansions of knowledge. This relation means that knowledge cannot follow a simply progressive or purely logical path. Giving an account of the world of the subject–object relation can be enormously complex, interesting and productive, especially when allied with modes of thinking drawing on the rich resources of understanding of modern and contemporary thinking or theory.
- Because of the determinations of significant objects in the field of education, there is always a political dimension to the pursuit of educational knowledge, if we understand politics as concerning forms of collective life and questions of how to live 'together'. Such a politics might be referred to as an onto-politics, as it, potentially, at least, calls into question familiar, established and powerful objects. This is politics of a more fundamental and revolutionary character than what usually passes as the politics of education mostly restricted to irrelevant questions of policy. Policy questions and the role of government are not well understood in educational research.
- Fundamental objects in education – including education itself – cry out for research attention but are mostly not addressed in educational research with any strong ontological intent.
- Questions concerning data are more complex and more interesting than research practice generally acknowledges. The unproblematic use of data as a term indicating decisive, indicative material – as well suggesting a discrete component of research – is symptomatic of much repetitive educational and social science research.
- Historically, the role of thinking in educational research has been dominated and restricted by a certain privilege that has been granted to the empirical.
- The philosophy of education has, historically, in its hegemonic form, refused to engage in fundamental thinking, preferring to rely on its very limited and ultimately conservative heritage. The philosophy of education has almost invariably seen itself as the servant of education, to whose transcendental status it bows.
- The dominant tendency of educational research is to be attached to an ethic of improvement or to an ethic of redemption. Both limit and distort possible modes of educational research.

- Metaphysics is an inescapable dimension of thinking, of writing and of knowledge. Research is always already metaphysical, freighted with ideas about its object, its world, the world. These ideas – this metaphysical dimension – can be more or less explicit.
- It follows that the idea of an empirical project that takes its starting point and its force from 'data' and only data is in danger of being misguided.
- Education research has eschewed questions concerning ontology. This is especially the case with educational philosophy that has, mostly, sought to act as an adjunct to an educational project that it takes for granted as a positive end-in-itself.
- Research projects often expend disproportionate energy on 'data' production. Methodology is often mistaken for an articulation, account or justification for method, when method is conceived of as data-producing technology. Apparatus questions are largely ignored in educational research, undermining the authority of much of the research conducted in relation to schooling and higher education, and invalidating, at the level of meaning much of the data accrued.
- What's more, data can never speak for itself. The discursive dimension is rich, complex and has been enormously enriched by a long and multifaceted tradition in modern thinking. The role of narrative in research is misunderstood by the separation of narrative into its own distinct, relatively minor mode. Narrative is always already in research, any research. Engaging with narrative promises powerful possibilities for the researcher.
- Modern thinking is alive and well. Formal philosophy is rich in resource and is challenging and exciting. What's more, deconstruction engages with modes of knowledge beyond the formal confines of philosophy to regenerate thinking and to vigorously, rigorously probe the big questions. These questions include returning to the enduring questions of the heritage of metaphysics; and the special, and especially challenging questions that confront 'we contemporaries'.

References

Abraham, N. (1994) *The Shell and the Kernel: Renewals of Psychoanalysis*. Chicago, Chicago University Press, 1994.

Adorno, T.W. (1990) *Negative Dialectics*. London, Routledge.

Agamben, G. (1997) *Homo Sacer*. Stanford, Stanford University Press.

Agamben, G. (2013) *The Highest Poverty*. Stanford, Stanford University Press.

Althusser, Louis (1984a) *Lenin and Philosophy*. London, Verso.

Althusser, L. (1984b) *Essays on Ideology*. London, Verso.

Anderson, P. (1992) *English Questions*. London, Verso.

Anderson, R. (2006) *British Universities Past and Present*. London, Continuum.

Appadurai, A. (1996) *Modernity at Large*. London, Minneapolis, University of Minnesota Press.

Apple, M. (2014) *Knowledge, Power and Education*. London, Routledge.

Arendt, H. (1958) *The Human Condition*. Chicago, University of Chicago Press.

Arendt, H. (1964) *Eichmann in Jerusalem*. New York, Viking Press.

Arthur, J., Kristjánsson, K., Harrison, T., Sanderse, W., Wright, D. (2016) Teaching Character and Virtue in Schools. London, Routledge.

Augustine (2016) *Confessions*, accessed from http://faculty.georgetown.edu/jod/augus-tine/conf.pdf

Ayer, A.J. (1971) *Language, Truth and Logic*. Harmondsworth, Penguin Books.

Bacon, F. (1620) *Novum Organum*. http://oll.libertyfund.org/titles/bacon-novum-organum

Badiou, A. (2007) *Being and Event*. London, Continuum.

Ball, S. (2004) 'Performativities and Fabrications in the Education Economy'. In Ball, S. (ed.) *The RoutledgeFalmer Reader in Sociology of Education*. London, RoutledgeFalmer, pp. 143–155.

Ball, S. (2005) *Education Policy and Social Class*. London, Routledge.

Ball, S. (2013) *The Education Debate*. Bristol, Policy Press.

Ball, S. (2013) *Foucault, Power and Education*. London, Routledge.

Barthes, R. (1973) *Mythologies*. London, Paladin.

Batsleer, J., Davies, T., O'Rourke R., and Weedon, C. (1985) *Rewriting English: Cultural Politics of Gender and Class*. London, Methuen.

Bauman, Z. (1991) *Modernity and the Holocaust*. Cambridge, Polity.

Bauman, Z. (2000) *Liquid Modernity*. Cambridge, Polity.

Bauman, Z. (2003) *Liquid Love*. Cambridge, Polity.

Bauman, Z. (2004) *Identity*. Cambridge, Polity.

Bauman, Z. (2005) *Liquid Life*. Cambridge, Polity.

Bauman, Z. (2006a) *Liquid Fear*. Cambridge, Polity.

Bauman, Z. (2006b) *Liquid Times*. Cambridge, Polity.

Bell, J. (with Waters, S.) (2014) *Doing Your Research Project*. Maidenhead, Open University Press.

Belsey, C. (1980) *Critical Practice* London, Methuen.

Belsey, C. (2005) *Culture and the Real*. Abingdon, Routledge.

Benjamin, W. (1999) 'Theses on the Philosophy of History'. In *Illuminations*. London, Pimlico, pp. 245–255.

Benvenuto, B. and Kennedy, R. (1986) *The Works of Jacques Lacan*. London, Free Association Books.

Berkeley, G. (2009) *A Treatise Concerning the Principles of Human Knowledge* in *Principles of Human Knowledge and Three Dialogues*. Oxford, Oxford University Press.

Bernstein, B. (1970) 'Education Cannot Compensate for Society'. *New Society*, 387, 344–347.

Bernstein B. (1971) *Class, Codes and Control*. London, Routledge and Kegan Paul.

Bernstein B. (ed.) (1973) *Class, Codes and Control: Vol. 2*. London, Routledge and Kegan Paul.

Bernstein, B. (1987) 'Class, Codes, and Communication'. In U. Ammon, N. Dittmar, K. Mattheier, P. Trudgill (eds.), *Sociolinguistics: An International Handbook of the Science of Language and Society*, vol. 1. Berlin, Walter de Gruyter, pp. 1287–1303.

Bernstein, B. (1995) *Pedagogy, Symbolic Control and Identity*. London, Taylor & Francis.

Bernstein, B. (1997) 'Class and Pedagogies: Visible and Invisible'. In A. H. Halsey, H. Lauder, P. Brown, A. Stuart Wells (eds.), *Education: Culture, Economy, Society*. Oxford, Oxford University Press, pp. 59–79.

Biesta, G. (2006) *Beyond Learning: Democratic Education for a Human Future*. Boulder, Paradigm.

Bonneuil, C. and Fressoz J.-B. (2016) *The Shock of the Anthropocene: The Earth, History and Us*. London, Verso.

Boothby, R. (2001) *Freud as Philosopher*. London, Routledge.

Bourdieu, P. (1991) *Language and Symbolic Power*. Cambridge, Polity.

Bourdieu, P. and Passeron, J.-C. (1970) *La Reproduction*. Paris, Editions de Minuit.

Bowles, S. and Gintis, H. (1976) *Schooling in Capitalist America*. London, Routledge and Kegan Paul.

Bracher, M. and Ragland-Sullivan, E. (eds.) (1991) *Lacan and the Subject of Language*. London, Routledge.

Brassier, R. (2007) *Nihil Unbound*. New York, Palgrave.

Brock, C. and Alexiadou, N. (2013) *Education Around the World*. London, Bloomsbury.

Brown, P. and Lauder, H. (2004) in Ball, S. (ed.) *Education, globalization and economic development The Routledge Falmer Reader in Sociology of Education*. London, RoutledgeFalmer, pp. 47–71.

Brown, P., Reay, D. and Vincent C. (eds.) (2015) *Education and Social Mobility*. London, Routledge.

Bryson, B. (2004) *A Short History of Nearly Everything*. London, Black Swan.

Bullock Report, The (1975) *A Language for Life*. London, H.M.S.O.

Burbules, N. and Torres, C. (eds.) (2000) *Globalization and Education. Critical Perspectives*. London, Routledge.

Butler, J. (1988) 'Performative Acts and Gender Constitution: An Essay in Phenomenology and Feminist Theory'. *Theatre Journal*, 40, 4.

Butler, J. (1990) *Gender Trouble*. New York, Routledge.

Butler, J. (1997) *Excitable Speech*. London, Routledge.

Butler, J. (2005) *Giving and Account of Oneself*. New York, Fordham University Press.

Calarco, M. (2008) *Zoographies*. New York, Columbia University Press.

Carr, D. (1998) *Education, Knowledge and Truth*. London, Routledge.

Carr, W. (2006) 'Education Without Theory'. *British Journal of Educational Studies*, 54 (2), 136–159.

Carr, W. (2007) 'Educational Research as a Practical Science'. *International Journal of Research and Method in Education*, 30 (3), 271–278.

Carson, A. (2009) *Grief Lessons: Four Plays by Euripides*. New York, NYRB Classics.

Castells, M. (2004) *The Power of Identity*. Oxford, Blackwell.

Cavarero, A. (1995) *In Spite of Plato*. New York, Routledge.

Cavarero, A. (2000) *Relating Narratives*. London, Routledge.

Cavarero, A. (2002) *Stately Bodies*. Ann Arbor, The University of Michigan Press.

Cavarero, A. (2005) *For More Than One Voice*. Stanford, Stanford University Press.

Cavarero, A. (2008) *Horrorism: Naming Contemporary Violence*. Columbia University Press.

Chaiklin, S. (2003) 'The Zone of Proximal Development in Vygotsky's Analysis of Learning and Instruction'. In A. Kozulin (ed.), *Vygotsky's Educational Theory in Cultural Context*. Cambridge, Cambridge University Press, pp. 39–63.

Chomsky, N. (1965) *Aspects of the Theory of Syntax*. Cambridge, MA, MIT Press.

Chomsky, N. (2000) *New Horizons in the Study of Language and Mind*. Cambridge, Cambridge University Press.

Christie F. (ed.) (1999) *Pedagogy and the Shaping of Consciousness: Linguistic and Social Processes*. London, Cassell.

Churchland, P.M. (1981) 'Eliminative Materialism and the Propositional Attitudes'. *The Journal of Philosophy*, 78 (2), 67–90.

Crotty, M.J. (1998) *The Foundations of Social Research*. London, Sage.

Darwin, C. (1860) *On the Origin of Species*. New York, Appleton and Co.

Delanty, G. (2005) 'The Sociology of the University and Higher Education: The Consequences of Globalization'. In Calhoun, C., Rojek, C. and Turner, B. (eds.) *Handbook of International Sociology*. London, Sage, pp. 530–545.

Delpit, L. (1988) 'The Silenced Dialogue'. *Harvard Educational Review*, 58, 280–298.

Delpit, L. (1995) *Other People's Children: Cultural Conflict in the Classroom*. New York, The New Press.

Denicolo, P. (2013) *Achieving Impact in Research*. London, Sage.

Derrida, J. (1976) *Of Grammatology*. London, The Johns Hopkins University Press.

Derrida, J. (1978) *Writing and Difference*. London, Routledge and Kegan Paul.

Derrida, J. (1980) 'The Law of Genre'. *Critical Inquiry*, 7, 1.

Derrida, J. (1981) *Dissemination*. London, University of Chicago Press.

Derrida, J. (1987) *Positions*. London, Athlone.

Derrida, J. (1993) *Aporias*. Stanford, CA, Stanford University Press.

Derrida, J. (1994) *Spectres of Marx*. London, Routledge.

Derrida, J. (1996) *Archive Fever*. Chicago, Chicago University Press.

Derrida, J. (1999) *Adieu to Emmanuel Levinas*. Stanford, CA, Stanford University Press.

Derrida, J. (2001) *Deconstruction Engaged: The Sydney Seminars*. Sydney, Power Publication.

Derrida, J. (2004) *The Animal That Therefore I Am*. New York, Fordham University Press.

DES (1998) *The Education Reform Act*. London, HMSO.

Dick & Kofman (2002) *Derrida*. Zeitgeist Films.

Dollimore, J. and Sinfield, A. (1985) *Political Shakespeare*. Manchester, Manchester University Press.

Donald, J. (1992) *Sentimental Education*. London, Verso.

Doyle, B. (1989) *English and Englishness*. London, Routledge.

Dreyfus, H. and Rabinow, P. (eds.) (1994) *The Foucault Reader*. New York, Pantheon Books, pp. 32–50.

Dylan, B. (2001) 'High Water' on *Love and Theft*.

Easthope, A. (1988) *British Post-Structuralism since 1968*. London, Routledge.

Easthope, A. (1991) *Literary into Cultural Studies*. London, Routledge.

Elias, N. (2000) *The Civilizing Process*. Oxford, Blackwell.

Feyerabend, P. (1975a) *Against Method*. New York, Humanities Press.

Feyerabend, P. (1975b) 'How to Defend Society Against Science'. *Radical Philosophy* 11, 3–8.

Foucault, M. (1977a) *Discipline and Punish*. London, Allen Lane.

Foucault, M. (1977b) *The Archaeology of Knowledge*. London, Routledge.

Foucault, M. (1981) 'The Order of Discourse'. In Robert Young (ed.), *Untying the Text*. London, Routledge and Kegan Paul, pp. 48–78.

Foucault, M. (1984) 'What Is Enlightenment?' In Paul Rabinow (ed.), *The Foucault Reader*, New York, Pantheon Books, pp. 32–50.

Foucault, M. (1988) 'What Is an Author'. In David Lodge (ed.), *Modern Criticism and Theory*. London, Longman, pp. 281–293.

Foucault, M. (1997) *Ethics, Subjectivity and Truth*. New York, New Press.

Foucault, M. (2005) *The Order of Things*. London, Routledge.

Foucault, M. (2009) *The History of Madness*. London, Routledge.

Freud, S. (1900) *The Interpretation of Dreams*. London, Hogarth Press.

Freud, S. (1901) *The Psychopathology of Everyday Life*. London, Hogarth Press.

Freud, S. (1921) *Beyond the Pleasure Principle*. London, Hogarth Press.

Fukuyama, F. (1992) *The End of History and the Last Man*. Harmondsworth, Penguin Books.

Fullan, M. (2001) *The New Meaning of Educational Change*. New York, Teachers College Press.

Fullan, M. and Hargreaves, A. (1998) *What's Worth Fighting for in Education*. New York, Teachers' College Press.

Gadamer, H.G. (1989) *Truth and Method*. London, Continuum.

Giroux, H. (2011) *On Critical Pedagogy*. London, Continuum.

Giroux, H. (2015) 'Where Is the Outrage? Critical Pedagogy in Dark Times', accessed from https://www.youtube.com/watch?v=CAxj87RRtsc

Gorard, S. (2002) *Creating a Learning Society*. Bristol, Policy Press.

Gorard, S. (2013) *Overcoming Disadvantage in Education*. London, Routledge.

Gorard, S. (2013) *Research Design*. London, Sage.

Gramsci, A. (1991) *Prison Notebooks*. New York, Columbia University Press.

Green, Andy (1997) *Education, Globalization and the Nation State*. London, Macmillan.

Greene, B. (2011) *The Elegant Universe*. New York, Vintage.

Grene, M. (1966) *The Knower and the Known*. Oakland, University of California Press.

Grosvenor, I. (1999) 'On Visualizing Past Classrooms'. In I. Grosvenor, M. Lawn and K. Rousmaniere (eds.), *Silences and Images*. New York, Peter Lang, pp. 85–104.

Habermas, J. (1984) *The Theory of Communicative Action*. London, Heinemann.

Habermas, J. (1987) 'The Idea of the University: Learning Processes'. *New German Critique*, 41, pp. 3–22.

Habermas, J. (1990) *Moral Consciousness and Communicative Action*. Cambridge, MA, MIT Press.

Halliday, M.A.K. (1973) *Explorations in the Functions of Language*. London, Arnold.

Halliday, M.A.K. (1979) *Language as Social Semiotic*. London, Edward Arnold.

Halliday, M.A.K. (2007) *Language and Society*. London, Continuum.

Hamilton, D. (1989) *Towards a Theory of Schooling*. London, Falmer.

Hammersley, M. (2007) 'The Issue of Quality in Qualitative Research'. *International Journal of Research and Method in Education*, 30 (3), 207–305.

Haraway, D. (2016) *Staying with the Trouble: Making Kin in the Chthulucene*. Durham, Duke University Press.

Harber, C. (2004) *Schooling as Violence*. Abingdon, RoutledgeFalmer.

Hardt, M. and Negri, A. (2000) *Empire*. Cambridge, Harvard University Press.

Hardt, M. and Negri, A. (2005) *Multitude*. Harmondsworth, Penguin.

Hardt, M. and Negri, A. (2009) *Commonwealth*. Cambridge, Harvard University Press.

Harland, R. (1987) *Superstructuralism: The Philosophy of Structuralism and Post-structuralism*. London, Routledge.

Harman, G. (2007) *Heidegger Explained*. Chicago, Open Court.

Harman, G. (2016) *Immaterialism: Objects and Social Theory*. Cambridge, Polity.

Harvey, D. (1991) *The Condition of Postmodernity*. Oxford, Blackwell.

Hatcher, R. (2001) 'Getting Down to the Business: Schooling in the globalized Economy', *Education and Social Justice*, 3, 2, pp. 45–59.

Hebdige, D. (1979) *Subculture: The Meaning of Style*. London, Methuen.

Hegel, G.W.F. (1998) *Phenomenology of Spirit*. Delhi, Motilal Barnarsidass.

Heidegger, M. (1962) *Being and Time*. Oxford, Blackwell.

Heidegger, M. (1967) *What Is a Thing?* Indiana, Gateway.

Heidegger, M. (1977) *The Question Concerning Technology*. New York, Harper & Row.

Heidegger, M. (1991a) *Nietzsche*: Volumes one and two. New York, Harper Collins.

Heidegger, M. (1991b) *The Principle of Reason*. Bloomington and Indianapolis, Indiana University Press.

Heidegger, M. (1993a) 'What Is Metaphysics?'. In *Martin Heidegger: Basic Writings*. London, Routledge, pp. 89–108.

Heidegger, M. (1993b) 'Letter on Humanism'. In *Martin Heidegger: Basic Writings*. London, Routledge, pp. 213–264.

Heidegger, M. (1993c) 'The Question concerning Technology'. In *Martin Heidegger: Basic Writings*. London, Routledge, pp. 307–341.

Heidegger, M. (1993d) 'The End of Philosophy and the Task of Thinking'. In *Martin Heidegger: Basic Writings*. London, Routledge, pp. 427–449.

Heidegger, M. (1993e) 'What Calls for Thinking'. In *Martin Heidegger: Basic Writings*. London, Routledge, pp. 369–391.

Heidegger, M. (1998) *Parmenides*. Bloomington and Indianapolis, Indiana University Press.

Heidegger, M. (2002) *The Essence of Truth*. London, Continuum.

Heisenberg, W. (1930) *The Physical Principles of the Quantum Theory*. Chicago, Chicago University Press.

Heisenberg, W. (1990) *Physics and Philosophy*. London, Penguin.

Herbst, J. (1999) 'The History of Education: State of the Art at the Turn of the Century in Europe and North America'. *Paedagogica Historica*, 35, 3.

Hirst, P. and Peters, R.S. (1970) *The Logic of Education*. London, Routledge.

Hochschild, A. (1999) *King Leopold's Ghost*. Boston, Mariner Books.

Hopkins, D. (2001) *School Improvement for Real*. London and New York, RoutledgeFalmer.

Howell, K.E. (2012) *The Philosophy of Methodology*. London, Sage.

Hull, J.M. (1975) *School Worship: An Obituary*. London, SCM Press.

Hunter, I. (1988) *Culture and Government*. London, Macmillan.

Hunter, I. (1994) *Rethinking the School*. Sydney, Allen & Unwin.

Husserl, E. (1970) *The Crisis of European Sciences and Transcendental Philosophy*. Evanston, Northwestern University Press.

Husserl, E. (1973) *Logical Investigations*. London, Routledge.

Irigaray, L. (1993) *Je, Tu, Nous: Towards a Culture of Difference*. London, Routledge.

Johnson, R. (1981) 'Really Useful Knowledge: Radical Education and Working Class Culture 1790–1848'. In R. Dale et al. (ed.), *Politics Patriarchy and Practice: Education and the State*. vol. 2. Basingstoke, Falmer Ford/OU Press, pp. 3–37.

Johnson, S. (1985) *The History of Rasselas, Prince of Abyssinia*. London, Penguin Books.

Jones, D. (1990) 'The Genealogy of the Urban Schoolteacher'. In S. Ball (ed.), *Foucault and Education: Disciplines and Knowledge*. London, Routledge, pp. 57–77.

Jones, D.K. (1977) *The Making of the Education System*. London, Routledge and Kegan Paul.

Jones, K. (2003) *Education in Britain*. Cambridge, Polity.

Jorgensen, M. (2002) *Discourse Analysis as Theory and Method*. London, Sage.

Kant, I. (1991) *Metaphysics of Morals*. Cambridge, Cambridge University Press.

Kant, I. (2003) *The Critique of Pure Reason*. New York, Dover.

Kant, I. (2014) *The Critique of Practical Reason*. Project Gutenberg: accessed at http://www.gutenberg.org/ebooks/5683, 2016.

Kuhn, T. (1959) *The Copernican Revolution*. New York, Random House.

Kuhn, T. (1970) *The Structure of Scientific Revolutions*. Chicago, Chicago University Press.

Labov, W. (2004) 'The Logic of Nonstandard English'. In O. Santa Ana (ed.), *Tongue-tied: The Lives of Multilingual Children in Public Education*. New York, Rowman and Littlefield, pp. 134–151.

Lacan J. (1977) *Ecrits: A Selection*. London, Tavistock.

Lacan, J. (1986) *The Four Fundamental Concepts of Psychoanalysis*. Harmondsworth, Peregrine.

Lacan, J. (2006) *Ecrits*. New York, Norton.

Latour, B. (2011) *Reassembling the Social: An Introduction to Actor-Network-Theory*. Oxford, Oxford University Press.

Latour, B. (2013) *An Inquiry into Modes of Existence*. Cambridge, MA, Harvard University Press.

Leavis, F.R. (1969) *English Literature in Our Time and the University*. London, Chatto and Windus.

Leavis, F.R. and Leavis, Q.D. (1970) *Dickens the Novelist*. London, Chatto and Windus.

Lindley, D. (2008) *Uncertainty*. New York, Anchor.

Lowe, R. (1997) *Schooling and Social Change, 1964–1990*. London, Routledge.

Lyotard, J.-F. (1986) *The Postmodern Condition*. Manchester, Manchester University Press.

Lyotard, J.-F. (1988) *The Differend*. Manchester, Manchester University Press.

Lyotard, J.-F. (1991) *The Inhuman Reflections on Time*. Stanford, CA, Stanford University Press.

Macdonell, D. (1991) *Theories of Discourse*. New York, Wiley.

Macherey, P. (1978) *A Theory of Literary Production*. London, Routledge and Kegan Paul.

Maclure, M. (2003) *Discourse in Educational and Social Research*. Buckingham, Open University Press.

Malabou, C. (2009) *Plasticity at the Dusk of* Writing. New York, Columbia University Press

Malabou, C. (2012) *Ontology of the Accident*. Cambridge, Polity.

Malabou, C. (2015) *Plastic Materialities*. Durham, Duke University Press.

Malabou, C. (2016) *The Anthropocene: A New History*. Castle Lecture Series, Durham Castle, Great Hall.

Malabou, C. (2016) *Before Tomorrow: Epigenesis and Rationality*. London, Polity.

Marcuse, H. (1964) *One-Dimensional Man*. Boston, Beacon Press.

Marx, K. (1970) *A Contribution to the Critique of Political Economy*. Moscow, Progress Publishers.

Marx, K. and Engels, F. (1848) *The Manifesto of the Communist Party*, accessed https://www.marxists.org/archive/marx/works/download/pdf/Manifesto.pdf, 2016.

Marx, K. and Engels, F. (2015) *The Communist Manifesto*. Harmondsworth, Penguin.

Masschelein, J. and Simons, M. (2013) *In Defence of the School*. Leuven, E-ducation, Culture & Society Publishers.

Mathieson, M. (1975) *The Preachers of Culture*. London, Allen and Unwin.

Maton, K. (2013) *Knowledge and Knowers: Towards a Realist Sociology of Education*. London, Routledge.

McLuhan, M. (1964) *Understanding Media*. New York, Mentor.

Meillassoux, Q. (2009) *After Finitude: An Essay on the Necessity of Finitude*. London, Continuum.

Merleau-Ponty, M. (2002) *Phenomenology of Perception*. New York, Routledge and Kegan Paul.

Mitchell, J. (1975) *Psychoanalysis and Feminism*. Harmondsworth, Penguin.

Moi, T. (1985) *Sexual/Textual Politics*. London, Methuen.

de Montaigne, M. (1993) *The Complete Essays*. London, Penguin Classics.

Moore, R. (2009) *Towards a Sociology of Truth*. London, Continuum.

Moran, D. (2000) *Introduction to Phenomenology*. London, Routledge.

Moreton, T. (2013) *Hyperobjects*. Minneapolis, University of Minnesota Press.

Muller J. and Young, M. (2007) 'Truth and Truthfulness in the Sociology of Educational Knowledge'. *Theory and Research in Education*, 5 (2), 173–201.

Murdoch, D.R. (1989) *Niels Bohr's Philosophy of Physics*. Cambridge, Cambridge University Press.

Newbolt Report (1921) *The Teaching of English in* England. London, H.M.S.O.

Nicolson, I. (2007) *Dark Side of the Universe: Dark Matter, Dark Energy, and the Fate of the Universe*. Bristol, Canopus.

Nietzsche, F. (1892) *Thus Spoke Zarathustra*, accessed from http://nationalvanguard.org/books/Thus-Spoke-Zarathustra-by-F.-Nietzsche.pdf, 2016.

Nietzsche, F. (1956) *The Birth of Tragedy and The Genealogy of Morals*. New York, Doubleday.

Nietzsche, F. (1976) *The Portable Nietzsche*. New York, Viking Press.

Nietzsche, F. (1990) *Ecce Homo*. New York, Vintage.

Nurse, P. (2016) 'Science as Revolution', public lecture accessed from https://rts.org.uk/event/rtsiet-public-lecture-sir-paul-nurse

Nybom, T. (2003) 'The Humboldt Legacy: Reflections on the Past, Present, and Future of the European University'. Higher Education Policy.

Obama, B. (2009) 'Promoting Innovation, Reform, and Excellence in America's Public Schools', accessed from http://www.whitehouse.gov/the-press-office/fact-sheet-race-top

Oho, S. (2012) *Critical Pedagogy and Social Change*. London, Routledge.

Parry J.H. (1990) *The Establishment of the European Hegemony: 1415–1715*. New York, Harper Collins.

Peim, N. (1993) *Critical Theory and the English Teacher*. London, Routledge.

Peim, N. (2001) 'The History of the Present: Towards a Contemporary Phenomenology of the School'. *History of Education*, 30 (2), 177–190.

Peim, N. (2003) *Changing English? Rethinking the Politics of English Teaching*. Sheffield, NATE.

Peim, N. (2005) 'The Life of Signs in Visual History', in U Mietzner K Myers, NA Peim, *Visualizing History: Images of Education*, Bern, Peter Lang, 7–34.

Peim, N. (2006) 'The Children's Fund and Schooling: changes in the governance topography', State of Knowledge Paper 7 on Governance and Engagement. The Joseph Rowntree Fund.

Peim, N. (2009) 'Activity Theory and Ontology'. *Educational Review*, 61, 2.

Peim, N. (2009) 'English and Literacy'. In D. Hill and L. Helavaara Robertson (eds.), *Equality in the Primary School: Promoting Good Practice Across the Curriculum*. London, Continuum, pp. 83–96.

Peim, N. (2009) 'Thinking Resources for Educational Research Methods and Methodology'. *International Journal of Research & Method in Education*, 32, 3.

Peim, N. (2010) 'What is a Thesis? Ghosts, Genre and the Archive'. *Nordic Studies in Education*, 30, 226–237.

Peim, N. (2011) 'Globalization'. In J. Arthur and A. Peterson (eds.), *Routledge Companion to Education*. London, Routledge, pp. 292–299.

Peim, N. (2013a) 'Education as Mythology'. In *Mythologies Today: Barthes Reimagined*. London, Routledge, pp. 132–140.

Peim, N. (2013b) 'Education, Schooling, Derrida's Marx and Democracy: Some Fundamental Questions'. *Studies in Philosophy and Education*, 32, 2.

Peim, N. (2016) 'Philosophy, Tragedy and Education: Thinking After Nihilism'. *Other Education*, 5, 2.

Peim, N. and Flint, K. (2011) *Rethinking the Improvement Agenda*. London, Continuum.

Peim, N. and Martin, G. (2011) 'Cross-Border Higher Education: Who Profits?'. *Journal for Critical Education Policy Studies*, 9, 1.

Pernecky, T. (2016) *Epistemology and Metaphysics for Qualitative Research*. London, Sage.

Petrović, G. (1983) 'Reification'. In T. Bottomore, L. Harris, V.G. Kiernan and R. Miliband (eds.), *A Dictionary of Marxist Thought*. Cambridge, MA, Harvard University Press, pp. 411–413.

Plato (1997) *The Complete Works*. Cambridge, MA, Hackett.

Polanyi, M. (2015) *Personal Knowledge*. Chicago, University of Chicago Press.

Popper, K. (1992) *The Logic of Scientific Discovery*. London, Routledge.

Pound, E. (2009) *Hugh Selwyn Mauberley*. Charleston, SC, Bibliolife.

Power. S. (2003) *Education and the Middle Class*. Buckingham, Oxford University Press.

Pring, R (2000) 'The False Dualisms of Educational Research'. *Journal of Philosophy of Education*, 34 (2), 247–260.

Pring, R. (2005) *Philosophy of Education*. London, Continuum.

Ranson, S. (1994) *Towards the Learning Society*. London, Cassell.

Reay, D. (2012) 'What Would a Socially Just Education System Look Like?'. *Journal of Education Policy*, 27, 5.

Reed, M. (2016) *The Research Impact Handbook*. London, Fast Track Impact.

Rhoads, R. and Torres, C. (2006) *The University, State, and Market: The Political Economy of Globalization*. Stanford, CA, Stanford University Press.

Ricoeur, P. (1990) *Time and Narrative*. Chicago, University of Chicago Press.

Ricoeur, P. and Kearny, R. (1978) 'Myth as the Bearer of Possible Worlds'. *The Crane Bag* 2, 1&2.

Robson, E. (1972) *School Architecture*. Reprinted by Leicester University Press, distributed by Humanities Press, New York.

Rose, J. (1982) *Feminine Sexuality: Jacques Lacan and the Ecole Freudienne*. London, Macmillan.

Roth, M. (2014) *Beyond the University*. London, Yale University Press.

Rothblatt, S. (1997) *The Modern University and its Discontents*. Cambridge, University Press.

Rottenberg, E. (2002) 'Introduction: Inheriting the Future'. In J. Derrida (ed.), *Negotiations*. Stanford, CA, Stanford University Press, pp. 1–7.

Russell, B. (1918) 'The Philosophy of Logical Atomism'. In R.C. Marsh (ed.), *Logic and Knowledge: Essays 1901–1950*. London, George Allen and Unwin 1956, pp. 177–281.

Sapir, E. (1929): 'The Status of Linguistics as a Science'. In E. Sapir (1958), D.G. Mandelbaum (eds.), *Culture, Language and Personality*. Berkeley, University of California Press, pp. 65–77.

de Saussure, F. (1922) *Cours de Linguistique Generale*. Paris, Payot.

Schopenhauer, A. (1883–1886) *The World As Will and Idea*, 3 vols. London, Routledge and Kegan Paul.

Scott, P. (1993) 'The Idea of the University in the 21st Century: A British Perspective'. *British Journal of Educational Studies*, 41, 4–25.

Shields, P. (2000) *Step-by-Step: Building a Research Paper.* Stillwater, OK, New Forums Press.

Simonti, C.N. (2016) The Phenotypic Legacy of Admixture between Modern Humans and Neandertals, accessed from science.sciencemag.org/cgi/doi/10.1126/science.aad2149

Singer, P. (1985) *In Defence of Animals*. Oxford, Blackwells.

Sloterdijk, P. (2011) *Bubbles*. New York, Semiotext(e).

Smitherman, G. (2000) *Talkin' That Talk: Language, Culture and Education in African America*. London, Routledge.

Stiegler, B. (2013) *What Makes Life Worth Living?* Cambridge, Polity.

Stringer, C. (2012) 'What Makes a Modern Human'. *Nature*, 485 (7396), 33–35.

Sun-keung Pang, N. (ed.) (2006) *Globalization: Educational Research,Change and Reform*. Hong Kong, Chinese University Press.

Susskind, L. (2005) *An Introduction to Black Holes, Information and the String Theory Revolution*. New York, World Scientific Publishing.

Swain, J. (ed.) (2017) *Designing Research in Education*. London, Sage.

Taylor, C. (1995) *Philosophical Arguments*. Cambridge, Harvard University Press.

Thomas, G. (2007) Education and Theory. Maidenhead, Open University Press.

Thomas, G. (2013) *How to Do Your Research Project*. London, Sage.

Thucydides (2000) *The History of the Peloponnesian War*. Harmondsworth, Penguin.

Tight, M. (2009) *Higher Education in the United Kingdom Since 1945*. Buckingham, Open University Press.

Tomlinson, J. (1991) *Cultural Imperialism*. London, Continuum.

Tooley, J. (2009) *The Beautiful Tree*. New Delhi, Penguin.

Uebel, T. (2016) 'Vienna Circle'. In E.N. Zalta (ed.), *The Stanford Encyclopedia of Philosophy* accessed from https://plato.stanford.edu/archives/spr2016/entries/vienna-circle/

Viswanathan, Gauri. (1989) *Masks of Conquest: Literary Study and British Rule in India*. New York, Columbia University Press.

Wardle, D. (1974) *Rise of the Schooled Society*. London, Routledge and Kegan Paul.

Weber, M. (1991) *Essays in Sociology*. London, Routledge.

Weedon, C. (1987) *Feminist Practice and Poststructuralist Theory*. Oxford, Blackwell.

Whorf, Benjamin (1956) *Language, Thought and Reality: Selected Writings of Benjamin Lee Whorf*. New York, Wiley.

Wilkinson, A. (1971) *The Foundations of Language*. Oxford, Oxford University Press.

Willett, J. (ed.) (1964) *Brecht on Theatre*. New York, Hill and Wang.

Williams, C. (2001) *Contemporary French Philosophy: Modernity and the Persistence of the Subject*. London, Athlone.

Willis, P. (1979) *Learning to Labour*. Aldershot, Gator.

Winnicott, D. (1953) 'Transitional Objects and Transitional Phenomena', *International Journal of Psychoanalysis*, 34, 89–97.

Wittgenstein, L. (1961) *Tractatus Logico-Philosophicus*. London, Routledge and Kegan Paul.

Wittgenstein, L. (1967) *Remarks on the Foundations of Mathematics*. Oxford, Blackwell.

Wittgenstein, L. (1968) *Philosophical Investigations*. Oxford, Blackwell.

Whorf, B.L. (1956) *Language, Thought and Reality*. Cambridge, MA, MIT Press.

Wolf, A. (2002) *Does Education Matter?* London, Penguin.

Yin, R. (2005) *Introducing the World of Education*. London, Sage.

Zizek, S. (1989) *The Sublime Object of Ideology*. London, Verso.

Zizek, S. (2004) 'What Rumsfeld Doesn't Know That He Knows' accessed from lacanian.ink website, http://www.lacan.com/zizekrumsfeld.htm

Zizek, S. (2009) *The Parallax View*. Boston, MIT Press.

Index